Best Hikes Near
Baltimore

HEATHER SANDERS CONNELLEE

FALCONGUIDES

GUILFORD, CONNECTICUT
HELENA, MONTANA

AN IMPRINT OF GLOBE PEQUOT PRESS

**To my parents, David and Dianne Sanders,
for their unconditional love and support.
I'm proud of who I am, and it's all because of them.**

To buy books in quantity for corporate use
or incentives, call **(800) 962–0973**
or e-mail **premiums@GlobePequot.com**.

FALCONGUIDES®

FalconGuides is an imprint of Globe Pequot Press.
Falcon, FalconGuides, and Outfit Your Mind are registered trademarks of Morris Book Publishing, LLC.

All photos are the author's unless otherwise indicated.

Text design: Sheryl P. Kober
Layout artist: Maggie Peterson
Project editor: Ellen Urban

Maps by Mapping Specialists Ltd. © Morris Book Publishing, LLC

Library of Congress Cataloging-in-Publication Data is available on file.

ISBN 978-0-7627-7930-7

Printed in the United States of America

10 9 8 7 6 5 4 3 2 1

Contents

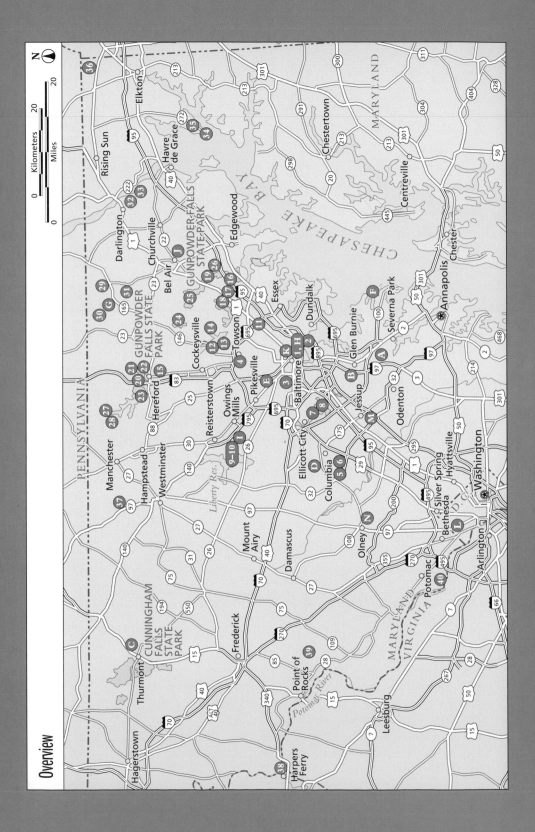

Overview

Acknowledgments

Let me start by thanking the many rangers and park staff who shared time and information to help make this book possible. Next, I'd like to thank the Baltimore hiking authors before me, especially Suzanne Meyer Mittenthal, Bryan Mackay, and Evan Balkan, who literally allowed me to follow in their footsteps and introduced me to some of my favorite trails back when I was a very young girl. To the thousands of volunteers who keep these trails open and accessible for all to enjoy, a big thank-you goes out to you! Keep up the amazing work. To my hiking partners Grant, Caroline, Rob, Petra, Beth, Jessi, Laura, Grace, and Paige, it was so nice to have someone to talk to other than my digital voice recorder!

To my childhood friends and their families who let me tag along on hiking, camping, and rafting trips, thank you! Thanks to Jessi for joining me on my first weekend backpack trip and first time on the Appalachian Trail . . . and to the long haired, bearded hiker we met on the trip: Thank you for telling me the trail went all the way to Maine! To the entire Sanders, Srnec, Poremski, and Connellee families for always taking an interest in my work and travels, thank you.

To Chuck, while writing this book was quite a big challenge, it's nothing compared to the challenge you are overcoming. You inspire me. To my grandfather Elmer and my late grandparents Alma, Walt, and Betty for taking me camping in Ocean City and Gettysburg—those memories are some of my fondest. To my godmother Bettie Jane and my aunt Pat for helping instill my love of nature and my sense of adventure, thank you. Thank you to my sister Kim for her constant support and encouraging words whenever I need them most. I'll always look up to you. To my mom and dad, who taught me everything I know, I am proud to have you as my parents! And to the greatest husband in the world . . . I wouldn't have made it through this book without your overwhelming love, patience, support, and encouragement. You waited on me hand and foot so I could dedicate all of my time to this book and for that I am grateful—I love you more!

Introduction

There's so much more to B-more than most will ever know! Do you know these phrases? How 'bout dem O's? What time is it, Ravens? . . . Game time! Charm City? Got crabs in Baltimore? Home of the Preakness Stakes. The burial place of Edgar Allen Poe. The birthplace of the "Star Spangled Banner"!

Of course, you can likely rattle off all of these iconic Baltimore phrases and claims to fame. But how many Baltimore hiking trails can you name?

Maybe hiking isn't the first thing that comes to mind when you think about blue-collar Baltimore. But that doesn't mean that the trails are anything less than fantastic. It just means that they are begging to be discovered. The largest city in the state of Maryland, Baltimore is located 100 miles from Philadelphia and 40 miles from Washington, DC. It's a working-class port town dubbed "a city of neighborhoods." Baltimore and the surrounding areas are home to rivers, reservoirs, covered bridges, national parks, rail trails, nature centers, gristmills, and lighthouses. All of these things can be found along the trails. Baltimore is located on a line between the Piedmont Plateau and the Atlantic Coastal Plain, and its number one natural resource is the Chesapeake Bay watershed.

Nope, they weren't kidding when they named this place Rocks State Park. You'll be fascinated by the giant boulders and rock formations along the trails in this park.

Baltimore is rich in recreation and history. While downtown Baltimore city is made up of concrete sidewalks, row homes, high-rises, boutique shops, and trendy neighborhood restaurants and pubs, there are hidden gems of lush parks and greenways secretly placed among the hustle and bustle. While the city goes rushing by, the trails stand still, awaiting your arrival. Baltimore County and surrounding counties are comprised of rolling hills, farmland, and vineyards offering much in the way of escaping the concrete jungle.

I get it, we're not talking about Mount McKinley or the Inca Trail, but don't dismiss the trails here or you are sure to miss out. The trails of Charm City and the surrounding areas will charm the hiking pants right off of you!

Weather

Baltimore's proximity to the Chesapeake Bay, the Atlantic Ocean to the east, and the Appalachian Mountains to the west means a moderate and humid climate with hot summers and mostly mild winters. Spring is warm and mostly dry with temperatures in the 60s and 70s. On average, July is the hottest and rainiest month of the year, with temperatures in the high 80s to mid-90s. But the summer heat certainly doesn't end there. It's not unusual for August and even early September to bring those same hot July temperatures. The fall will dip down into the 50s and 60s. While summer and early fall are thunderstorm and hurricane seasons, fall and spring are still the best times to hike, with cooler temperatures, spring blossoms, and fall foliage. The average annual snowfall in Baltimore is 20 inches. And remember, there is no such thing as bad weather—only bad gear. So, if you want an enjoyable hike, do your homework, check the weather, wear appropriate clothing, and always be prepared.

Safety and Preparation

While you don't have to be worried about deadly crocodiles or polar bears in the Baltimore hiking vicinity, there are other safety hazards to be aware of. Especially in the summer months, poison ivy, poison oak, and poison sumac grow well in Baltimore's moist, humid climate. Poison ivy is the most common poisonous plant. It grows as a vine or a shrub and typically has three groups of leaves growing off of one stem, with a pointed or almond shape and somewhat shiny surface. It ranges in color, based on the season, from light green and dark green to red, orange, or yellow. Contact with this plant results in itching or poisonous rash. Although annoying, the result generally isn't serious. It typically goes away within a few weeks and treatment includes over-the-counter anti-itch medications.

Ticks are prevalent from early spring to fall and are known to transmit Lyme disease. Wear light-colored clothing so you can easily spot any tick hitchhikers and check your clothing and body after your hike. If a tick has gotten under your skin, remove it by using tweezers and grip the tick from behind the head and as close to the skin as you can get. Gently pull it off. Do not smash or burn it. Clean the tick bite with antiseptic.

The copperhead snake is the only venomous snake found in Baltimore and the surrounding counties. It can be identified by its triangular-shaped head and solid copper color and often has an hourglass pattern with dark lines crisscrossing over a lighter background. Their colors range from pinkish, tan, and brown to rust. They are especially found in rocky areas. A copperhead bite is seldom fatal.

And a few last tips on safety and preparedness:

Wear sturdy shoes to protect your feet and ankles and to keep your feet dry. Several hikes listed in this book do not have public facilities, so be sure to carry extra water and food. Dress in layers and always tell someone where you are going and when you expect to return. Carrying a cell phone is recommended, but it should be used only in emergency situations. Always be prepared for any situation, and think about packing the items on American Hiking Society's list of ten essentials of hiking. Learn more at americanhiking.org.

Old-growth trees, a carpet of green, and pops of blue wildlflowers (bluebells) make for a gorgeous backdrop for a hiking adventure along the Gunpowder.

Ten Essentials of Hiking
1. Appropriate footwear
2. Map and compass/GPS
3. Water
4. Extra food
5. Rain gear and extra layers
6. Safety items: fire, light, and whistle
7. First-aid kit
8. Knife
9. Sunscreen/sunglasses
10. Daypack

Leave No Trace
Some trails in the Baltimore area and neighboring counties can be heavily used year-round, some with sensitive ecosystems. We, as trail users and advocates, must be especially vigilant to make sure our passage leaves no lasting mark. Here are some basic guidelines for preserving trails in the region:

- Be prepared. Bring or wear clothes to protect you from cold, heat, or rain. Use maps to navigate (and do not rely solely on the maps included in this book).
- Avoid damaging trailside soils and plants by remaining on the established route. This is also a good rule of thumb for avoiding trailside irritants like poison ivy.
- Pack out all your own trash, including biodegradable items like orange peels. You might also pack out garbage left by less considerate hikers. Use outhouses at trailheads or along the trail, and keep water sources clean.
- Don't pick wildflowers or gather rocks, antlers, feathers, and other treasures along the trail. Removing these items will only take away from the next hiker's experience.
- Be careful with fire. Use a camp stove for cooking. Be sure it's okay to build a campfire in the area you're visiting. Use an existing fire ring and keep your fire small. Use sticks from the ground as kindling. Burn all the wood to ash and be sure the fire is completely out and cold before leaving.
- Don't approach or feed any wild creatures—the ground squirrel eyeing your snack food is best able to survive if it remains self-reliant. Control pets at all times.
- Be kind to other visitors. Be courteous by not making loud noises while hiking and be aware that you share the trail with others. Yield to other trail users when appropriate.

For more information, visit LNT.org.

How to Use This Guide

This guide is designed to be simple and easy to use. The overview map at the beginning of the book shows the location of each hike by number, keyed to the table of contents. Each hike is accompanied by a route map that shows access roads, the highlighted featured route, and directional arrows to point you in the right direction. It indicates the general outline of the hike. Due to scale restrictions, it is not as detailed as a park map might be or even as our "Miles and Directions" are. While most of the hikes are on clearly designated paths, use these route maps in conjunction with other resources.

Each hike begins with summary information that delivers the trail's vital statistics including length, difficulty, fees and permits, park hours, canine compatibility, and trail contacts. Directions to the trailhead are also provided, along with a general description of what you'll see along the way. A detailed route finder ("Miles and Directions") sets forth mileages between significant landmarks along the trail.

Outdoors lovers of all types, from hikers to fishermen, find the
Gunpowder River banks appealing.

Difficulty Ratings

These hikes range from easy to difficult. Some would argue that there are no mountains in Baltimore and therefore all hikes must be easy. While the trails are not nearly as rugged as the mountainous terrain of the West, you will still encounter challenges like uphill climbs, rock scrambles, long distances, extreme heat, and exposed areas. To aid in the selection of a hike that suits particular needs and abilities, each is rated easy, moderate, or difficult. Bear in mind that even most challenging routes can be made easy by hiking within your limits and taking rests when you need them.

Easy hikes are generally short and flat and take 1 to 2 hours to complete.

Moderate hikes involve increased distance and relatively mild changes in elevation and will take more than 2 hours to complete.

Difficult hikes feature some difficult terrain, greater distances, and steep ups and downs, and generally take longer than 2 hours to complete.

These are completely subjective ratings—consider that what you think is easy is entirely dependent on your level of fitness and the adequacy of your gear

Lots of flat rocks make for a great spot to take a rest or throw out a line.

(primarily shoes). If you are hiking with a group, you should select a hike with a rating that's appropriate for the least fit and prepared in your party.

Hiking times are approximate and based on the assumption that on flat ground, most walkers average 2 mph. Adjust that rate by the steepness of the terrain and your level of fitness (subtract time if you hike like it's your business and add time if you're hiking with kids), and you have a ballpark hiking duration. Be sure to add more time if you plan to picnic or take part in other activities like bird watching or photography.

Hike Selection

This guide has a trail for every hiker ranging in difficulty from a few miles on flat rail trails to all-day adventures with long distances and intense climbs. The hikes range from less than 1 mile to 14 miles in length. While these trails are the best near Baltimore, keep in mind that nearby trails, often in the same park or preserve, may offer options better suited to your needs. I've sought to space hikes throughout Baltimore city and county and the surrounding area, so wherever your starting point, you'll find a great hike nearby. The intention was to "keep it real" by making sure that the majority of hikes in the book are on natural surfaces and through a natural environment.

The author's husband takes in a bird's-eye view of the Potomac River from Weverton Cliffs.

Trail Finder

Hike No.	Hike Name	Best Hikes for Waterfalls	Best Hikes for Great Views	Best Hikes for History Lovers	Best Hikes for Children	Best Hikes for Dogs	Best Hikes for Birders	Best Hikes for Urbanites	Best Hikes for Lake and Pond Lovers	Best Hikes for River Views
1	Baltimore Waterfront Promenade: Canton Waterfront Park to Fells Point							●		
2	Fort McHenry National Monument and Historic Shrine: Seawall Trail			●				●		
3	Gwynns Falls Trail			●				●		
4	Robert E. Lee Park					●		●	●	
5	Middle Patuxent Environmental Area: South Wind Trail				●		●			
6	Patapsco Valley State Park: Switchback and McKeldin Rapids Loop									●
7	Patapsco Valley State Park: Orange Avalon Loop	●								
8	Patapsco Valley State Park: Sawmill Buzzards Rock Loop		●							
9	Soldiers Delight: Serpentine Trail									
10	Soldiers Delight: Choate Mine Loop									
11	Double Rock Park: Yellow Loop							●		
12	Oregon Ridge: Loggers Red and Ivy Hill / S. James Campbell Yellow Loop								●	
13	Loch Raven Reservoir: Merryman Trail									●

Trail Finder

Hike No.	Hike Name	Best Hikes for Waterfalls	Best Hikes for Great Views	Best Hikes for History Lovers	Best Hikes for Children	Best Hikes for Dogs	Best Hikes for Birders	Best Hikes for Urbanites	Best Hikes for Lake and Pond Lovers	Best Hikes for River Views
14	Loch Raven Reservoir: Jessops Circuit with Spur		●							
15	Torrey C. Brown Rail Trail (NCR): Paper Mill to Monkton			●		●				
16	Gunpowder: Lost Pond Trail									●
17	Gunpowder: Wildlands Sweathouse Loop									●
18	Big Gunpowder Trail: Belair Road to Harford Road									●
19	Gunpowder: Jerusalem Village with Jericho Covered Bridge			●						
20	Gunpowder: Bunker Hill and Mingo Fork Loop									●
21	Gunpowder: Panther Branch Loop	●								
22	Gunpowder: North and South Circuit									●
23	Gunpowder: Highland Loop									●
24	Gunpowder: Sweet Air Loop								●	
25	Gunpowder: Pleasantville and Bottom Loop									●
26	Little Gunpowder Trail: Sherwood Loop			●						

Trail Finder

Hike No.	Hike Name	Best Hikes for Waterfalls	Best Hikes for Great Views	Best Hikes for History Lovers	Best Hikes for Children	Best Hikes for Dogs	Best Hikes for Birders	Best Hikes for Urbanites	Best Hikes for Lake and Pond Lovers	Best Hikes for River Views
27	Prettyboy Reservoir: Hemlock Gorge									●
28	Prettyboy Reservoir: Gunpowder Loop									●
29	Rocks State Park: Falling Branch	●			●					
30	Rocks State Park: Hidden Valley				●					
31	Rocks State Park: White Trail Loop		●							
32	Susquehanna State Park: LSHG to Trestle Bridge					●				
33	Susquehanna State Park Loop			●						
34	Elk Neck State Park: Lighthouse Trail		●	●	●		●			
35	Elk Neck State Park: Beaver Marsh Loop								●	
36	Fair Hill NRMA: Orange Loop								●	
37	Hashawha Environmental Appreciation Area: Perimeter Loop						●		●	
38	Appalachian Trail: Gathland State Park to Harpers Ferry		●							
39	Sugarloaf Mountain: Northern Peaks and Mountain Loop		●							
40	Billy Goat Trail Section A	●	●	●						

Map Legend

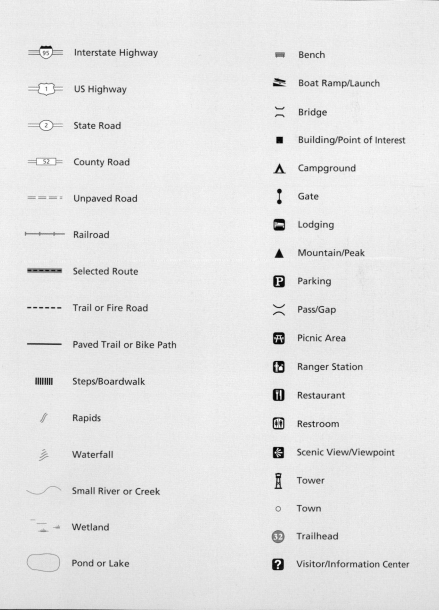

Interstate Highway

US Highway

State Road

County Road

Unpaved Road

Railroad

Selected Route

Trail or Fire Road

Paved Trail or Bike Path

Steps/Boardwalk

Rapids

Waterfall

Small River or Creek

Wetland

Pond or Lake

Bench

Boat Ramp/Launch

Bridge

Building/Point of Interest

Campground

Gate

Lodging

Mountain/Peak

Parking

Pass/Gap

Picnic Area

Ranger Station

Restaurant

Restroom

Scenic View/Viewpoint

Tower

Town

Trailhead

Visitor/Information Center

Baltimore Waterfront Promenade: Canton Waterfront Park to Fells Point

An urban hike through the heart of downtown Baltimore's tourist center takes you past restaurants and pubs, boutique shops, attractions, and marinas. Meander through the historic town of Fells Point or continue on the trail to the Inner Harbor, Baltimore's tourist mecca, all while enjoying the view of the water.

Start: Water taxi dock at Canton Waterfront Park
Distance: 4.3 miles out and back
Hiking time: About 2 hours
Difficulty: Easy
Trail surface: Paved walkway
Best season: Year-round
Other trail users: Runners, bikers, in-line skaters
Canine compatibility: Leashed dogs permitted
Land status: Baltimore city
Fees and permits: None
Schedule: Promenade always open
Maps: Waterfront Walking Map, waterfrontpartnership.org/water-front-walking-map
Trail contacts: Waterfront Partnership of Baltimore, 650 S. Exeter St., #200, Baltimore, MD 21202; (443) 743-3308; waterfrontpartnership.org
Other: Restaurants, cafe, boutique shops are along the way. Baltimore water taxi information and schedule at baltimorewatertaxi.com.
Special considerations: Be especially careful after dark—you are in a city, after all.

Finding the trailhead: From I-95, take exit 57 for Boston Street. Canton Waterfront Park is on your left in the 3000 block of Boston Street. A parking lot and street parking are available. **GPS:** N39 16.626' / W76 34.358'

THE HIKE

This path is the epitome of urban hiking. Soak in some Baltimore culture while seeing the sights, taking in great views, and getting some exercise. The entire length of the trail is 7.0 miles running from Fort McHenry to the Canton Waterfront Park, with some disconnected sections, boardwalk, brick, and sidewalk. This hike describes a well-marked section of the trail from Canton Waterfront Park to the Fells Point pier. Large green signs with the waterfront promenade logo appear along the way. On this section you will pass by several marinas, residences, and restaurants where you can be sure to get a whiff of steamed crabs and fresh seafood. At Canton Waterfront Park you'll often see locals with rod in hand, out for a fresh catch of fish or blue crabs. This park is also a popular spot for Baltimoreans to play Frisbee with their dogs or throw down a blanket to sunbathe, picnic, or enjoy a good book.

As you meander along the water's edge, eye up the sailboats and yachts, hear outdoor diners clanking plates and forks, and notice the numerous pubs. Think about stopping in one of the art galleries, gelato or ice cream shops, or clothing and gift boutiques as you enter the historic neighborhood of Fells Point, famous for its maritime history. "Fells," as the neighborhood is referred to

A view of Baltimore's famous Inner Harbor, one of the city's top tourist attractions. Bart Viguers

by locals, was founded in 1730 by William Fell. It became a major port and hub for shipbuilding. Baltimore's famous Clipper Ships were built in Fells Point. The homes you see today were once the residences of sailmakers and local seamen. Along the cobblestone streets you may see the Urban Pirate Ship docked, soon followed by what looks to be an abandoned police station. This structure was used specifically for the filming of the network police drama *Homicide: Life on the Street.*

No doubt, it's an urban trail so expect to see trash and construction along the way. The floating trash that gathers in some sections along the way is quite disturbing. But the positives of this hike most certainly outweigh the negatives. It's refreshing to see so many city folks using this path, whether it's to get in a long run, take a walk with their dogs, or to get from point to point (or bar to bar) on foot. If you choose to continue the trail past the suggested turnaround point at Fells Point, you will eventually circle through the Inner Harbor and past famous attractions such as Harbor Place, the Science Center, and the National Aquarium. Fells Point is also a water taxi stop so you may choose to do your return trip by hopping onboard a taxi back to Canton Waterfront Park.

MILES AND DIRECTIONS

0.0   Begin trail at Canton Waterfront Park, just steps from the Canton water taxi dock.

0.1   When you are facing the water, go right to follow the brick path.

0.2   Pass by the outdoor dining area of Bay Café restaurant and begin walking along the marina.

0.3   Pass by Bo Brooks restaurant and crab house as you hug the water on the left.

0.5   Pass the pier, where you will often see Baltimore's *Black-Eyed Susan* paddle-boat docked.

0.7   Cross a wooden bridge.

1.1   Captain James Landing restaurant and taxi dock come into view. Follow the trail behind the restaurant and continue on the brick-paved path.

1.2   The trail changes briefly from brick to boardwalk and then concrete.

1.3   Briefly walk through a parking lot and turn left to rejoin the boardwalk.

1.7   Come upon the Inn at Henderson's Wharf. Walk through the parking round-about to continue on the brick path.

1.8   The trail becomes boardwalk again.

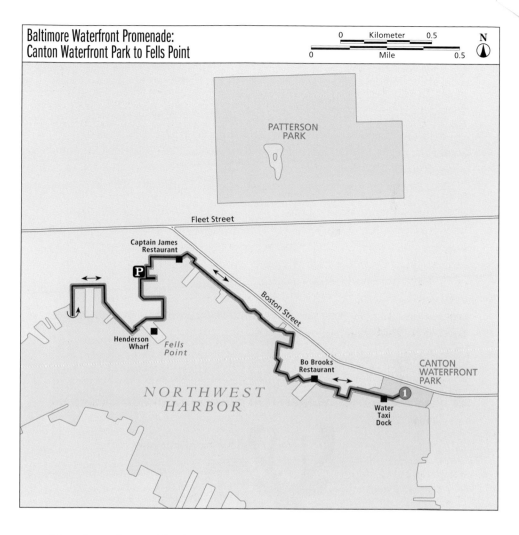

1.9 Enter the neighborhood of Fells Point. Turn left on Thames Street to follow the brick sidewalk.

2.0 Reach the film set for *Homicide: Life on the Street,* which looks like a police station.

2.1 Come to the Fells Point water taxi dock.

2.2 Follow the path to the end of the pier, which juts out into the water. Turn around and retrace your route to the beginning.

4.3 Arrive back at Canton Waterfront Park.

Options: Should you choose to continue past Fells Point, you can walk all the way to Fort McHenry. The length in total, one-way, is roughly 7.0 miles.

HIKE INFORMATION

Local attractions: You are near all Baltimore Inner Harbor attractions as well as the neighborhoods of Canton and Fells Point.

Maryland Science Center, 601 Light St. Baltimore; (410) 685-2370; mdsci.org

National Aquarium, 501 E. Pratt St., Baltimore; (410) 576-3800; aqua.org

Good eats: Nacho Mamas, located in Canton Square, 2907 O'Donnell St., Baltimore; (410) 675-0898; mamasmd.com

Blue Moon Café is famous for breakfast (expect a long wait); 1621 Aliceanna St., Baltimore; (410) 522-3490; bluemoonbaltimore.com.

Berthas, 734 S. Broadway, Baltimore; (410) 327-5795; berthas.com

🍂 Green Tip:
Observe wildlife from a distance. Never feed wild animals under any circumstances. You may damage their health and expose yourself (and them) to danger.

Fort McHenry National Monument and Historic Shrine: Seawall Trail

The American flag waves above as you hike the Seawall Trail, a short trail that circles an eighteenth-century star-shaped fort. Birthplace of the national anthem, Fort McHenry's perimeter trail follows along the seawall of Baltimore's harbor, affording expansive views of the city's waterfront, skyline, and industrial areas.

Start: Begin at the visitor center.
Distance: 0.9-mile loop
Hiking time: About 30 minutes
Difficulty: Easy
Trail surface: Paved surface
Best season: Year-round
Other trail users: Bikers
Canine compatibility: Dogs are permitted on the grounds but not in the historic areas or visitor center. Dogs must be on a leash at all times.
Land status: National Park Service
Fees and permits: None required to hike the Seawall Trail. Small fee for those 16 or older to visit the National Monument and Historic Shrine.

Schedule: Daily, park open 8 a.m. to 5 p.m., fort and visitor center open 8 a.m. to 4:45 p.m. Park, fort, and visitor center open at 9 a.m. from September to May. Closed Thanksgiving, Christmas, and New Year's Day.
Maps: No maps available
Trail contacts: Fort McHenry, 2400 E. Fort Ave., Baltimore, MD; (410) 962-4290; nps.gov/fomc
Other: Fort McHenry can be reached by water taxi. Information and schedule can be found at baltimorewatertaxi.com.

Finding the trailhead: On I-95, take exit 55 to Key Highway. From Key Highway turn left on Lawrence Street, then left on Fort Avenue. Proceed 1 mile to the park. **GPS:** N39 15.907' / W76 34.787'

THE HIKE

Located in Federal Hill next to Baltimore's Inner Harbor, walk in the steps of our brave countrymen on a historical hike around the star-shaped Fort McHenry, where Francis Scott Key wrote the national anthem. In the early morning of September 13, 1814, British ships launched an attack on Fort McHenry during the War of 1812. The fort defended Baltimore's harbor from attacks. Key witnessed the 25-hour bombardment and the strong defense during this Battle of Baltimore. With a successful defeat, a 30-by-42-foot American flag was hoisted. These events inspired Key to write "The Star-Spangled Banner."

Take a tour of the grounds (fee). Stop by the visitor center to watch an orientation film, see exhibits, and visit the gift shop. Then take a self-guided tour of the fort. When you're ready to pound out some patriotic steps, hop on the gray-brick sidewalk located in front of the Visitor and Education Center and next to the parking area. Facing the center, take the trail to the right to head toward the statue of Colonel George Armistead. The statue and the fort and flag are on your left. Armistead was the commander of the fort during the British bombardment. You'll

Built in 1864, this building was once a Civil War magazine used for safe storage of additional gunpowder and ammunition for the cannons.

be paralleling the entrance road for a few steps until you reach the official NPS sign. Take a left here to follow the path through the lawn, toward the picnic area.

Ahead, you won't be able to miss the larger-than-life statue of a man holding a harp. The bronze statue is not of Francis Scott Key, as many would assume. Rather, it represents Orpheus, the artful poet, musician, and singer of Greek mythology. The monument marks the centennial of the writing of "The Star-Spangled Banner" and the defense of Baltimore. Standing 24 feet tall, the statue's base has a medallion honoring Francis Scott Key. Take note of the trees lining the path, each dedicated to various colonels, majors, generals, and other heroes who played important roles in the battle.

Once you reach the picnic area, notice the redbrick building set to the right. This was once a Civil War magazine building used for safe storage of additional gunpowder and ammunition for the cannons. Built it 1864, the structure was converted into a rifle range during World War I. The fort served as an active military post into the 1900s.

After the picnic area you'll veer to the left to follow along the water and seawall. Choppy waves lap against the wall, the smell of salt lingers in the cool breeze from the water, and the sound of a CSX train whistle is common in the background. Be sure not to walk on the seawall! On your left pass a memorial grove of Japanese cherry trees, originally planted in 1931, the same year "The Star-Spangled Banner" became the official national anthem. As you come to a bend in the trail, the Key Bridge stands straight ahead as numerous freight and

Trees and plaques dedicated to those who played important roles in the Battle of Fort McHenry line the trail.

car-carry ships like the *Wallenius Wilhelmser,* sailboats, and personal watercraft float peacefully. More and more cannons come into sight by the fort, and a grandiose American flag stands tall and flies proud.

Now, on the final leg of the loop, the 1st Mariner Bank Tower hovers over many city buildings, the Natty Boh beer sign is perched on a building just behind the tower, and a line of boat masts can be seen across the way. Just before you approach the backside of the visitor center, the taxi pier comes into view. Bear right to return to your starting point and revel in the glory you will feel from this historical hike.

MILES AND DIRECTIONS

0.0   Facing the visitor center, take the gray-brick path to the right, heading toward the Armistead Statue. You will reach the statue in just a few steps.

0.1   Reach the official National Park Service sign for Fort McHenry. Take a left to head toward the picnic area and giant statue of Orpheus.

0.2   Veer to the left to follow along the water and seawall.

0.3   Reach the Memorial Japanese Cherry Grove.

0.6   You'll be directly across from the Canton industrial area.

0.8   Reach the backside of the visitor center and the side path to the water taxi pier.

0.9   Arrive back at the start of the hike.

Fort McHenry and the Star-Spangled Banner

Built between 1799 and 1802, Fort McHenry is shaped like a star with five points and surrounded by a moat. This was a popular design during that era. It was designed by Frenchman Jean Foncin for the purpose of defending the Port of Baltimore. In the War of 1812, Francis Scott Key witnessed the bombardment of Fort McHenry under British attack during the Battle of Fort McHenry. When the young poet and lawyer saw the American flag still flying over the fort the next morning, he was moved to write the poem "Defense of Fort McHenry." It later was set to music and eventually became a well-known patriotic song. On March 3, 1931, it was made the national anthem, a resolution signed by President Herbert Hoover.

0   Kilometer 0.25

0   Mile   0.25

N

NORTHWEST
HARBOR

East Fort Ave

Armistead
Statue

Fort
McHenry

Fort McHenry Tunnel

95

Harbor Tunnel

895

HIKE INFORMATION

Local attractions: There is a plethora of restaurants and shops in nearby Federal Hill.

Maryland Science Center, 601 Light St., Baltimore; (410) 685-2370; mdsci.org

National Aquarium, 501 E. Pratt St., Baltimore; (410) 576-3800; aqua.org

Good eats: Rusty Scupper Restaurant and Bar, 402 Key Highway; (401) 727-3678; rusty-scupper.com

Gwynns Falls Trail

As urban as trails around Baltimore come, one section of the 15-mile Gwynns Falls Trail—from Leon Day Park to Windsor Mill Road—will surprise you with thick tree canopy, river views, historical structures, and a variety of plant and animal species. The environment on the trail is a sharp contrast from the urban neighborhoods of west and southwest Baltimore city that the trail connects.

Start: Begin by crossing a wood bridge from Leon Day Park.

Distance: 3.6 miles out and back

Hiking time: About 2 hours

Difficulty: Moderate due to the distance

Trail surface: Gravel, crushed stone

Best season: Year-round

Other trail users: Bikers, skaters, birders

Canine compatibility: Leashed dogs permitted

Land status: Publicly owned land

Fees and permits: None

Schedule: Dawn–dusk daily. Note that it is possible for trailhead parking areas with gates to sometimes stay locked until 8 or 9 a.m.

Maps: Trail map available at http://gwynnsfallstrail.org/images/pics/GFTMapForWeb.pdf

Trail contacts: Gwynns Falls Trail, 800 Wyman Park Dr., Suite 010, Baltimore, MD 21211; (410) 448-5663; gwynnsfallstrail.org

Other: While this section of the trail is gravel, the rest of the trail is paved.

Special considerations: The Gwynns Falls Trail travels through some rough parts of the city. Use common sense and always have a hiking partner.

Finding the trailhead: From I-695 take exit 16 for I-70 East / Local Traffic / Park & Ride. Exit at I-70 exit 94 (Security Boulevard). Stay in the right lane and turn right at the Ingleside Avenue traffic light. Cross the bridge and turn right at the top of the bridge (just before the Franklintown sign). Proceed 1 block to the stop sign at Franklintown Road and turn left. Proceed on Franklintown Road approximately 1.5 miles past the intersection with Winans Way, and the Winans Meadow trailhead is around the bend on the left. Continue for another 1.5 miles and reach the Leon Day Park trailhead and parking lot on the right. **GPS:** N39 18.009′ / W76 40.303′

THE HIKE

Hiding among row homes, concrete sidewalks, and traffic congestion, the 15-mile Gwynns Falls Trail brings some green to the otherwise gray surroundings. This linear greenway trail travels through west and southwest Baltimore city along the Gwynns Falls stream valley, a continuous trail that connects thirty neighborhoods. The section of trail from Leon Day Park to Windsor Mill Road, the only gravel, nonpaved section, follows the route of an early 1800s millrace that carried water to power five mills. These mills turned Baltimore into one of the leading flour and textile producers in the nation. Along the hike, learn about the history of the stream valley and the natural habitat through interpretive signs and historical heritage exhibits. You'll encounter hardwood species like white oak, American beech (uncommon in cities and urban areas), tulip poplar, sycamore, northern catalpa, and pin oak. You'll see locals fishing in the stream, out for a run or bike ride, or doing some bird watching.

Bridges span the Gwynns Falls stream valley.

3

Begin the trail at Leon Day Park, named for Leon Day, a southwest Baltimore resident and ballplayer in the Negro Leagues who was inducted into the National Baseball Hall of Fame in 1995, six days before he died. Among other teams, he played for the Baltimore Black Sox in 1934 when African Americans were not allowed to play in the Majors or Minors. Today, the park facilities include a baseball field, playground, and pavilion.

From the parking lot, begin the trail by crossing a wood bridge. You'll see green ovals painted on the ground with "GF Trail" in white writing. Follow the oval markers as you cross over Franklintown Road and then Morris Road. The path climbs uphill on Morris Road as it takes a turn back to head into the woods. This is the point where the city fades into the background and the forest welcomes you on a wide, well-maintained, lush trail. The traffic noise is obvious in the beginning but soon becomes distant as the sound of the river grows stronger. Your hike from Trailhead 4 (Leon Day Park) to Trailhead 3 (Windsor Mills) will have benches for resting and a nice picnic table overlooking the river rapids below. Enjoy the city's green scene, truly a diamond in the rough!

MILES AND DIRECTIONS

0.0   Begin the trail at the Leon Day Park trailhead.

0.1   Cross over Franklintown Road.

0.3   Cross over Morris Road. The trail heads uphill on Morris Road before entering the woods.

0.4   The trail takes a sharp U-turn to head into the woods.

0.9   Reach the first small trickle of a spring.

1.0   Reach a second spring.

1.3   Come to the intersection with the Jastrow Trail.

1.4   Reach an interpretive sign about Olmstead.

1.5   Cross a bridge surface.

1.7   Come to a picnic table with a view of the rapids below soon followed by the Millstream interpretive sign.

1.8   Arrive at Windsor Mill trailhead. Turn around and retrace your route to Leon Day Park.

3.6   Arrive back at the parking lot and Leon Day Park trailhead.

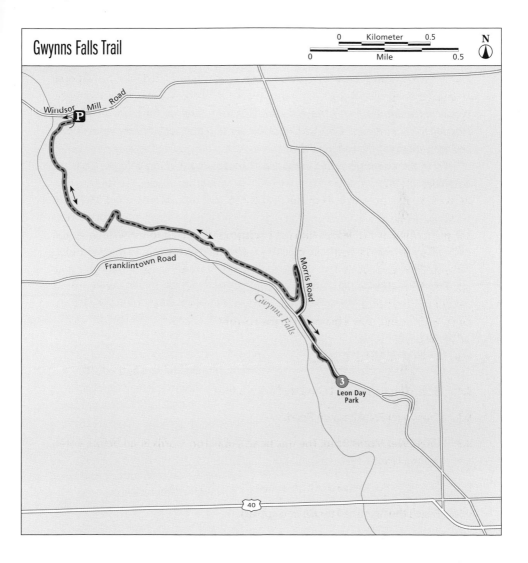

Options: With 9 trailheads (listed on the website), there are many options for hiking sections of the 15-mile trail. For example, start at the Inner Harbor (trailhead 7) and hike or bike 6.2 miles to Waterview Ave (trailhead 8). This is the longest section between trailheads.

> 🌿 **Green Tip:**
> *Don't take souvenirs home with you. This means natural materials such as plants, rocks, shells, and driftwood as well as historic artifacts such as fossils and arrowheads.*

Follow the red Rail Trail (aka the main trail), which parallels the Jones Falls before crossing the Lake Roland Dam and hooking up to a trail around Lake Roland that passes by arguably the best view in the park. Along the way you'll enjoy rare species of wildlife, railroad history, and exceptional scenery located just minutes from the Baltimore city line.

Start: From the Falls Road parking lot, begin on the rail trail that starts at a black gate.
Distance: 4.1 miles point to point with shuttle, or 6.7 miles out and back
Hiking time: About 2 hours
Difficulty: Rail Trail portion—easy; Woodbrook Trail portion—moderate
Trail surface: Natural surface, packed dirt, some paved
Best season: Year-round
Other trail users: Bikers, trail runners
Canine compatibility: Leashed (strictly enforced) dogs permitted
Land status: County park
Fees and permits: None
Schedule: Sunrise–sunset daily
Maps: Trail maps available online and at the ranger station
Trail contacts: Robert E. Lee Park, 1000 Lakeside Dr., Baltimore, MD 21209; (410) 887-4156; relpnc.org; baltimorecountymd.gov/Agencies/recreation/programdivision/naturearea/relpark/index.htm
Other: Facilities include pavilions, portable toilets, picnic tables, boat launch, and fishing platform. The park is accessible by light-rail train. Light-rail trains run often, and you will be crossing the tracks on this hike. Nature and educational programs, kayak tours, and campouts available. Fee for annual membership to the dog park, Paw Point.
Special considerations: Do not swim or wade in the Jones Falls or Lake Roland. Boat rules: nonmotorized boats only, lifejackets must be worn, launch at the dock only.

Finding the trailhead: **To Falls Road lot:** Take I-83 to the exit for Northern Parkway east. From above, turn left on Falls Road. Continue on Falls Road for several miles and reach a gravel parking area / pull-off on the right side of Falls Road. Start from here. **GPS:** N39 23.776' / W76 39.802'

To Robert E. Lee lot: Follow signs for the light-rail and turn right into the Light-Rail parking lot. Bear right to enter the park. The entrance road, Lakeside Drive, takes you past the dam to the left and dead-ends at the parking area. You'll walk the entrance road back to the dam to reach the dam bridge, where your hike will begin. Visitors may also park in the Light-Rail parking lot and follow the boardwalk to the park. To do a one-way hike, drop off a car here. **GPS:** N39 22.673' / W76 38.650'

THE HIKE

This park has come a long way, baby, and Robert E. Lee just keeps getting better and better! After much neglect the 453-acre park fell into disrepair and closed to the public. It reopened in 2011, after being leased to Baltimore County, which gave it a major overhaul. The land area encompassing Robert E. Lee Park was originally part of late-seventeenth- and early-eighteenth-century land grants from Lord Baltimore to a number of Maryland families. It's now a sanctuary for outdoors lovers that's close to the city. From new trail systems, park programs, the inclusion of accessible areas, and upgraded facilities, the improvements in this park just keep coming.

Snapping turtles, green frogs, and largemouth bass call Lake Roland home. Hummingbirds are also included in the roster of wild inhabitants of Robert E. Lee Park. Photo by Bart Viguers

Looking back, by 1832 the Baltimore and Susquehanna Railroad entered the Jones Falls valley. Today, much of its rail bed remains, as well as those of the former Northern Central Railroad, which are evident throughout the park trail system and the currently operating light-rail. The trail described here follows the red-blazed Rail Trail. It begins from the parking area on Falls Road on a wide rail trail following the Jones Falls (also paralleling Falls Road) and passing nice rock formations under a canopy of trees. It goes on to cross a beautiful bridge over an old railroad trestle, past an old railroad mileage marker, while paralleling old rail tracks on the left. Eventually it crosses over the light-rail tracks to enter the main park area of Robert E. Lee. The light-rail tracks are the official end to the Rail Trail. These tracks are also the old Hollins Station and the mileage marker you pass indicates 1 mile to this stop. Note there are some muddy spots and lots of poison ivy.

Cross the light-rail tracks and meet up with the paved park road, passing a butterfly enclosure, pavilions, and picnic tables as you are now in the hub of the park. The trail continues on the other side, but first you will encounter the heart and soul of Robert E Lee Park: Lake Roland. In the 1850s the lake was formed by the impoundment of three streams—Jones Falls, Roland Run, and Towson Run—to create a reservoir for the city of Baltimore. By 1915 Lake Roland no longer provided an adequate supply of drinking water for a growing city, but it remained a recreational spot.

The trail affords scenic views of calm and peaceful Lake Roland.

During the 1940s the land surrounding the lake, which had been largely tracts of privately owned properties, was consolidated to form a Baltimore city park. In 1944 Robert Garrett, then president of the Baltimore and Ohio Railroad and chairman of the Baltimore Department of Parks and Recreation, led an effort to establish the park as a memorial to General Robert E. Lee. The Garrett money was used to increase the amount of land already owned by the city, set up a picnic area, erect a footbridge below the dam, and add signs identifying the newly enlarged park as the Robert E. Lee Memorial Park.

Just before you reach the Lake Roland dam, the point where Lake Roland flows into the Jones Falls, take notice of the Ranger Station and a boardwalk on your right. The boardwalk is an excellent spot for bird watching and it leads to the Light-Rail parking lot. On the other side of the dam, pass the pump house, which was built in 1861.

The lake experience doesn't end here. Once you've reached the back parking lot, the trail takes the Woodbrook Trail, to eventually skirt the edge of Lake Roland. This trail was first cleared in 2013 for your hiking pleasure. Pass old foundations, walk the former Woodbrook Road, cross a scenic feeder creek, and enjoy 180-degree views from a peninsula.

At the point where the trail dead-ends into Woodbrook Road, follow a narrow path downhill to the left. The trail goes on to hug the water, passing by arguably the best view in the park from a rock outcropping, called the Cave, overlooking the lake and pump house. You could encounter a spectacle of wild inhabitants. The park is home to, get ready . . . wood ducks, beaver, monarch butterflies, deer, green frogs, eagles, woodpeckers, hummingbirds, snapping turtles, sliders, red-belly turtles, sunfish, largemouth bass, smallmouth bass, bullhead catfish, crappy, northern water snakes, black rat snakes, garter snakes, and milk snakes. And that's just to name a few! Plus, see if you can spot mica rock, jewelweed spicebush, Indian strawberries, and honeysuckle.

Finally, this lake trail dead-ends at the light-rail tracks. Do not cross or follow the tracks. *Turn around!* Retrace your steps to the parking area inside Robert E. Lee. You'll fall in love and be sure to return.

MILES AND DIRECTIONS

0.0 Begin at the trailhead on Falls Road behind a black gate on a wide, flat, rail-trail path.

0.7 See the intersection with the first obvious trail downhill on the left. (This trail follows the Jones Falls and ends at a field.) Then, cross over a new bridge / old trestle over the Jones Falls.

0.8 Pass a trail on the left and downhill and another trail on right.

0.9 Pass a trail on the right. Immediately after, come to a split and follow the red Rail Trail straight and slightly right. The other side of the split is the Ridge Trail. These trails parallel each other.

1.2 The Ridge Trail and the Rail Trail meet here. Bear right and immediately after, come to a Y split and make a left.

1.4 Again intersect with the ridge trail. At this intersection you start to get views of Lake Roland off to your left.

1.6 The old rail tracks come into view on the left side.

2.0 Cross over the light-rail tracks (be cautious of frequent trains!) and up the stairs on the opposite side. With a pavilion straight ahead, make a right on the paved park road/loop path.

2.2 Reach another pavilion on the left, set above the dam, and follow the path downhill.

2.3 Reach the ranger station and the boardwalk that leads to Falls Road Light-Rail Station. Cross the dam and make a left on Lakeside Drive, the entrance road to the park. Pass the pump house on your left.

2.5 Reach the park's parking lot and follow the trail closest to the water, near the boat/fishing dock.

2.6 A side trail leads to a campfire ring. See an old parking lot, no longer in use. Make a left, crossing a paved section to follow a wide natural dirt path, formerly Woodbrook Road.

2.7 Cross over the bridge above a wide scenic creek with several water spills and rocks perfect to play on.

2.8 Take the side trail left to a peninsula with a great view.

2.9 The trail dead-ends into Woodbrook Road. Head downhill to the left on a narrow dirt trail located at a park sign.

3.1 The trail takes you over the Cave, a giant boulder, offering by far the best view in the park, overlooking Lake Roland and the pump house. The underside of the rock is a great cave/overhang.

3.4 Reach the light-rail tracks and retrace your steps to the main parking lot. **Do not pass this point**—turn around!!

4.1 Arrive back at the main lot.

Options: Hike this trail as an out-and-back for a total of 6.7 miles or a point-to-point.

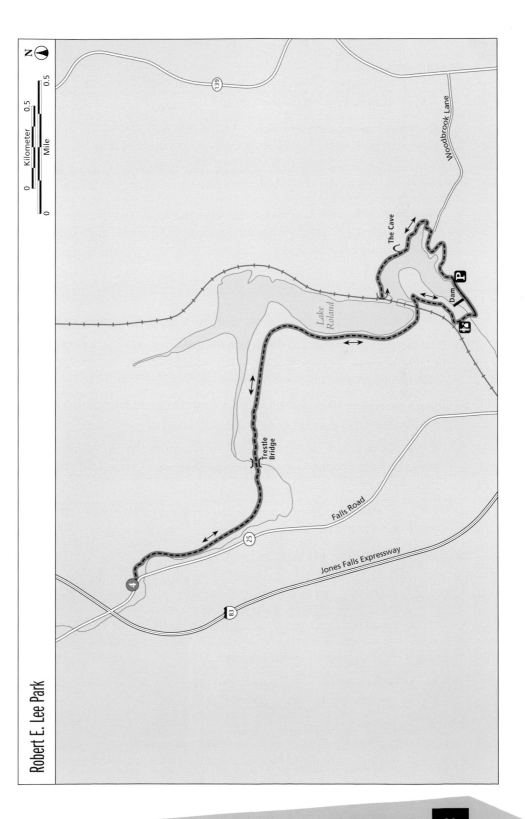

Robert E. Lee Park

N

0 Kilometer 0.5
0 Mile 0.5

139

Woodbrook Lane

The Cave

Lake Roland

Dam

P

Trestle Bridge

Falls Road

25

Jones Falls Expressway

83

HIKE INFORMATION

You can slice and dice this trail several ways in addition to hiking it one way with a shuttle:

1. Hike the red trail only out and back.
2. Begin from the Robert E. Lee parking lot to hike in either direction.
3. Do a full out-and back from Falls Road for a total of 6.7 miles

Good eats: Mt. Washington Tavern, 5700 Newbury St.; (410) 367-6903; mt washingtontavern.com

The Haute Dog Carte, 6070 Falls Rd.; (410) 608-3500; hautedogcarte.com

Earth, Wood and Fire, 1407 Clarkview Rd.; (410) 825-3473; earthwoodfire.com

Local outdoor stores: Princeton Sports Bike and Ski Shop, 6239 Falls Rd., Baltimore; (410) 828-1127; princetonsports.com

Joe's Bike Shop, 5813 Falls Rd., Baltimore; (410) 323-2788; joesbikeshop.com

What's Wild in Baltimore?

Wildlife is not the first thing that comes to mind when you think of Baltimore city . . . or drive through Baltimore city, or even when you've lived in Baltimore your entire life, like I have. Well, think again. Park ranger and amateur photographer Bart Viguers has captured some shots of wildlife at its best in Robert E. Lee Park, located in Baltimore County, on the edge of the city line. Take a visit to the park to see for yourself. Look for owls, woodpeckers, beaver, deer, and oh so much more! Go to relpnc.org for more information.

Middle Patuxent Environmental Area: South Wind Trail

This short and stunning hike packed with sights gives you just a taste of what Middle Patuxent Environmental Area's 5-plus miles of trail have to offer, leaving you wanting more. Before you go, print out the online interpretive nature walk from the website to match up the numbers with the posts along the way to create your own self-guided hike.

Start: Begin at a wood post with a Howard County park sign and a sign about leashed pets.
Distance: 1.4-mile lollipop loop
Hiking time: About 40 minutes
Difficulty: Easy
Trail surface: Natural surface
Best season: Year-round
Other trail users: Trail runners
Canine compatibility: Leashed dogs permitted
Land status: Howard County Park
Fees and permits: None
Schedule: Dawn–dusk daily

Maps: *Interpretive Nature Walk* brochure and trail map of South Wind Trail and Wildlife Loop are available at howardcounty md.gov/MPEA.htm and in the brochure boxes at the trailheads.
Other: Foot trail only, no camping, no swimming, no facilities at the trailhead
Trail contacts: Middle Patuxent Environmental Area, 5795 Trotter Rd., Clarksville, (410) 313-4726; howardcountymd.gov/MPEA.htm

Finding the trailhead: Take I-695 to I-70 west. Continue to MD 29 south and then MD 108 west toward Clarksville. Go 5 miles and make a left onto Trotter Road. In a half mile look for a gravel parking area on the left. (This is the MPEA main entrance and trailhead for the Wildlife Loop Trail.) You may park here if you choose to pick up trails that connect to the South Wind Trail. Continue past the gravel lot for 0.1 mile to reach a traffic circle. Take your second right onto South Wind Circle and take the road through a housing community. In 0.5 mile from the circle, look to the left for a wide grass path and wood post with a park sign—you will see this just before you reach Misty Top Pass (road) on your right. Park curbside on the street. **GPS:** N39 12.392' / W76 54.858'

THE HIKE

The Middle Patuxent Environmental Area encompasses 1,021 acres in Clarksville, Howard County, Maryland. Established in 1996, this educational, environmental, and wildlife habitat isn't well known like Gunpowder or Patapsco. But quite frankly, that's what makes this place great. The serene landscape of flowing water, green open meadows, and pristine trails combined with some solitude will have you hooked after your first visit. Even the couple backyards you pass by don't take away from the experience. The South Wind Trail is a total of 2.3 miles, however, the trail described here is a short 1.4-mile loop section of the trail.

You'll pick up this trail in a quiet housing community with street parking, giving new meaning to the term "curbside pickup." From the curb, you can see a wide grassy path that leads to a trail information kiosk in about 100 feet. This is your trailhead. At the kiosk you can view a map of the park. The brochure box should contain trail brochures and a bird checklist for the MPEA. Middle Patuxent is also a very popular spot for birders.

Continue on the grassy wide path, past two posts with a chain strung across. This is a hikers-only trail, so you don't have to share! The numbered markers you see along the trail coordinate with the *Interpretive Nature Walk* brochure you

Perch yourself on a fallen log and enjoy the views of Cricket Creek.

can pick up at the kiosk or download from the park website. The first numbered marker you reach, #1, describes the border known as the "edge habitat." This is where the field and forest meet. A short distance ahead, you can see the wood post with a #2. Not only does it mark a meadow of persimmon trees, but you will also see your first trail marker here, a blue circle with a silver arrow directing you to continue straight. In another 70 feet, the grassy path continues straight and two dirt trails head off to the right into the forest. Take the first trail, off to the right, but note that you will complete this loop and return to this spot via the second trail heading slightly left. (I prefer to hike this trail counterclockwise, but note that if you are following along with the *Interpretive Nature Walk* brochure, this means the numbers will go in reverse.) Immediately after you pick up this dirt path, stay straight and slightly to the right at a Y intersection.

At a T intersection you'll begin to hear the rush of the water from Cricket Creek, the largest tributary that flows into the Middle Patuxent River, before coming to a short path that leads to its edge. This is a gorgeous sight with the most perfect flat rock to perch on and fallen logs that span the creek. The trail parallels the creek. Just when you think you've lost your water view, you get nice clear overlook of the Middle Patuxent River. This river flows nearly 24 miles through Howard County into the Little Patuxent River.

In addition to persimmon trees, you can look for an abundance of ferns and spicebush, but stay away from the poison ivy. Critters to keep an eye out for include eastern cottontail rabbits, raccoons, opossums, flying squirrels, skinks (lizards), mink, cardinals, deer, box turtles, woodcock, and even copperhead snakes. The trail goes from being a wider grass path to a narrow packed-dirt path as it meanders through the undeveloped land. When you close the loop, retrace your steps to the left to return to the trailhead. If you haven't gotten enough of this awesome area, take a right to walk the other half of the South Wind Trail, a lollipop-shaped hike. The blue trail also connects to the red Wildlife Loop via the orange Connector Trail. In total the area offers 5.4 miles of hiking trails.

MILES AND DIRECTIONS

0.0 Start at a wide grassy path that begins curbside in a small housing community. A trail kiosk can be seen about 100 feet ahead on the trail.

0.1 Past the trail kiosk are two metal posts with a chain and white pipe strung across. Walk around it and continue on the wide path.

0.2 Reach a trail marker labeled #1. Ahead see a second post labeled #2. Continue straight for 70 feet and make a right on the first of two blue trails. The second blue trail is the return leg of the loop. Immediately after taking the first trail, stay far right at a Y intersection.

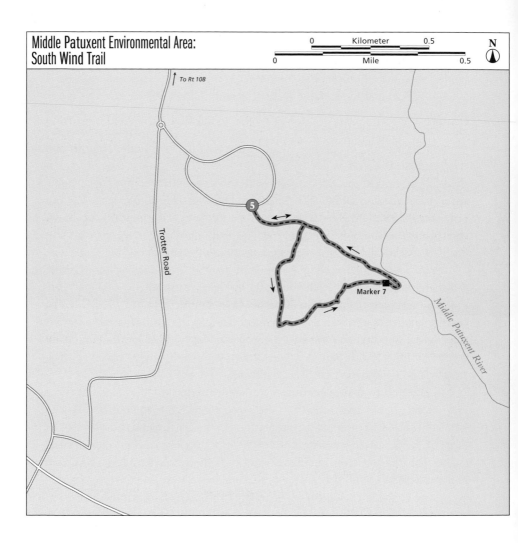

0.5 Make a left at a T intersection. The right side is a cleared path for a sewer pipeline.

0.6 Take a short side trail on the right to Cricket Creek. Back on the blue trail, reach an intersection where a shortcut trail goes left. Continue straight. The trail then bears left, while another sewer line path continues straight.

0.8 Reach trail marker #7, with views of Cricket Creek.

0.9 The trail curves left and leaves the river briefly. Stay straight and slightly left, passing a barely worn trail that heads to the right.

1.0 Come to a bench and a view of Middle Patuxent River.

1.2 See trail marker #3 and close the loop. Head left to retrace your steps.

1.4 Arrive back at the trailhead.

Options: Add the red Wildlife Loop (2.4 miles) to the blue South Wind Trail, using the orange connector trail to reach both. Start either from South Wind Circle or the gravel parking lot on Trotter Road (see "Finding the trailhead" above).

HIKE INFORMATION

Local attractions: Clark Elioak's Farm offers hayrides and a petting zoo in an enchanted forest; 10500 Clarksville Pike, Ellicott City; (410) 730-4049; open late Mar to early Nov; small admission fee; clarklandfarm.com.

Centennial Park offers a paved loop hike around Centennial Lake, paddling, and many park facilities; 10000 Route 108; centennialmd.org.

Robinson Nature Center, 6692 Cedar Ln., Columbia; (410) 313-0400; howard countymd.gov/robinsonnaturecenter.htm

Good eats: Iron Bridge Wine Company serves lunch and dinner; 10435 State Route 108; (410) 997-3456; ironbridgewines.com.

Baltimore Oriole

Everyone knows the Baltimore Orioles, Maryland's professional baseball team. And yes, the Baltimore oriole (*Icterus galbula*) is the official state bird, designated in 1947. Supposedly, the bird got its name because the colors of the male resemble the coat of arms of Lord Baltimore. The professional ball team adopted the name in 1954 in honor of the state bird.

The males have vibrant orange-gold colors on their chests and shoulders, with a black head and wings. The colors of the females are not quite as brilliant, with a lighter orange on the breast and gray-brown on the head and back. They are a medium-size bird and are more often heard than seen. You can only find them in this area typically during the summer months. Visit state symbolsusa.org/Maryland/baltimore_oriole.html for more information.

6

Patapsco Valley State Park: Switchback and McKeldin Rapids Loop

Follow the south branch of the Patapsco River to the confluence of the north and south branches. Combine the Switchback Trail with the McKeldin Rapids Loop for views of wild rapids, ending with a stiff climb and an overlook of Liberty Dam.

Start: Begin near the entrance station at the brown park sign that reads SWITCHBACK TRAIL.

Distance: 3.9-mile loop

Hiking time: About 2 hours

Difficulty: Easy with 1 strenuous climb

Trail surface: Natural surface

Best season: Year-round

Other trail users: Mountain bikers, trail runners, horseback riders

Canine compatibility: Leashed pets permitted

Land status: State park

Fees and permits: Small per-car fee; discounted for Maryland residents

Schedule: 9 a.m. to sunset daily

Maps: Trail maps available at ranger station

Trail contacts: Patapsco Valley State Park, 8020 Baltimore National Pike, Ellicott City, MD 21043; (410) 461-5005; dnr.state .md.us/publiclands/central/ patapsco.asp

Other: Fishing, picnic shelters, disc golf course, playgrounds, ball fields, basketball court

Special considerations: Swimming is allowed in the river except in the rapids area and the pool below the rapids due to dangerous currents.

Finding the trailhead: From I-695/I-70 west take I-70 to Marriottsville Road (exit 83). Go north on Marriottsville Road for 4.0 miles to the park entrance on the right. On your drive in, the trailhead is on your right just before you reach the entrance gate. **GPS:** N39 21.519′ / W76 53.402′

THE HIKE

The McKeldin area is the most northern portion of Patapsco State Park, and the Switchback Trail is one of the most popular trails in the McKeldin area. It follows the south branch of the Patapsco River down to the confluence of the north and south branches of the Patapsco. The trail then follows the north branch up a steep switchback to a ridge with an overlook of Liberty Dam. This hike combines the white-blazed Switchback Trail with the orange-blazed McKeldin Rapids Trail. Most of the trail follows the river.

You will pass the trailhead on your right just before you reach the entrance gate. A brown sign reads SWITCHBACK TRAIL. There are also signs in very close proximity for the trailheads of Tall Poplar Trail and Spring Glen Trail.

You may not be impressed with the scenery initially since you'll have to parallel Marriottsville Road for a bit, but don't let that discourage you. The sound of traffic soon fades and the scenery gets better and better along the way as

Follow the trail through a lowland floodplain, following the north branch of the Patapsco River.

you enter a lowland floodplain littered with skunk cabbage and wildflowers. The trail can get very muddy here. The purple and white trails share a path through this section, following the south branch of the river, with train tracks on the opposite side.

After leaving the purple trail, the white-blazed trail heads uphill and becomes much more narrow and rocky, passes a thick stand of bamboo, and soon crosses a park road. (The paved road downhill will take you to the rapids viewing area.) Here a restroom building is on your right. As you cross the park road, there are two trails blazed in white. The one on the left has a brown park sign labeling the Switchback Trail. Do not take that trail. This takes you into the upland area, where you'll find white blazes heading in many directions. Instead, take the path directly on the other side of the road that begins as a white gravel path. It leads downhill to reach the orange McKeldin Rapids Trail just steps later.

Here, leave the white trail behind for now and follow the orange trail. Once on the orange trail, at the bottom of the hill at the water's edge, follow the trail to the left (or take the orange trail right to extend your hike and pass a large rapids viewing area), immediately hopping over some large boulders and traversing one large, steep slanted rock. The trail described here follows the orange trail for less than 0.5 mile before again rejoining the white-blazed Switchback Trail. When you reach the intersection with the Switchback Trail, head right to continue to hug the water. White blazes head off to the left as well, again heading into a maze of trails in the upland. Stay along the river as it makes a bend and becomes more still. From here, the walk is easy and flat as it continues to follow the river's edge, but you may have to dodge some horse poo. If you hear the sound of repeated gunshots, don't be too concerned: They are coming from the nearby Associated Gun Club Trap Range. A train whistle occasionally breaks the silence as well.

Just when you thought you were getting off easy on this stroll-of-a-river walk, the trail becomes narrow and rocky before making a turn left and uphill on a steep "sucking wind" switchback climb, for which the trail was named. The trail dead-ends into a park road, and you will now follow this paved road past a restroom facility, several picnic pavilions, and basketball and volleyball courts. Definitely take a rest at the first pavilion you see on your right-hand side for a fantastic view of Liberty Dam. When you see a playground on the left, head toward it to pick up the sidewalk, which will take you back to the lot where you parked.

MILES AND DIRECTIONS

0.0   Just near the entrance station, see a brown park sign that labels the Switchback Trail and white blazes.

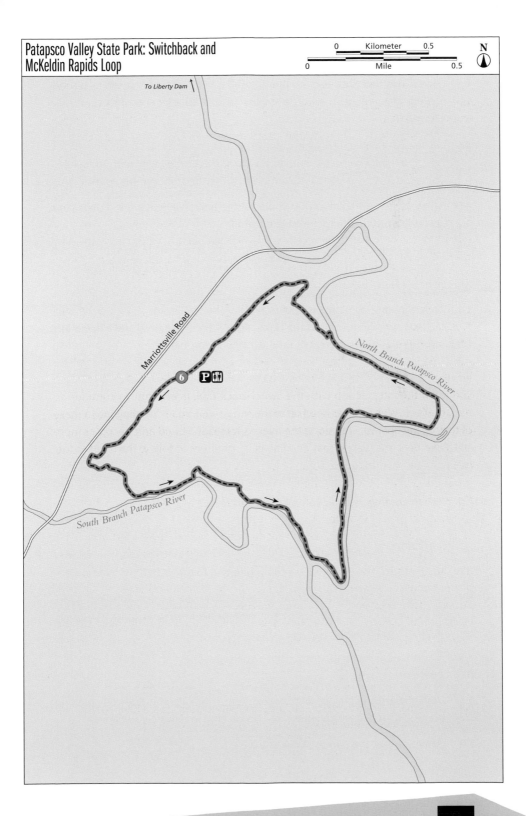

0.5 Parallel Marriottsville Road on your right side just before seeing a trail kiosk and a side trail that leads to Marriottsville Road. Follow the white-blazed trail as it curves to the left, and pass by the intersection with the blue-blazed trail.

0.6 Reach an intersection with the purple Tall Poplar Trail, which goes both left and right. The purple path to the right shares the route with the white-blazed trail. Continue to follow the white-blazed trail, heading right.

0.9 The purple trail splits off from the white trail and heads left. Follow the white-blazed trail to the right and uphill.

1.0 Cross a park road. Follow the white-blazed trail directly in front of you that starts as a white stone path. Do not take the white-blazed trail to the left labeled Switchback Trail.

1.1 Reach an intersection with the orange McKeldin Rapids (hikers-only) trail. Follow the orange trail to the right. When the orange trail splits both left and right at the river's edge, take the trail to the left.

1.5 The orange trail intersects with the white trail. Rejoin the white-blazed path, taking the trail to the right and hugging the water.

1.7 An intersection with a white-blazed trail comes in from your left. Stay straight, bearing slightly to the right to hug the river.

2.2 Reach a Y intersection with the red trail. Continue to follow the white blazes to the right. You will see red blazes too as the white and red share this path.

2.4 Reach another intersection with the red trail.

3.0 The trail comes to a Y split. Follow the white blazes left up a steep switchback climb.

3.2 At the top of the climb, follow the white trail to the right.

3.4 The trail ends at a park road with a restroom facility on the right and a row of picnic pavilions. The first picnic area pavilion on your right has a nice view of Liberty dam.

3.6 When the paved road splits, stay to the right. Off to the left are basketball courts.

3.8 Walk toward the playground on your left to pick up the sidewalk, passing some restrooms, which leads into the parking lot where you parked.

3.9 Arrive back at the parking lot and trailhead.

Patapsco Valley State Park: Orange Avalon Loop

Although the area tends to have swarms of mountain bikers, the scenery is certainly a must-see, beginning with cascading falls and ending with ridgeline views.

Start: Follow the blue-blaze trail on the opposite side of the road from the Swinging Bridge.

Distance: 6.7-mile loop

Hiking time: About 3.5 hours

Difficulty: Moderate

Trail surface: Natural surface

Best season: Year-round

Other trail users: Bikers, runners, equestrians; portions are hikers-only trails

Canine compatibility: Leashed dogs permitted

Land status: State park

Fees and permits: Small per-car fee, which is discounted for Maryland residents

Schedule: 9 a.m. to sunset daily

Maps: Trail maps available at ranger station

Trail contacts: Patapsco Valley State Park, 8020 Baltimore National Pike, Ellicott City, MD 21043; (410) 461-5005; dnr.state.md.us/publiclands/central/patapsco.asp

Other: Playground, restrooms, water fountain

Finding the trailhead: From the Beltway I-695, take Route 1 exit 12-A toward Elkridge. Follow Route 1 south about 3.0 miles to South Street. Turn right. The park entrance is on the left. Park in the lot across from the Swinging Bridge. **GPS:** N39 14.461' / W76 44.997'

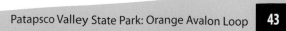

THE HIKE

While the scenery is spectacular on the trails of Patapsco, as a hiker you must be warned to watch your back! This area especially is extremely popular for mountain biking, and bikers sometimes come fast and furious around a corner on a narrow trail. Most trail enthusiasts are considerate users, but it never hurts to be on the lookout.

This hike combines the blue Cascade Falls Trail, the yellow Morning Choice Trail, the purple Rockburn Branch Trail, the white Valley View Trail, and the orange Ridge Trail to make a big loop around the Avalon and Orange Grove areas of Patapsco Valley State Park.

Begin your hike on the hikers-only path of the Cascade Falls Trail, just across from the Swinging Bridge, where you'll almost immediately be rewarded with a series of waterfalls tumbling over large rocks and a pool of water at the base. This is definitely a photo-op spot. As you cross the creek at the base of the falls and walk to the top of the incline, you will come to a T intersection labeled for the Ridge Trail (orange) on the left and the blue Cascade Falls Trail, which heads to the right. The hike continues on the blue trail to the right, but note that you will return to this same spot to complete the loop via the orange trail on the left.

This loop hike immediately rewards you with waterfall views on the Cascade Falls Trail portion of the loop.

As you parallel the creek of Cascade Falls, it's sure hard to beat this scenery of tumbling waterfalls and natural spills under a canopy of trees. You'll cross this creek several times via rocks and boardwalks.

The yellow Morning Choice Trail intersects with the red Old Track Loop in four spots and opens up to a wide-open meadow, following the perimeter near the Belmont Research Conference Center. Also on yellow, you'll pass by a rusted old tractor and the remains of an old house as it winds through mature trees and a stand of bamboos on a mostly level trail. Just keep a safe distance from the falling-down structure. There are more ruins that you can see through the trees, but this hike does not take you pass them.

You'll hang a right on the purple Rockburn Branch Trail, a wooded loop path that adds 1.2 miles to the overall circuit. It loops off of the yellow trail before connecting with the orange Ridge Trail. If you wish to shorten your trek, you can cut out the purple loop altogether and take a quick left on the purple trail in order to connect with the orange Ridge Trail and then the white Valley View Trail.

The Swinging Bridge, a highlight of the park, is directly across from the start of the trail. While you don't cross the bridge for the Orange Avalon Loop, you will cross it to reach the Grist Mill Trail and the Sawmill Buzzards Rock hike.

After completing the purple loop, hang a right to walk briefly on the orange trail in order to connect with the white Valley View Trail, a foot-traffic only path. But don't let your guard down—not everyone follows the hikers-only rule! Regardless, the white trail is a nice break from bike traffic. The white trail intersects with the orange Ridge Trail in several spots so you can't go wrong here. Once you connect with orange, walk the ridgeline past a few old foundations and a gazebo until again reaching the intersection with the blue trail at the site of the Cascade Falls. Although the section of Patapsco isn't ideal for solitude, it's certainly refreshing to see so many people out and active. Patapsco Valley is Maryland's oldest state park, with roughly 16,000 acres for recreating.

MILES AND DIRECTIONS

0.0 Begin the blue-blazed trail across from the Swinging Bridge at a brown sign that reads CASCADE FALLS TRAIL. Walk up the stairs.

0.1 At the top of the hill, make a left at the T intersection.

0.2 Reach a series of waterfalls. Cross over the creek at the base of the falls and reach a T intersection on the other side. The orange trail on the left will be our return trail. Go right on the blue trail.

0.7 The blue trail splits at a Y. Follow the left side over a wooden bridge. The right blue split loops you back to the start of Cascade Falls Trail.

0.9 Follow the blue trail to the left and up the hill. At the next split take a left to follow the yellow Morning Choice Trail uphill to the left.

1.1 The yellow trail crosses a gravel park road and continues on the opposite side.

1.3 Cross the park road (Norris Lane) and bear left. An unmarked trail goes off to the right. At a Y split with the red Old Track Loop, follow the yellow trail right. Yellow and red trails share a path for a few feet.

1.5 Come to another yellow Y split. The right side goes to Landing Road. Follow the trail to the left. Look for arrows painted on the tree.

1.6 Reach a meadow and soon after you'll see a rusted old tractor on the left.

1.9 Follow the yellow trail as it takes a sharp right downhill.

2.1 Following the meadow on the right, pass near the Belmont Research Conference Center.

Patapsco Valley State Park: Orange Avalon Loop

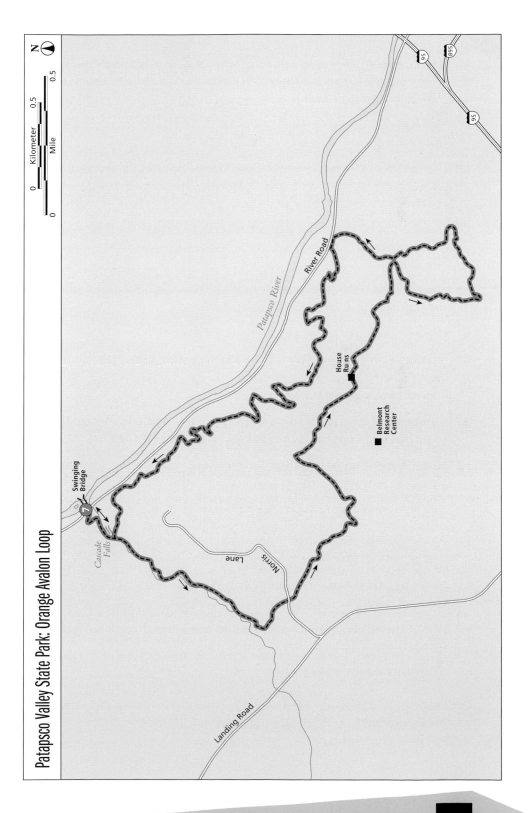

2.3 See the ruins of a home on your left, though it is not safe to explore. Just after the house ruins, see a connector shortcut trail on the left. Stay right, heading toward the meadow.

2.8 Reach a four-way intersection with the purple Rockburn Branch Trail. Take a right to make a full loop back to this spot.

3.9 Arrive back at the purple intersection. Make a right on the purple trail to reach the orange-blazed trail. Follow the orange trail straight and downhill to connect with the white trail.

4.1 Nearing the bottom of hill, see a trail kiosk and gravel road on right. Straight ahead is River Road. Follow the orange trail left and over a boardwalk bridge.

4.2 At a three-sided shelter on your left, head uphill and left to follow the white blazes, immediately followed by a steep climb.

4.4 The white trail splits left and right. Stay to the right.

4.9 Come to a T intersection. Follow the orange/white trail to the right.

5.1 See the last intersection with the white trail on the right. Follow the orange trail.

5.3 The orange trail splits. Head right and downhill. (Note that some of the orange blazes on this trail look more gold/yellow.)

5.6 Several old foundations can be seen on your right.

6.0 The trail crosses a wooden bridge followed by a square gazebo on your right.

6.2 The orange trail comes to a Y split. The right side leads to River Road. Follow the left split to soon reconnect with the Cascade Trail.

6.5 Arrive back at the blue Cascade Falls Trail intersection. Head right and downhill toward the waterfall to retrace your steps.

6.6 Don't forget to take the right downhill and down steps to reach Swinging Bridge and the parking lot at the bottom.

6.7 Arrive back at the trailhead.

Options: At the 2.8 mile 4-way intersection. You may choose to skip the purple Rockburn Branch Trail loop, which would shorten your hike by 1.2 miles.

Patapsco Valley State Park: Sawmill Buzzards Rock Loop

In the midst of a metropolitan area, this Patapsco Park trail crosses the Swinging Bridge across the Patapsco River and then follows an old railroad bed to connect to the Hilton-area trails of Sawmill and Buzzards Rocks, where you will enjoy a dramatic overlook from a rock outcropping.

Start: Begin your hike by crossing the Swinging Bridge

Distance: 3.0-mile lollipop loop

Hiking time: About 1.5 hours

Difficulty: Moderate

Trail surface: Natural surface with paved portion

Best season: Year-round

Other trail users: Bikers, runners, equestrians; portions are hikers-only trails

Canine compatibility: Leashed dogs permitted

Land status: State park

Fees and permits: Small per-car fee, which is discounted for Maryland residents

Schedule: 9 a.m. to sunset daily

Maps: Trail maps available for purchase at ranger station

Trail contacts: Patapsco Valley State Park, 8020 Baltimore National Pike, Ellicott City, MD 21043; (410) 461-5005; dnr.state .md.us/publiclands/central/ patapsco.asp

Other: Playground, restrooms, water fountains

Finding the trailhead: From the Beltway I-695, take Route 1 exit 12-A toward Elkridge. Follow Route 1 south about 3.0 miles to South Street. Turn right. The park entrance is on the left. Park in the lot across from the Swinging Bridge. **GPS:** N39 14.458′ / W76 44.992′

THE HIKE

Who doesn't love walking over a swinging bridge? Our inner child aches to jump and make it sway! Well, you get a swinging-bridge start on this combination hike of the Grist Mill Trail, the Sawmill Trail, and the Buzzards Rock Trail.

Cross the Swinging Bridge over the Patapsco River to the Hilton area of the park. Prior suspension footbridges at this location allowed residents of the Orange Grove mill town to cross the river to Baltimore County to work in the five-story Orange Grove Flower Mill of the C. A. Gambrill Manufacturing Company. This mill burned on May 1, 1905. Once you reach the other side of the bridge, you'll see the ruins of the mill site. Orange Grove flour was sold in white bags tied with string with labels that read "Patapsco Superlative Flour." Read the educational sign at this site to learn more about the flour-making process.

Hang a left on the wide, flat, paved Grist Mill Trail, which follows the river on the left and an old railroad bed on the right. The Grist Mill path follows the original rail bed of the Baltimore & Ohio Railroad. The river has sandy shorelines and a small rock beach. Small side trails cut away from the main path to get a

Leave the Grist Mill Trail to follow the red- and blue-blazed trail through the tunnel.

closer look at the river. The Patapsco is home to yellow perch, largemouth bass, smallmouth bass, brook trout, rainbow trout, walleye, bluegill, and brown trout.

Before you cross a small bridge, see a tunnel on your right as well as painted blue and red blazes. Make a right off the paved path and walk through the tunnel. As you pop out on the other side, cross the creek and head uphill to follow the red and yellow blazes and see signs for the Buzzards Rock Trail and the Sawmill Branch Trail. Then hop on the red-blazed Sawmill Branch Trail and follow the branch and its scenic pools and glades as you rock-hop through the water.

The red trail then meets up with the yellow Buzzards Rock Trail, a path along the ridgetop that will take you to the Ilchester Rocks overlook. The green side trail to Ilchester Rocks is a steep loop with views of rock cliffs above the water, overlooking the train tracks and train bridge. A sign reads CAUTION: TRAIL LEADS TO STEEP ROCK OVERLOOK, PROCEED AT YOUR OWN RISK. This is a popular spot for rock climbers.

After your visit to the rocks, continue on a long downhill path on the yellow Buzzards Rock Trail until you reach the flat path along the river at the bottom of the hill. From here, you will have views of Bloede Dam. Bloede Dam is believed to be the world's first submerged electrical generating plant that was housed underwater inside the shell of a dam. This unique hydroelectric dam is now listed

Rapids, chutes, and whirlpools make for a wild and wonderful hike.

on the National Register of Historic Places. Several small trail cuts lead to the river for better views of the dam. Be extremely careful as people have drowned playing in the water in this area.

Make a left on the flat river path, still blazed in yellow. It officially turns back into the Grist Mill Trail near the tunnel and trailhead for Sawmill Branch. Retrace your steps to the Swinging Bridge, enjoying the views and educational signs along the way.

MILES AND DIRECTIONS

0.0   Begin the hike at the Swinging Bridge and cross over the Patapsco River. On the opposite side make a left on the paved Grist Mill Trail.

0.4   Before crossing the next small bridge, make a right to walk through the tunnel following the blue and red blazes. On the opposite side of the tunnel, cross the creek, head uphill, and follow the red-blazed Sawmill Branch Trail to the right.

0.8   Cross under power lines.

0.9   At a split in the trail, the "foot traffic only" path has ended. Follow the red blazes uphill and to the left. (The Santee Branch Trail heads right, crossing a creek.)

1.3   Reach the intersection with yellow Buzzards Rock Trail. The left path will take you back to the tunnel on a "foot traffic only" trail. Head right to follow the yellow trail to Ilchester Rocks overlook.

1.5   Come to a parking lot, passing a trail kiosk and blue house on the right, and reenter the woods on other side of the lot.

1.8   Take the green-blazed side trail loop to the Ilchester Rocks overlook. Return to the yellow trail and make a right to continue on your loop.

2.1   Reach the flat, riverside Grist Mill Trail (officially still the yellow trail in this section) and make a left to return to the Swinging Bridge. First get a good look at Bloede Dam.

2.6   Read the educational sign about the first railroad before passing by the tunnel now on your left. Retrace your steps on the Grist Mill Trail.

3.0   After making a right to cross over the Swinging Bridge, arrive back at your car on the opposite side of the river.

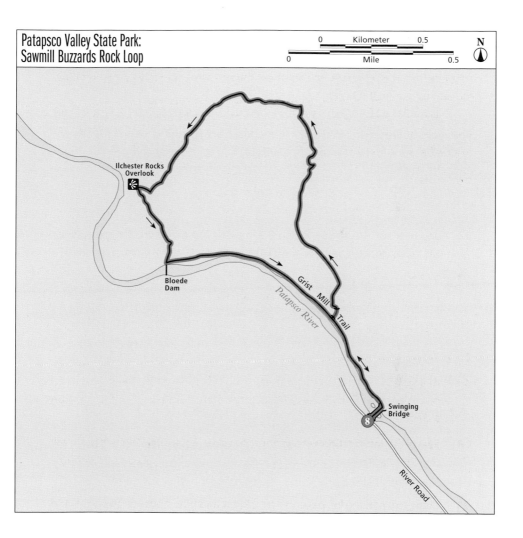

Patapsco Valley State Park:
Sawmill Buzzards Rock Loop

0   Kilometer   0.5
0   Mile   0.5

N

Ilchester Rocks
Overlook

Bloede
Dam

Patapsco River

Grist Mill Trail

8

Swinging
Bridge

River Road

What is the difference between a damselfly and a dragonfly? Damselflies hold their wings up when they land. Dragonflies hold their wings out.

Soldiers Delight: Serpentine Trail

For a hiking experience unlike any other in the area, hit the trails at Soldiers Delight Natural Environment Area and take in this endangered ecosystem along the Serpentine Trail. Learn why it was named "serpentine" and enjoy the unique geological features and rare habitat.

Start: With Deer Park Road facing your back, follow the trail left toward the visitor center.
Distance: 2.5-mile loop
Hiking time: About 1 hour
Difficulty: Moderate due to exposure
Trail surface: Natural surface and rock fragments
Best season: Year-round
Other trail users: Hikers only
Canine compatibility: Leashed dogs allowed
Land status: Natural Environment Area
Fees and permits: None
Schedule: Daily sunrise–sunset. Visitor center open Sat–Sun 11 a.m. to 3 p.m., Mon–Fri open by request—call ahead.

Maps: Trail map available at park headquarters and at dnr.state.md.us/publiclands/central/soldiers map.asp
Trail contacts: Soldiers Delight Natural Environment Area, 5100 Deer Park Rd., Owings Mills, MD 21117; (410) 922-3044; dnr.state.md.us/publiclands/central/soldiersdelight.asp
Other: The aviary is not open to the public, but there are enclosures that you may view if a staff member is available. Audio files available for download at dnr.maryland.gov/parkquest/soldiersdelight.asp for 10 stations throughout Soldiers Delight.
Special considerations: The hike is very open and exposed to the elements.

Finding the trailhead: From I-695 west, take exit I-795. Take exit 7B for Franklin Boulevard west. In 0.8 mile, make a right at Church Road. In 1.2 miles, turn left on Deer Park Road. In 1 mile, use the parking lot on your left on Deer Park Road, which has room for about twenty cars, not the lot adjacent to the visitor center. **GPS:** N39 24.857' / W76 50.136'

THE HIKE

Don't get spooked by the snakelike reference! "Serpentine" actually refers to a type of rock formation likely named for its olive, gray, and green scaly appearance, which you will find on the trail.

In total the Soldiers Delight Natural Environment Area encompasses 1,987 acres and nearly 6.0 miles of hiking trails. It was named an NEA in 1968. The visitor center will give a peek into the history of the area and this sensitive ecosystem with unique features. It's a protected area due to the serpentine soil and nearly forty endangered plant species, as well as insects, rocks, and minerals that can all be found here. The Serpentine Grassland and Oak Savanna Ecosystem were part of the Great Maryland Barrens, an expansive area bare of timber. These barrens once covered more than 100,000 acres in Maryland, but today cover fewer than 1,000 acres. Serpentine rock is high in magnesium, originating 500 million years ago as a result of magma from under the ocean. It's dissolved by rainfall.

The restoration of this sensitive area is ongoing and trail reroutes may be in place. Prescribed burns are taking place to help rehabilitate the area and restore it back to its natural serpentine habitat. Be sure to stay on the trail at all times. This Natural Environment Area protects the largest undeveloped mass of serpentine bedrock in the eastern United States.

The trailheads are well marked beginning on a wide barren path.

Soon after you start the trail from the very large parking lot, you'll pass by the visitor center, followed by an intersection with the Red Dog Lodge, once used as a hunting lodge and vacation getaway. The white-blazed path is well marked and easy to follow, but be warned that much of the trail is extremely open and exposed. Along the way the wide path flops between forest, wetlands, and grassland habitats. Walk on jagged rocks, look for tadpoles in the creek crossing, and rock-hop your way across a small stream. Be sure to look for the white wildflowers called serpentine chickweed, and read up on the area's ecosystem at the various educational signs.

Not only is Soldiers Delight a rare habitat, it also was the site of military encounters during the Civil War between Maryland Volunteers of the Confederate Army and the troops of the Union Army. An area rich in history but not in soil! Enjoy hiking in this unique habitat located practically in your backyard.

MILES AND DIRECTIONS

0.0 Begin the trail by heading left toward the visitor center.

0.2 Reach a burned field.

0.3 Reach the visitor center and another parking area.

0.4 At the intersection with trail to Red Dog Lodge, the trail continues to the right, but take a moment to visit the lodge, straight ahead.

0.5 Head under power lines.

0.7 Second eco information sign.

1.0 See a barbed wire fence on the left.

1.2 Take a quick hop across a small creek.

1.3 Rock-hop across a second stream.

1.8 Pass another eco information sign.

1.9 Cross power lines a second time.

2.3 Approach information sign about serpentine rock.

2.5 Arrive back at the parking area.

Options: Combine this hike with the Choate Mine Loop (Hike 10).

Soldiers Delight: Serpentine Trail

HIKE INFORMATION

Local attractions: Nearby Owings Mills Mall has shopping, dining, and a theater; 10300 Mill Run Circle; (410) 363-7000; owingsmillsmall.com. While it's not necessarily an attraction, you are just down the road from the Baltimore Ravens Training Camp, which might be worth a drive by; 1 Winning Dr., Owings Mills; (410) 701-4000.

Soldiers Delight: Choate Mine Loop

This trail ends at an old mine, but first experience extremely diverse ecosystems on this loop, which jumps between an exposed desertlike environment to a densely wooded forest. Combine this with the Serpentine Trail to lengthen your hike.

Start: Begin at the brown Choate Mine sign and a post marked #8.
Distance: 3.1-mile loop
Hiking time: About 2 hours
Difficulty: Moderate due to exposure
Trail surface: Natural surface and rock fragments
Best season: Year-round
Other trail users: Hikers only
Canine compatibility: Leashed dogs allowed
Land status: Natural Environmental Area
Fees and permits: None
Schedule: Daily sunrise–sunset. Visitor center open Sat–Sun 11 a.m. to 3 p.m., Mon–Fri by request—call ahead.

Maps: Trail map available at park headquarters and at dnr.state.md .us/publiclands/central/soldiers map.asp
Trail contacts: Soldiers Delight Natural Environment Area, 5100 Deer Park Rd., Owings Mills, MD 21117; (410) 922-3044; dnr.state .md.us/publiclands/central/ soldiersdelight.asp
Other: The aviary is not open to the public, but there are enclo- sures that you may view if a staff member is available. Audio files available for download at dnr .maryland.gov/parkquest/ soldiersdelight.asp for 10 stations throughout Soldiers Delight.

Finding the trailhead: From I-695 west, take exit I-795. Take exit 7B for Franklin Boulevard west. In 0.8 mile, make a right at Church Road. In 1.2 miles, turn left on Deer Park Road. In 1 mile, use the parking lot on your left on Deer Park Road, which has room for about twenty cars, not the lot adjacent to the visitor center. **GPS:** N39 24.874′ / W76 50.150′

THE HIKE

On the opposite side of the road from the Serpentine Trailhead is the trailhead for the red-blazed Choate Mine Trail. One of the trails on the more than 1,900 acres of serpentine barrens, the Choate Mine Loop has similar characteristics of the Serpentine Trail. However, what is interesting about this particular hike is not only the remains of the Choate chromite mine, but the abrupt transition from the exposed serpentine barrens to a shaded oak forest.

Maryland was the chrome-producing center of the world for a period of time. Chromite was first discovered and mined on Isaac Tyson Jr.'s farm, followed by the discovery of chromite in Soldiers Delight 1827.

There are three trails on the east side of Deer Park Road: the orange-blazed Red Run Trail, the red-blazed Choate Mine Trail, and the yellow-blazed Dolfield Trail. The Serpentine Trail is on the west side of the road.

Begin from the parking lot by crossing over Deer Park Road and walking to the left to pick up the trailhead for Choate Mine. There is a brown park sign labeling the trailhead. Several hundred feet down the road, near the opposite end of the parking lot, is another sign that reads CHOATE MINE. This is where you will end your hike.

The barren landscape along the trail makes you feel like you are somewhere far, far away.

The hike begins as your typical-looking trail with trees and shrubs lining a packed-dirt path. The trees get less dense until you reach an open field and the path turns into a rocky scree-like surface surrounded by managed burn areas, tall grass, and orange-clay-tan-colored rocks.

At an intersection with the orange-blazed trail, leave the red-blazed trail, which continues straight, and take a left, now following the orange-blazed trail. You'll cross a creek just before leaving the exposed area and entering a forest setting, followed by another creek crossing. Look for deer and listen for woodpeckers and frogs on the trails, which are lined with post oak, serpentine chickweed, Indian grass, and blue gentian.

The orange-blazed trail is well marked so ignore any side trails. Follow a stream on your left, and look for fish and minnows. You may be able to see an open field with hay barrels off to your left through the trees. Soon enough, the trail bears off to the right following newly painted orange blazes. On the left a very faint orange blaze can be seen as well as a not-so-well-worn path. This may confuse you for a brief moment but just keep following those well-marked blazes. You'll also pass by the Trout Transit Trail, heading off to the left.

The backyards of some homes come into view on the left as you make your way uphill, soon to intersect with the yellow Dolfield Trail. You'll reach this obvious intersection with the yellow-blazed trail at 1.3 miles, labeled with a professional brown sign directing the orange trail to the right and the yellow trail straight ahead and slightly left. The trail continues to meander through the forest, where you come upon a small, still, and stagnant pond on your right. Soon enough the trail again leads you to an open and exposed area with grassy meadows and a rocky footpath over layered rocks that look like scales.

Cross a couple more creeks until you reach a wide-open area, the junction of all three trails, with brown park signs labeling each. Here, we want to rejoin the Choate Mine Trail, though there are two Choate Mine paths to choose from. One heads straight and one heads to the left. The path straight ahead takes you back to the trail you started on, retracing your steps to the trailhead. You'll want to take the trail to the left in order to hike by the Choate Mine, certainly a highlight of this hike.

Arriving at the mine at around 3.0 miles, you'll see two markers labeling audio stop #7 and #8. The #7 marks a small but deep pit, the Choate Mine Air Shaft, named after the operator of the mine and holder of the lease from Isaac Tyson. The #8 mine has an old track that leads to a cave-like pit. Both are enclosed with a chain fence but you can still get good views of them from a safe distance. Leaving the mine, the trail bends to the right to continue on the red-blazed trail to exit again onto Deer Park Road.

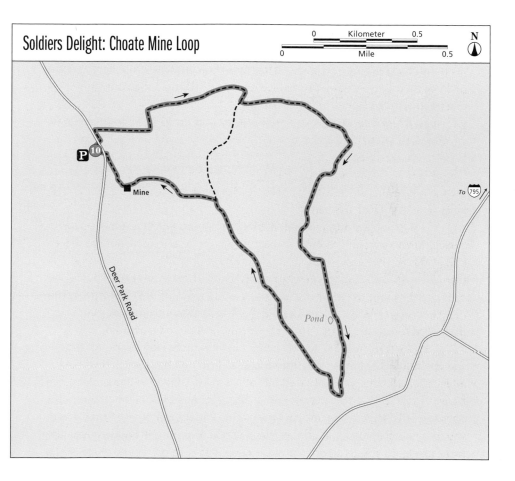

Soldiers Delight: Choate Mine Loop

MILES AND DIRECTIONS

0.0   Start at the trailhead, labeled with a large brown park sign and a red blaze on a wooden post marked with a #8.

0.3   Reach an open field where the trail turns to a rocky scree and gravel surface.

0.6   Arrive at the intersection with the orange (Red Run) trail. A post marks stop #6.

0.8   Leave the open field and enter a forest setting followed by a creek crossing.

0.9   Here you may be able to see a field on the left through the trees with hay barrels scattered about.

1.0 Follow the very well-marked orange blazes bearing right, heading uphill. Then pass the intersection with the Trout Transit Trail.

1.1 You may begin to see the backyards of some homes on the left side.

1.3 Reach the intersection with the yellow trail (Dolfield Trail) and take it straight ahead.

1.5 Leave the woods, walk a mowed grass path through an open field for 0.1 mile, and come to Dolfield Road. The trail continues on the opposite side of the road.

1.7 Look for a pond on your right.

1.8 A slightly worn path heads to the right (it's a shortcut to where the trail will eventually go).

1.9 A path heads to the left toward a road. Take the right split, almost making a U-turn, and walk the trail, which looks like a dried-up creek bed.

2.0 Cross a creek.

2.1 Briefly step back into a forested area.

2.2 Cross a creek.

2.6 Arrive at the junction of all three trails. Here, rejoin the red trail. The red trail has two paths to choose from. One heads straight and the other to the left. Take the left path, which will take you to the mine.

2.9 Arrive at the Choate Mine. Bear right to finish the loop.

3.1 Arrive back at the start after exiting the trail at a yellow gate on Deer Park Road. (Use the crosswalk to return to the parking lot.)

Options: Combine this hike with the Serpentine Trail (Hike 9).

HIKE INFORMATION

Local attractions: Nearby Owings Mills Mall has shopping, dining, and a theater; 10300 Mill Run Circle; (410) 363-7000; owingsmillsmall.com.

While it's not necessarily an attraction, you are just down the road from the Baltimore Ravens Training Camp, which might be worth a drive by; 1 Winning Dr., Owings Mills; (410) 701-4000.

Double Rock Park: Yellow Loop

This is a treat of a trail located right in town between Parkville and Overlea. Despite some unfortunate vandalism, the hiking trails in this park offer a much needed natural respite from the highways and urban sprawl that surround it. You'll encounter several scenic stream crossings on the forested loop hike with some unexpected ups and downs. Stemmers Run, flowing through crevices and over moss-covered rocks, is certainly a highlight.

Start: From the top parking lot, begin at a wide gravel path with a cable strung across the trailhead.

Distance: 1.6-mile loop

Hiking time: About 45 minutes

Difficulty: Easy

Trail surface: Natural surface with short paved portion

Best season: Year-round

Other trail users: Mountain bikers, trail runners

Canine compatibility: Leashed dogs permitted

Land status: Baltimore County Recreation and Parks

Fees and permits: None

Schedule: Sunrise–sunset daily

Maps: No maps available. You can view the map posted at the trail kiosk.

Trail contacts: Double Rock Park, 8211 Glen Rd., Parkville, MD 21234; (410) 887-5300; baltimorecountymd.gov/Agencies/recreation/countyparks/cntyparkslist.html

Finding the trailhead: From I-695, take exit 64 toward Towson. Take exit 32B to Belair Road / US 1 north. Turn left on Rossville Boulevard, which becomes Putty Hill Avenue. In 0.5 mile, turn left onto Wendell Avenue. Take the second right onto Hiss Avenue. Take the first left onto Glen Road. Park in the top lot as soon as you enter the park. **GPS:** N39 22.326' / W76 31.658'

THE HIKE

Double Rock Park is a little urban oasis with 100-plus acres in Baltimore County. The yellow-blazed loop trail begins on a wide gravel path with a cable strung across it, from the top parking lot, located just to the right of the trail kiosk with the trail map. You'll immediately be rewarded with the sight of scenic Stemmers Run, with its water flowing over and around large boulders. Cross over Stemmers Run and bear right. The path is well-marked . . . almost too well. Sometimes there are so many yellow blazes that they might confuse you for a moment.

Rock-hop your way across Stemmers Run.

The first portion of the mostly shaded hike follows a rusty chain-link fence while traversing several ups and downs through of mature forest of tall oaks and maple trees. Look for wildlife like woodpeckers, squirrels, fox, possums, owls, black rat snakes, and water-loving creatures like frogs, turtles, and fish. The gurgling sounds from the creek are pleasant, but they don't completely drown out the sound of the traffic. The ideal season for a hike here is fall, when there is much foliage to help block the backsides of houses and buildings that can be seen through the trees. Don't be surprised to see many downed trees in the area, though the trail itself is usually clear. Due to its location right in town, this beautiful trail does fall victim to some vandalism. Many trees are inscribed with the names of local teens, and a small amount of graffiti and some trash may be seen along the way. But don't let that discourage you from making a visit to the park.

The several water crossings are most certainly highlights of this hike. The flow of water seems to be extra playful, dancing over rocks, and especially scenic compared to the neighboring urban sprawl. The trail takes you through a gazebo-like pavilion, also covered with graffiti art, before passing behind a red building that houses bathrooms (but they are locked), then bearing left to stay in the woods. There are a couple sharp turns but keep following the yellow blazes to complete your loop.

Toward the end you'll reach the Rich Pavilion and the Alexia Pavilion (with restrooms). The pavilion area has about twenty-five picnic tables with a parking area. There is much more activity here in summer, with groups hosting parties and occupying the pavilions. Just past the pavilions are ball fields. At this point the yellow blazes disappear and you will follow the paved road up and to the right, hugging the ball fields, which are on your left. Portable toilets and a bathroom building are located at the ball fields. Pass yet another playground and pavilion. At this point you can see the lot where you parked up above.

Managed by the Baltimore County Department of Recreation and Parks, the park was purchased by the Lions Club of Parkville in 1945, dedicated to the people of the community in 1947, and deeded to Baltimore County Department of Recreation in 1952.

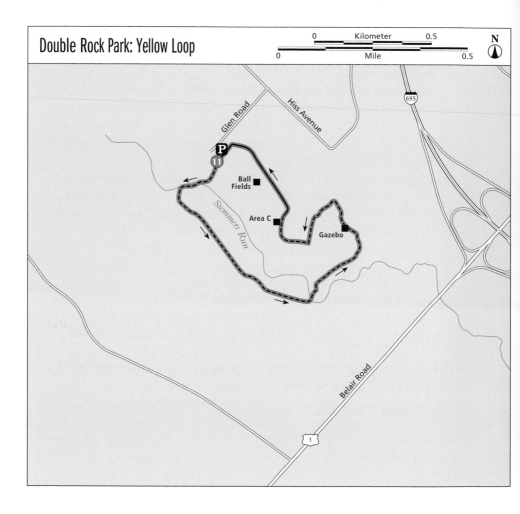

Double Rock Park: Yellow Loop

Ball
Fields

Area C

Gazebo

Stemmers Run

Glen Road

Hiss Avenue

Belair Road

🌰 **Green Tip:**
Even if it says it's biodegradable, don't put soap into streams or lakes. If you need to use soap, bring the water to you.

0.0 Begin the trail at the top parking lot on a wide gravel path with a cable strung across. In a few steps cross Stemmers Run.

0.1 The trail bears to the left.

0.5 The trail bears to the right.

0.7 Cross the creek.

0.9 Reach a gazebo. Then take a quick right, then left, to find yourself behind a red building at the edge of a field that houses restrooms (they are locked).

1.1 The trail takes a sharp turn right and downhill to cross Stemmers Run Creek, followed by an immediate short uphill climb.

1.2 Reach the Rich Pavilion and picnic area. The yellow blazes disappear here.

1.3 Area C is on your left with the Alexia Pavilion and restrooms. Follow the paved road, hugging the ball fields on your left.

1.5 Notice another playground and the Rock Pavilion on your left. The lot where you parked comes into sight up ahead.

1.6 Arrive back at the trailhead and parking lot.

12 Oregon Ridge: Loggers Red and Ivy Hill / S. James Campbell Yellow Loop

This loop hike is a combination of two of the park's trails on the 1,043 acres of land that was once an active iron-ore- and marble-mining operation during the mid-nineteenth century. Pass by a nature center, swimming lake and beach, pond, and overlooks. Hop your way across several stream crossings and walk a few ups and downs through a second-growth forest on old logging roads.

Start: Begin at the bridge next to the nature center.
Distance: 4.1-mile loop
Hiking time: About 2 hours
Difficulty: Moderate
Trail surface: Natural surface
Best season: Year-round
Other trail users: Hikers only
Canine compatibility: Leashed dogs permitted on trails (not permitted at the beach and concession area)
Land status: Baltimore County Park
Fees and permits: None
Schedule: Park grounds open daily dawn–dusk; nature center open 9 a.m. to 5 p.m. Tues–Sun, closed Mon
Maps: Trail map available at oregonridgenaturecenter.org/ trailmap.html as well in the nature center and boxes outside the nature center
Trail contacts: Oregon Ridge Nature Center, 13555 Beaver Dam Rd., Cockeysville, MD; (410) 887-1815 for the nature center, (410) 887-1818 for the office, (410) 887-1817 for the beach; oregonridge naturecenter.org
Other: Nature center with history, wildlife, and natural environment exhibits, and gift shop. Swimming allowed at Oregon Ridge Beach Memorial Day through Labor Day; fee for ages 12 and up. Educational tours, programs, and festivals.
Special considerations: Copperhead snakes inhabit the park.

Finding the trailhead: Coming from I-83, take Shawan Road west, then make a left turn on Beaver Dam Road at the Oregon Grill. Just past the Oregon Grill, you will see a small red hut with signs in front of it directing you to the various areas of the park. Make a right following the arrow to the nature center. The trail begins at the bridge, to the left of the nature center. **GPS:** N39 29.620' / W76 41.518'

THE HIKE

A little slice of heaven in Baltimore County! The land where the Oregon Ridge Nature Center now sits was an iron-ore- and marble-mining operation during the mid-nineteenth century. The forest that stood here during that time was clear-cut and sold for firewood. What you see now is a second-growth forest. The trails you see today were once logging roads used to drag out the trees after being cut. The nature center was built in 1963 and houses displays on the history, wildlife, and environment of the park. It also has a library and gift shop. Oregon Ridge was also a downhill-ski area in the 1960s.

In total the Cockeysville park has 1,043 acres for recreation. This hike combines the Loggers Red Trail with the Ivy Hill Yellow / S. James Campbell Yellow Trail to give you a good taste of what the Oregon Ridge trails have to offer. To the left of the nature center, begin your hike by heading over the bridge, where you'll be greeted by a sign that says WELCOME TO THE EASTERN DECIDUOUS FOREST. Follow the well-marked red-blazed trail to the right to hike this trail counterclockwise. But take a quick look to the left as this will be where you'll end the loop. Along the way, pass educational signs about chestnut trees and forest sustainability. Plants

Take in views of the valley at this scenic overlook along the Loggers Red Trail.

and flowers to look for include spicebush, jewelweed, chicory, and goldenrod, and little critters like wood frogs, monarch butterflies, and spring peepers can also be found here.

Parallel a scenic creek for a good ways in the beginning of the hike as you make your way gradually uphill. At the top of the hill, you'll reach an intersection with the Ridge Tan Trail, which heads to the left, passing a gazebo. The Tan Trail will take you back to the start of the Red Trail. Instead, head to the right to continue to enjoy the spectacular forest that Oregon Ridge has to offer.

Continuing on, the trail follows a gas-line cut before taking a sharp left back into the forest. (You will cross a gas-line cut four times on this hike.) After making this sharp left, take the very first trail you see that heads to the right. This is the Short Cut Trail, blazed in white, which will lead you to the Ivy Hill Yellow Trail. If you do miss it, you'll come to another intersection with the Ivy Hill Trail soon after.

On the Ivy Hill Trail, at 1.8 miles, a scenic creek on your left feeds Balsam Run, a nice water flow on your right. The yellow trail bears to the right here, but first follow the feeder creek uphill to a scenic pond. As you continue on the yellow trail, you have four water crossings over Balsam Run. At least one or two of these crossings could leave you with wet feet, so wear waterproof shoes.

After a third gas-line crossing, the yellow trail, now named the S. James Campbell Trail, again intersects with the Loggers Red Trail. Bear right to follow the red blazes of the Loggers Red Trail and arrive at the scenic overlook in just 0.1 mile. The view from this former ski slope overlooks Hunt Valley.

In 0.4 mile, after the overlook, the trail has one short section that could trick you up. At a T intersection look for a red blaze and make a left. (At the time of this writing, the tree that has a directional sign has fallen over.) After that left, immediately make another left to walk up the gas line, followed by an immediate right to leave the gas line and briefly dip into a wooded section before reaching an open area with a playground and picnic area. Frog Pond is on your right just before you cut through the picnic area and volleyball courts.

The beach and lake, a former quarry, are now on your left. Enjoy some summer fun and take a swim, but be sure to pay the fee. The red blazes disappear in this short section as you walk between the beach and the concession building and bathhouse. The trail exits the lake area out the gate at the far side of the concession building. Note that the gate is often locked in season. You may need to exit through the bath and concessions building. On the other side you'll see the parking area. You can head to your car from here or skirt the perimeter of the parking lot following the wooded red trail to complete the loop and arrive back at the nature center.

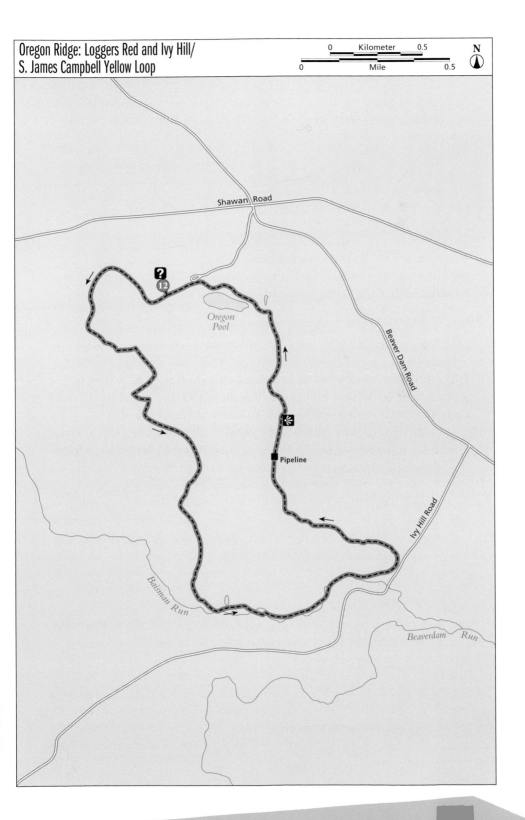

0   Kilometer   0.5

0   Mile   0.5

N

Shawan Road

12

Oregon
Pool

Beaver Dam Road

Pipeline

Ivy Hill Road

Baisman Run

Beaverdam Run

Oregon Ridge

MILES AND DIRECTIONS

0.0   Start the trail at the bridge to the left of the nature center. On the other side of the bridge, red blazes go left and right. Hang a right.

0.1   At a Y intersection follow the sign that reads LOGGER TRAIL with a red arrow pointing to the right and a NATURE TRAIL sign also pointing to the right. The trail heading left is the Ridge Tan Trail.

0.2   A path to the right leads to the accessible trail. Stay straight.

0.5   Pass an unmarked trail on your right with a map return box. Stay straight, heading uphill.

0.7   Reach the top of the hill and a T intersection with the Tan Ridge Trail that heads left. Hang a right to continue on the red trail.

0.8   Make a right following the red blazes down a cleared path, a gas-line cut.

0.9   Leave the gas-line path and take a sharp left into the woods to follow the red blazes.

1.0   Reach the white-blazed shortcut trail on the right. The red trail continues straight. Take the shortcut trail, which leads to the Ivy Hill Trail. This is the first right-hand trail intersection you come to after leaving the gas line.

1.2   Arrive at the intersection with the yellow Ivy Hill Trail, which heads both left and right. Make a right on the Ivy Hill Trail.

1.5   Cross over another gas-line cut and continue the yellow trail on the opposite side.

1.8   Notice a wooden bridge on your right that crosses Balsam Run. Stay straight—do not cross this wooden bridge.

1.9   Reach a split in the trail. The yellow trail goes to the right, but first head left to reach a pond.

2.0   At a Y split, a gravel trail heads uphill to the right. Bear left to follow the S. James Campbell Trail, still blazed in yellow, and cross Balsam Run.

2.3   A wooden bench here displays the message "Let us then be up and doing with a heart for any fate, still achieving still pursuing learn to labor and to wait." Cross a creek to continue on the yellow trail.

3.1   Cross a gas line for the third time.

3.2 An arrow points to the left for the Virginia Pine Green Trail. Bear right to again follow the Loggers Red Trail and the red blazes.

3.3 Walk an unmarked path on the right to the overlook.

3.7 Come to a T intersection. Make a left and look carefully for a red blaze. Immediately after that left, take another left and walk uphill on a gas-line cut. After a few feet, make a sharp right into woods to follow red blazes past Frog Pond.

3.8 Cut through the playground and picnic area. Walk between the beach (left) and concessions/bathhouses (right). In season, exit through the concession area, or continue past the concession stand and exit through a door in the fence on the other side of the concession building. A red blaze is painted on the gate fence.

4.0 After exiting through the gate, the parking area is straight ahead. Hug the parking lot on your right. At a fork in the trail, the Laurel Blue Trail heads left. Bear right to continue on the red trail. Make a right and retrace your steps across the bridge.

4.1 Arrive back at the nature center and the start of your hike.

Options: Hike only the red loop, or combine other trails to make your own loop.

HIKE INFORMATION

Local attractions: Nearby Hunt Valley Towne Center off of Shawan Road has shops, restaurants, a grocery store, and a movie theater; shophuntvalley.com.
Good eats: The Oregon Grille, a fine-dining restaurant, 1201 Shawan Rd., Cockeysville; (410) 771-0505; theoregongrille.com

Loch Raven Reservoir: Merryman Trail

An unmarked out-and-back trail hugs the edge of the Loch Raven Reservoir for a majority of this trip. Highlights include old stone foundations, vast reservoir views, and a picturesque creek that pours over mossy boulders as it makes its way to the reservoir.

Start: Begin in the middle of the grassy area at a metal post and a tree with an orange blaze.
Distance: 5.3 miles out and back
Hiking time: About 2.5 hours
Difficulty: Moderate
Trail surface: Natural surface
Best season: Year-round
Other trail users: Trail runners
Canine compatibility: Leashed dogs permitted
Land status: Watershed Management Area

Fees and permits: None
Schedule: Sunrise–sunset daily
Maps: No trail maps available for the Loch Raven Reservoir Water Quality Management Area
Trail contacts: City of Baltimore Department of Public Works, Reservoir Natural Resources Section, 5685 Oakland Rd., Eldersburg, MD 21784; (410) 795-6151; baltimore city.gov

Finding the trailhead: Take I-695 to exit 27, Dulaney Valley Road north. In 3.5 miles the parking area is on the left just before the bridge over Loch Raven Reservoir. The trail begins in the center of the grassy area in front of the parking lot on a narrow path. A metal post in the ground and orange blaze on a tree mark the spot. There is also a sign that says No Trail with a circle and line, depicting no biking or equestrian use, nailed to the tree. **GPS:** N39 27.772' / W76 35.188'

THE HIKE

Eat, hike, and be merry on Loch Raven Reservoir's Merryman Trail! There are certainly many features to be happy about on this trail, which hugs the reservoir for most of the distance. From the parking lot, there is a trail on the far right and off to the left, but cut straight through the middle of the open grassy area in front of the parking lot to begin your hike. You might have to look for it since the area can get a bit overgrown. Some of the highlights include remains of old foundations, vast reservoir views, scenic creeks, and a resident eagle.

This trail is very popular and you'll see it reviewed in several other hiking guidebooks. However, it is often suggested as a hike from Dulaney Valley Road with the end point being Warren Road. Problem is, the last 1-mile stretch of this path takes hikers through private property, which is simply not allowed. There are tree stands, which indicate the likelihood of owners hunting on their property. Therefore, it also a danger to hikers to hike this path all the way to Warren Road. But still, this trail is not to be missed. Instead, this hike description ends your journey around Merryman Point. You get all the same beauty without a killer climb near Warren Road. It's a win-win!

In addition to reservoir views, hikers will see several foundation remains along the trail.

Speaking of beauty, around 0.9 mile start looking for an eagle's nest high above and off to the right of the trail. Locals refers to the bird as "the eagle," meaning it's a resident eagle. So here's hoping the bird likes this spot so we can enjoy seeing it again and again.

In another 0.2 mile the trail crosses a picture-perfect stream with moss-covered boulders and stepped rocks that create little falls and spills as it makes its way downhill into the reservoir. On the other side of this stream, take a hard right to follow a trail next to the creek and downstream where you'll see it pour into Loch Raven Reservoir. At that confluence is a small sandy and rocky beach and a large rock formation. Both are great spots to have a snack and enjoy the five-star view. From here, the trail hugs the reservoir on your right. Ignore any small side trails, likely made by bikes, that shoot off from the main path.

The trail passes by some old foundations including an old stone wall that is now covered in bright graffiti. You'll have to stay on the lookout for all of these features as they are sometimes overgrown with vegetation. Look right for open views of the Dulaney Valley Road bridge over the reservoir in the distance. You'll get a few fantastic views looking back at the reservoir bridge. Fall colors really make this view a sight to see!

Try to spot more old foundations on the right side of the trail, including the remains of three sides of a structure and a fireplace in the middle. This is Merryman Point, for which the trail got its name, and once you arrive, you'll know your journey is nearing it's end. You can't help but wonder what it was like here back in the day. Today this waterfront view would be prime real estate.

After crossing a second open field while paralleling the power lines, reach a small cove where you can watch the logs and driftwood, backwash from the eddies, bob up and down along the shore. From here, turn around and retrace your steps.

MILES AND DIRECTIONS

0.0 Take the narrow path that starts in the center of the field from the parking lot. A metal post in the ground and an orange blaze on the tree mark the spot.

0.1 At the first split, the trail to the right heads to the water and the trail to the left is the high road. Both of these trails meet back up but this hike describes the route following the high road to the left.

0.2 The trail that headed to the water meets back up with the high road here.

0.3 The trail splits. Follow the trail to the right. A very faint orange arrow painted on a tree points you to the right.

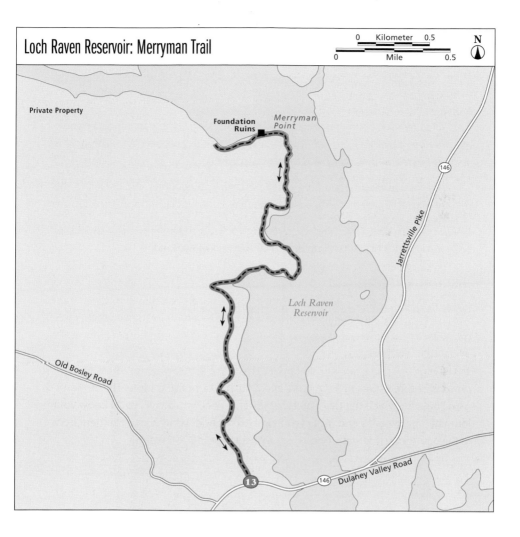

0.5 Take two rock-hops across a feeder creek.

0.9 Come to an intersection with a wide trail that heads both left and right, as well as a trail directly across. Take a right on the wider well-worn trail. Take note of this spot as it may be easy to miss on your return trip. A few steps after taking a right, look to the right of the trail for an eagle's nest.

1.0 Cross a wide creek with mossy boulders. On the other side make a sharp right to follow the creek downstream.

1.2 See a rock outcropping on your left where the creek flows into the reservoir.

1.3 A short side trail to the left leads to an old foundation followed by an old stone wall covered in graffiti.

1.5 Reach a scenic point with nice views behind you of the bridge.

2.3 Cross under power lines that extend from one side of the reservoir to the other.

2.6 Pass by foundation remains with three sides and a fireplace in the middle before paralleling power lines for a few steps in an open field. This area is Merryman Point, for which the trail is named.

2.7 Walk through an open field, paralleling the power lines. Dip back into the woods to enjoy a cove filled with bobbing driftwood. Retrace your steps to the start.

5.3 Arrive back at the parking area on Dulaney Valley Road.

HIKE INFORMATION

Good eats: The Grille at Peerce's, 12460 Dulaney Valley Rd., Phoenix; (410) 252-7111; thegrilleatpeerces.com

A resident bald eagle watches hikers from its perch high above the reservoir.

Loch Raven Reservoir: Jessops Circuit with Spur

A short and sweet loop hike on a ridgeline affords you an overlook view of the reservoir as well as views of a peaceful lowland cove of the Loch Raven Reservoir.

Start: Begin at 2 wooden posts with a cable strung across with a sign that reads "814 Paper Mill Rd."
Distance: 2.2-mile lollipop loop
Hiking time: About 1 hour
Difficulty: Moderate
Trail surface: Natural surface
Best season: Year-round
Other trail users: Trail runners
Canine compatibility: Leashed dogs permitted
Land status: Watershed Management Area

Fees and permits: None
Schedule: Sunrise–sunset daily
Maps: No trail maps available for the Loch Raven Reservoir Water Quality Management Area
Trail contacts: City of Baltimore Department of Public Works, Reservoir Natural Resources Section, 5685 Oakland Rd., Eldersburg, MD 21784; (410) 795-6151; baltimorecity.gov

Finding the trailhead: Take York Road (Route 45) to Cockeysville (exit 18 off I-83). Turn right (east) on Ashland Road. Bear left onto Paper Mill Road. Go less than 0.5 mile. Look for the parking lot on your left. Park in the NCR parking lot (fifty cars) on the left side of the road if you are heading east on Paper Mill Road. The trailhead is east of the NCR parking lot by about 100 yards on the opposite side of the road from the parking lot. Look for two wooden posts with a wire cable strung across and a sign that reads "814 Paper Mill Rd." **GPS:** N39 30.074' / W76 38.001'

THE HIKE

Just steps away from the popular Torrey C. Brown Trail (formerly the NCR) is a little-known loop hike through a forest of pine trees and hardwoods in the Loch Raven watershed. Little-known does *not* mean little to love. There is something about this place that is calm and peaceful even though you aren't far from Paper Mill Road on the first half of the loop. From ridgeline views to wetlands and wildlife, this hike offers a variety of natural features in a short distance.

You'll need to park in the Torrey C. Brown (NCR) parking lot on Paper Mill, but cross over Paper Mill and walk east on the road about 100 yards to reach the trailhead. A sign on the shoulder says ENTERING WATERSHED PROPERTY. There is a gravel pull-off at the site of the trailhead but there is also a No Parking sign there. Take great caution walking the grassy shoulder of Paper Mill Road.

The hike begins on a very short paved portion of what looks like a fire road until it becomes a natural surface just steps later. About 30 feet after it turns into a dirt path, you'll notice a narrow trail that heads to the right and a wider trail heading gradually uphill to the left. The narrow path is a spur trail to a wetland

A peaceful cove awaits you at the end of a spur trail along the Jessops Circuit loop trail.

area. We'll take this spur at the very end of the hike. But for now head uphill to the left. At a second Y split, the trail continues to bear left and uphill. Do not take the trail to the right at this time as this will be our return loop. You'll arrive back at this same spot to complete the loop.

The trail parallels Paper Mill Road in the distance off to your left as you make your way uphill on a wide wooded path. As you near the top of the climb, a very short path on your left leads to a rock outcropping, with a dramatic view overlooking the bridge and reservoir below. Continue on the ridgeline loop trail, where you will see yet another trail off to the left. This one leads downhill to get a closer view of the water.

Several other trails head off to the right, crisscrossing back and forth over the top of the hill, as well as a few more trails that shoot off to the left and downhill. Continue to follow the obvious wide path around the ridgetop to complete the loop.

The trail consists of a few gradual ups and downs, but a significant portion is flat and level. Once you complete the loop and return to the same spot where the loop began, you'll now head to the left toward the trail split that takes you to the wetland spur trail that we noted at the very start of the hike. From this split, you can see Paper Mill Road off to the right, and you may choose to end your hike here. But if you have the time to spare, definitely take the spur trail to the left for a quick out-and-back to a small cove of Loch Raven Reservoir. The 0.3-mile spur trail is a great spot to see deer and wildflowers, ferns, and dogwoods. Walk the path until the trail deadends, ignoring a few trails that head off to the right. Once you reach the marshy cove, enjoy the quiet and solitude, watch ducks slice the calm water, and listen to their calls. Once you've had your fill, retrace your steps.

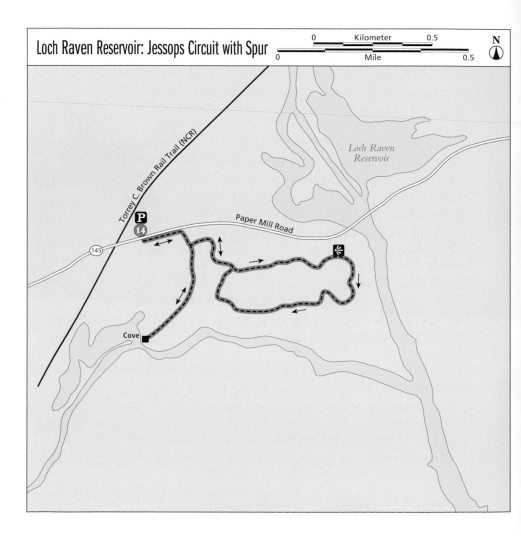

Loch Raven Reservoir: Jessops Circuit with Spur

Loch Raven Reservoir

Torrey C. Brown Rail Trail (NCR)

Paper Mill Road

145

Cove

MILES AND DIRECTIONS

0.0 Begin your hike from the parking lot for the Torrey C. Brown (NCR) Trail.

0.1 After walking east from the parking lot on the opposite side of Paper Mill Road, begin your hike on a fire road marked by two wood posts and a cable strung across. It begins as a paved path for a few feet before turning to a natural surface.

0.2 Immediately come to a split. A narrow path heads off to the right and a wider path heads slightly uphill to the left. Take note of the path to the right as we will walk this path at the end of the hike, but first take the trail to the left.

0.4 Come to another Y split. Keep to the left, but do not take the trail on the right as this will be your return loop.

0.6 A short path to the left leads to a rock formation and scenic overlook of the reservoir and bridge below.

0.8 Intersect with a trail on the left, which leads downhill to a water view.

1.3 Close the loop at this point, returning to the same intersection you were at at 0.4 mile. Now head left to retrace your steps.

1.5 When you again arrive at the first split, take the trail left this time.

1.8 Reach the end of this spur trail at a water cove. Retrace your steps to the start.

2.1 Make a left to walk Paper Mill Road back to the parking lot.

2.2 Arrive back at the parking lot and your car.

HIKE INFORMATION

Local attractions: Nearby Hunt Valley Towne Center off of Shawan Road has shops, restaurants, a grocery store, and a movie theater; shophuntvalley.com.

Torrey C. Brown Rail Trail (NCR): Paper Mill to Monkton

Hike a popular section of this 20-mile crushed-stone abandoned railroad that starts in Cockeysville and ends just past the Pennsylvania line in New Freedom. Mostly covered by tree canopy, the trail parallels the Gunpowder River and offers recreational, historical, and educational features.

Start: Begin at the far back corner of the parking lot off of Paper Mill Road near a trail kiosk.

Distance: 6.8 miles one way

Hiking time: About 2.5 hours

Difficulty: Moderate due to distance

Trail surface: Crushed stone

Best season: Year-round

Other trail users: Runners, bikers, horseback riders

Canine compatibility: Leashed dogs permitted

Land status: State park

Fees and permits: None

Schedule: Sunrise–sunset daily. The Monkton Station is open Wed–Sun from Memorial Day to Labor Day and weekends in the spring and fall.

Maps: Trail map available at dnr .state.md.us/greenways/ncrt_trail .html. Maps can be purchased online at http://shopdnr.com/ centraltrailguides.aspx.

Trail contacts: Gunpowder Falls State Park, 2813 Jerusalem Rd., Kingsville, MD; (410) 592-2897; dnr.state.md.us/publiclands/ central/tcb.asp

Other: Tubing, fishing

Special considerations: The parking lots fill up fast on weekends and holidays.

Finding the trailhead: Directions to Monkton parking: Take I-695 to I-83 north. Take I-83 north to exit 27, MD 137 / Mt. Carmel Road. Turn right onto Mt. Carmel Road. In 0.4 mile turn right at the traffic light onto MD 45 / York Road. Make an immediate left at the next light onto MD 138 / Monkton Road. Proceed 2.9 miles to the trail crossing and the parking lot on the left. The Monkton parking lot is one of the most popular on the trail. On weekends between Memorial Day and Labor Day, part of the lot is closed for the safety of bikers; street parking is limited and often fills early in the morning.

Directions to Paper Mill parking: Take York Road (Route 45) to Cockeysville (exit 18 off I-83). Turn right (east) on Ashland Road. Bear left onto Paper Mill Road. Go less than 0.5 mile and look for the parking lot on your left. Pick up the trail at the back corner of the parking lot. **GPS:** N39 30.106' / W76 38.023'

THE HIKE

This rail trail is typically referred to as the NCR or the Northern Central Railway Trail, as it was named prior to the dedication to Torrey C. Brown. Dr. Brown, the third secretary of the Maryland Department of Natural Resources, had the vision for this multirecreational trail, which was constructed in 1984.

The Northern Central Railway was built in 1832 and operated until 1872. It transported goods like flour, paper, milk, and coal from the small rural towns all the way up to York, linking them to Baltimore city. Abraham Lincoln rode this rail on his way to give the Gettysburg Address, and his body was delivered to Illinois via the NCR after his assassination.

The wide, flat, crushed-stone path is paradise for outdoor enthusiasts. In peak weather don't be surprised to see crowds of people at the parking area unloading bikes, strapping on water belts, lacing up their hiking shoes, and rolling inner tubes down the road to get in on a piece of outdoor action. Under a shaded canopy of tall oaks, maples, and birch trees, hike alongside the Gunpowder Falls. On a hot day visitors splash in swimming holes and tubers float downstream. This trail has rewards around every corner, from bridges and scenic overlooks to ruins

Signs along the trail educate hikers about historical happenings.

and rapids. The wildlife seems to like it here as well. It's not uncommon for a rabbit to hop across the trail, while pileated woodpeckers sound out their rhythmic song, and an eagle perches on a tree limb, standing tall and proud.

The section closest to Baltimore begins in Cockeysville, just a half mile shy of the southernmost terminus. Parking at that terminus has room for only ten cars so it's best to begin from the larger parking lot on Paper Mill Road. Head north on a 10-foot-wide abandoned rail bed to find wildflowers, rock outcroppings, benches, picnic tables, the occasional educational sign, and yes, even portable toilets. At half a mile pass the remains of a lime kiln built into the hillside, likely constructed in the late 1800s. The educational sign details the purpose of the lime and how it was extracted. In less than a mile, you'll cross the Big Gunpowder River and parallel it for scenic water views.

One of several road crossings along this stretch is the Sparks Road crossing, with a parking lot and the Sparks Bank Nature Center on your right. The center once featured interpretive displays and held family activities. It was closed in 2011 due to storm damage, and volunteers are currently working to restore it. For more information on Sparks Bank Nature Center, call (410) 592-2897. Along the way, look for the white posts marked with a W. In the days of railroad operation, these whistle stops instructed engineers to sound their horns or whistles as they approached a crossing. You may also see white posts with painted black numbers. These mile markers indicated the distance to the next stop or station.

This section hike ends in Monkton, the site of the restored Monkton Station, a historic train station now converted to a museum with exhibits about animals, tools, and the history of the railroad. It also houses a gift shop, ranger station, water fountains, flush toilets, and educational displays.

At the end of your long hike, reward yourself with a sandwich and ice cream from the carryout restaurant and cafe located at the parking area. Here you can rent bikes, tubes, and kayaks.

The Torrey C. Brown Trail is part of the larger Grand History Trail route, which connects the historic cities of Annapolis, Baltimore, Frederick, Gettysburg, Washington, and York. It is also part of the East Coast Greenway, which extends from Florida to Maine.

MILES AND DIRECTIONS

0.0   On the far end, back side of the parking lot, take the short path that leads to the main trail.

0.5   Come to an educational sign on the left about the lime kiln.

0.6   Cross over the river for the first time on a bridge with metal fencing. Two portable toilets are located here.

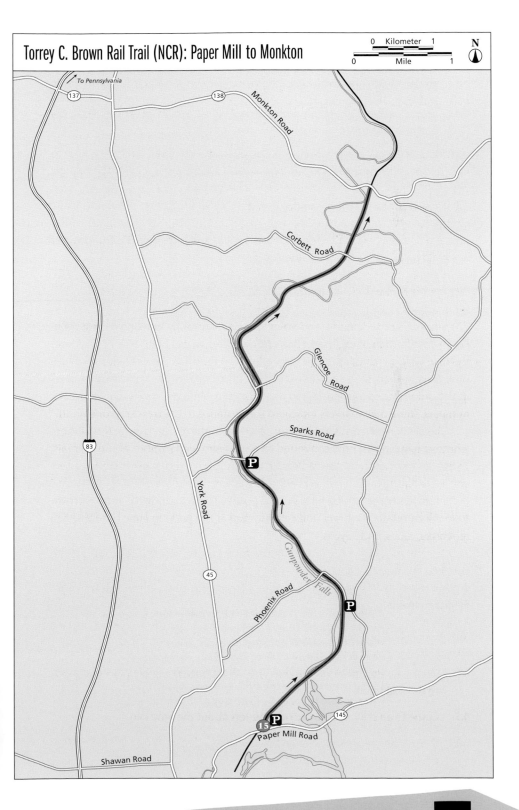

To Pennsylvania

137

138

Monkton Road

Corbett Road

Glencoe Road

Sparks Road

83

York Road

45

Gunpowder Falls

Phoenix Road

145

15

Paper Mill Road

Shawan Road

0   Kilometer   1

0   Mile   1

N

1.5 Reach the Phoenix Road crossing and parking lot.

2.5 See the mile marker post designating mile 3.

3.4 Cross Sparks Road and a parking area and the Sparks Bank Nature Center and portable toilet.

3.5 See the mile marker post designating mile 4.

4.2 Cross Glencoe Road. There is no parking here.

4.6 See the mile marker post designating mile 5.

5.5 Cross over another bridge.

5.6 See the mile marker post designating mile 6.

6.1 Cross over Corbett Road. There is no parking here.

6.3 Another bridge crosses the river. (Try to spot an eagle here.)

6.6 See the mile marker post designating mile 7.

6.8 Arrive at Monkton.

Options: This hike describes only one section of the 20-mile hike. Start and end at any parking area of your choice and choose your own length.

HIKE INFORMATION

Local attractions: Bike, Tube, and Kayak Rental, 1900 Monkton Rd., Monkton; (443) 212-5951; monktonbike.com

Good eats: Monkton Cafe, 1900 Monkton Rd., Monkton; (443) 212-5951; monkton bike.com

> *Along the Torrey C. Brown Trail, formerly the Northern Central Railroad Trail, you'll see white posts with W painted on them. In the days of the railroad, these signs were designed to remind the engineer and the firefighters to sound the whistle or the bell. This was done to warn people to get out of the way of the train.*

East Coast Greenway (ECG)

The East Coast Greenway is a work in progress; a developing trail system between Canada and Key West. The 3,000-mile trail project links all the major cities on the Eastern Seaboard, much of it using trails that are already in place or are in the planning phase. The route in Maryland is 166 miles long, and 32 percent of the path is completed as off-road trail. The trail enters Maryland in the north, beginning in Elkton, Maryland. The route travels south to the mouth of the Susquehanna River, though it offers no pedestrian or bicycle access across the bridge over the river. Therefore, the only way to safely cross at this time is via MTA bus service over the Hatem Bridge. Continuing on, the Greenway travels through Harford County to Monkton, where it picks up the Torrey C. Brown Rail Trail. After another road section, the path joins many Baltimore-area and Annapolis trails to complete the Maryland section. These city trails include the Gwynns Falls Trail, BWI Trail, and the B&A Trail, to name just a few. The end result is a 100 percent traffic-free, linear park for self-powered recreation. It's referred to as "the nation's most ambitious long-distance urban trail project." Learn more at greenway.org.

The bald eagle population declined during the twentieth century because of hunting, habitat loss, and pollution. But they have made a significant comeback due to recent measures to protect the species. They are attracted to rivers with an abundance of fish.

Gunpowder: Lost Pond Trail

The pond truly is lost, but other highlights like views of the Gunpowder River, the Pot Rocks rapids, and large boulders, can all be seen on the floodplain before heading upward into the forest. The location of this hike, just off of Belair Road, makes it an easy trail to access for a quick outdoor fix.

Start: Begin the hike from the back parking lot, walking down steps to the river.
Distance: 4.2-mile lollipop loop
Hiking time: About 2 hours
Difficulty: Moderate
Trail surface: Natural surface
Best season: Year-round
Other trail users: Trail runners, horseback riders, mountain bikers
Canine compatibility: Leashed pets permitted
Land status: State park
Fees and permits: None
Schedule: Sunrise–sunset daily

Maps: To date, there is not a formal published map of the area. However, a hand-drawn map is available for free at park headquarters and at dnr.state.md.us/publiclands/central/gunpowder central.asp.
Trail contacts: Gunpowder Falls State Park, 2813 Jerusalem Rd., Kingsville, MD 21087; (410) 592-2897; dnr.state.md.us/publiclands/central/gunpowder.asp
Other: There are no facilities at the trailhead.

Finding the trailhead: Take I-695 to exit 32, MD 1 north (Belair Road), and drive 5.5 miles. Cross the Gunpowder Falls and immediately look for the parking lot on your right. Continue through the first lot to reach a second adjacent lot. Facing the river, see a cutout in the fence and wooden steps leading downhill to the river. **GPS:** N39 25.637' / W76 26.595'

THE HIKE

People driving cars up and down the busy Route 1 corridor on Belair Road have no clue that the peaceful and scenic Lost Pond Trail lies just off in the distance, transporting hikers like us a world away from that rat race only steps away. Lost Pond Trail is just one of several trails that begin from this parking area on Belair Road.

Follow the blue-blazed trail down the stairs to the water and head left on a trail that starts as a sand and packed-dirt path. Paralleling the gorge of Gunpowder Falls on your right, enjoy a walk along the floodplain. Following the well-marked path, you'll pass cool rock formations, bold rapids, wood footbridges, creeks, and wildlife to boot. Look for mallard ducks, herons, beavers, squirrels, deer, and oh, watch out for horse poop!

You will come to an intersection with the yellow Sawmill Trail heading off to the left, but continue to stay straight on the Lost Pond Trail. Should you choose, you can add the yellow Sawmill Trail on your return to add some distance to the hike. Much of the path along the floodplain is flat and unobstructed, with only occasional rocks and roots in the trail. A wide creek has well-placed rocks to help you across.

Pull up a rock and take in the views of Pot Rocks rapids.

When you reach the intersection for Pot Rocks and the Overlook, keep straight/slightly right but do note this spot, as this will be the end point of the loop and you will return to this point. Continue to follow the trail along the water.

Just after this junction you'll be graced with impressive rocks and boulders that jut out into the river, and flat rocks that beckon you to run around on them. Here you can get up close and personal with the river. You may want to linger longer and have yourself a picnic party. This rapids area is named Pot Rocks because of the deep potholes in the riverbed rock due to erosion. Blue blazes are painted on the rocks here so you can find your way across the rocks, continuing to follow the trail.

At about the time that the blue trail intersects with the red trail off to left, you may find the hike a bit overgrown. Keep following the trail with the river on your right. The path becomes quite narrow for a short bit with a tiny creek hop. Less than a mile from Pot Rocks, you'll reach an intersection for Lost Pond, which you'll arrive at in another half mile. Take the trail left for Lost Pond.

Now the trail has a gradual incline with some ankle-turning rocks to navigate. At a T intersection follow the newly painted blue blazes toward the left. There are two trees next to each other, both with blue blazes. If you look to the right, there is also a path with some old blue blazes. You do not want to head right. Head left to make your loop back toward the direction you came from, followed by five rock hops across the creek you crossed over previously.

Now you are high on a ridge, enjoying the sights and sounds of the upland forest, and the river is out of sight. When you finally arrive at Lost Pond, for which the trail is named, you won't see much more than a big empty field overgrown with brush, with a small trickle of water running through the middle. This wetland area of the abandoned mill pond is a good place for birding. The trail then circles around to the other side of the pond and the trail takes a steep downhill climb as the river comes back into view, though your view may be obstructed when the trees are full. At an intersection with the red trail, continue straight on the blue-blazed trail to reach the parking lot in 1.1 miles. The left trail takes you back to the Pot Rocks.

Making your way around the loop, a small trail on the left with large flat rocks will lead you to a dramatic overlook of the river and rapids. Take in the view before again reaching the intersection where you first started the loop. From here, retrace your steps to the parking lot. And to all those cars whizzing by on Belair Road . . . just say "Suckers!"

MILES AND DIRECTIONS

0.0   Begin your hike on a blue-blazed trail heading down the stairs to the river. Reach the river at the bottom of the hill and head left, walking downriver.

Gunpowder: Lost Pond Trail

0.4   Reach the intersection with the yellow Sawmill Trail, heading off to the left. Stay straight on the blue-blazed Lost Pond Trail.

0.8   Cross a wide creek with well-placed rocks to aid your crossing.

0.9   Cross a small wooden footbridge.

1.0   Arrive at the intersection for Pot Rocks and the Overlook. The trail loops around and eventually comes back to this spot. Continue to hug the river, arriving at the Pot Rocks rapids.

1.1   An intersection with the red trail heads off to the left. Continue following the blue blazes.

1.4   Hop over a small creek.

1.9   Reach an intersection for Lost Pond and take the trail left.

2.0   At a T intersection head to the left.

2.4   Arrive at Lost Pond.

2.7   The trail bears to the left.

3.1   Reach the intersection with the red trail and continue straight, heading back to the parking lot.

3.2   A short path on the left leads you to an overlook of the rapids.

4.2   Arrive back at the trailhead and parking area.

Options: Add the yellow Sawmill Loop to extend this hike. Or combine this hike with the Gunpowder Wildlands Sweathouse Loop for a total hike of about 9.0 miles.

HIKE INFORMATION

Good eats: Gunpowder Lodge, 10092 Belair Rd., Kingsville; (410) 256-2626; the gunpowderlodge.com. A neighborhood restaurant and bar with outdoor seating.

Start: Begin at the trail kiosk and walk through the culvert under Belair Road.

Distance: 4.9-mile loop

Hiking time: About 2.5 hours

Difficulty: Moderate

Trail surface: Natural surface, gravel, crushed stone

Best season: Year-round

Other trail users: Trail runners, horseback riders

Canine compatibility: Leashed dogs permitted

Land status: State park

Fees and permits: None

Schedule: Sunrise–sunset daily

Maps: To date, there is not a formal published map of the area. However, a hand-drawn map is available for free at park headquarters and at dnr.state.md.us/publiclands/central/gunpowdercentral.asp.

Trail contacts: Gunpowder Falls State Park, 2813 Jerusalem Rd., Kingsville, MD 21087; (410) 592-2897; dnr.state.md.us/publiclands/central/gunpowder.asp

Finding the trailhead: Take I-695 to exit 32, MD 1 north (Belair Road) and drive 5.5 miles. Cross the Gunpowder Falls and immediately look for the parking lot on your right. Begin your hike near the trail kiosk, starting at the green gate. Head downhill and through the culvert under Belair Road. **GPS:** N39 25.652'/ W76 26.611'

"The woods are lovely, dark and deep. But I have promises to keep and miles to go before I sleep," wrote Robert Frost. A lovely quote for a lovely hike. A sign displaying these words greets you at the entrance of the Sweathouse Branch Wildlands Area of Gunpowder Falls State Park.

Our hike starts out as a wide stone and gravel path just beyond the trail kiosk and green gate, heading downhill and crossing through the culvert under Belair Road. On the other side of the culvert, enter this scenic Piedmont river valley along Gunpowder Falls. Almost immediately, leave the wide gravel and dirt path, which is the blue Stocksdale Trail, and take the pink Wildlands Trail on your right. Don't worry, you'll get your fill of river walking on the homestretch. Begin heading uphill on the narrow dirt path to the upland forest. The pink Wildlands Trail takes us over creeks, past an unmarked trail or two, and through a remarkable section where towering pine trees line the path and provide shade for the trail. Underfoot is a cushion of pine needles, and the scent of Christmas fills the air.

Soon enough we leave the pink trail and reach an intersection with the blue-blazed Stocksdale Trail, which we follow to the right. The blue trail also heads to the left and back down to the river, however, there is much more to see in this forest. The trails on this hike are well marked and easy to follow.

The trail takes hikers through an almost magical stand of towering pine trees.

The next intersection is with the yellow Sweathouse Trail. The blue Stocksdale Trail continues straight, but make a right on the Sweathouse Trail, heading slightly downhill to keep the fun going a little longer. At the bottom of the hill, you'll cross Sweathouse Run and walk the trail, heading downstream, on the opposite side for a short bit until you cross Sweathouse Run yet again and again once more.

At about 3.0 miles, heading downhill, you may notice that the trail comes to a Y. A very narrow and lightly worn path heads off to the right and steeply downhill to a swimming hole. You can take this path if you wish, but there is an easier route to this swimming hole ahead.

Once you reach the bottom of the hill, the trail levels out and a path heads both left and right. The river is 100 feet in front of you but not easily seen. The yellow trail crosses Sweathouse Run on your left one last time to meet back up with the Gunpowder River and head back in the direction of the trailhead. First, however, follow the wide, clear path on your right (unmarked), and in less than 0.2 mile, reach a swimming hole on the tributary of Long Green Creek with small spills of water, flat rocks perfect for a picnic, and boulders to climb on. Stay and play, and enjoy nature's finest features. Long Green Creek is one of the best runs in Maryland for whitewater paddlers when the water levels are just right, which isn't terribly often.

Have your fun and then retrace your steps, this time crossing over the Sweathouse Run one last time, heading downstream, before meeting back up with the Gunpowder to follow it downriver and complete the loop. The yellow trail turns back into the blue-blazed Stocksdale Trail. Passing the pink Wildlands Trailhead on your left, the traffic will snap you back to reality real quick, but savor the experience, knowing that the trail will wait for your return.

MILES AND DIRECTIONS

0.0 Start at the trail kiosk and green gate to head downhill and through the culvert under Belair Road.

0.1 On the other side of the tunnel, stay straight on a wide path (the blue Stocksdale Trail) very briefly and then take the pink Wildlands Trail on your right.

0.9 Cross a scenic creek and continue the trail on the other side just slightly uphill.

1.0 Cross another creek.

1.1 A trail, not terribly worn, heads off to the right. Continue on the pink trail, entering a section of trail lined with towering pine trees.

Gunpowder: Wildlands Sweathouse Loop

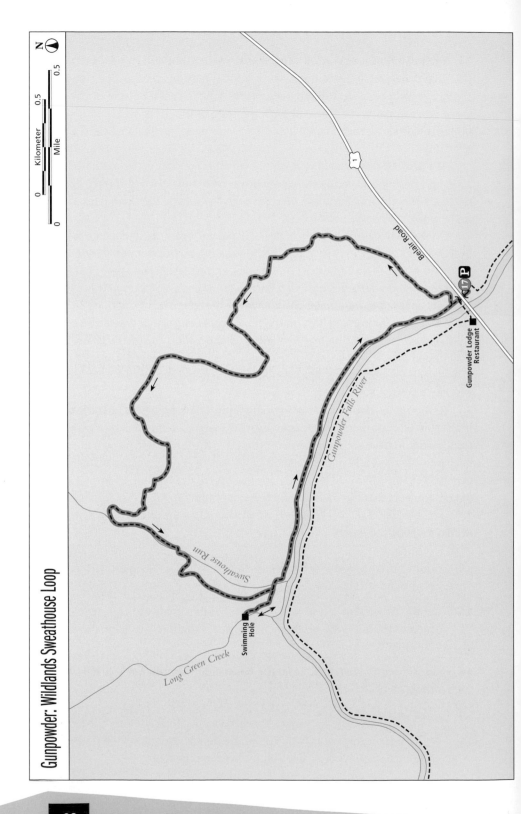

N

Kilometer
0   0.5

Mile
0   0.5

1

Belair Road

P
147

Gunpowder Lodge
Restaurant

Gunpowder Falls River

Sweathouse Run

Long Green Creek

Swimming
Hole

1.3   Reach a Y intersection with the blue Stocksdale Trail, which heads left and right. Bear to the right.

1.8   Cross a small creek.

2.1   Reach an intersection with the yellow Sweathouse Trail off to the right. The Stockdale Trail continues straight. Make a right on the yellow trail. Head slightly downhill.

2.5   At the bottom of a hill, cross Sweathouse Run and look for the yellow blaze on the opposite side of the creek.

2.6   Cross back over to the other side of Sweathouse Run.

2.8   Cross over Sweathouse Run for the third time on the yellow trail.

3.1   A small unmarked narrow path splits off to the right taking you steeply downhill to a swimming hole, but there is an easier path. Continue straight, slightly left, on the yellow trail.

3.2   At the bottom of the hill, the yellow trail continues across Sweathouse Run to the left. First, take an unmarked, flat, and very well-worn trail to the right to reach the swimming hole.

3.4   Arrive at the swimming hole on Long Green Creek. Turn around and retrace your steps to the yellow-blazed trail.

3.6   Now cross Sweathouse Run to head back in the direction of your car on the yellow path, heading downstream for several hundred feet until it meets up with the Gunpowder River.

4.8   Pass by the trailhead for the pink trail where we started our loop. Again, cross under Belair Road via the culvert.

4.9   Arrive back at the trailhead and parking lot.

Option: Combine this hike with the Gunpowder Lost Pond Loop (Hike 16) for a total hike of about 9.0 miles.

HIKE INFORMATION

Good eats: Gunpowder Lodge, 10092 Belair Rd., Kingsville; (410) 256-2626; thegunpowderlodge.com. A neighborhood restaurant and bar with outdoor seating.

Big Gunpowder Trail: Belair Road to Harford Road

Its length aside, this trail is a cakewalk. It's amazing that this natural beauty of land and river lies between two of the busiest routes in Baltimore. The walk along the bank of the Gunpowder River is big on scenery.

Start: Begin at the parking lot and trail kiosk.

Distance: 9.8 miles out and back

Hiking time: About 4 hours

Difficulty: Moderate due to distance

Trail surface: Natural surface

Best season: Year-round

Other trail users: Trail runners, horseback riders

Canine compatibility: Leashed pets permitted

Land status: State park

Fees and permits: None

Schedule: Sunrise–sunset daily

Maps: Trail maps available at park headquarters and the park's website: dnr.state.md.us/publiclands/pdfs/GFSP_big2.pdf

Trail contacts: Gunpowder Falls State Park, 2813 Jerusalem Rd., Kingsville, MD 21087; (410) 592-2897; dnr.state.md.us/publiclands/central/gunpowder.asp

Finding the trailhead: To Belair Road trailhead: Take I-695 to exit 32, MD 1 north (Belair Road) and drive 5.5 miles. Cross the Gunpowder Falls and immediately look for the parking lot on your right. Begin your hike near the trail kiosk, starting at the green gate. Head downhill and through the culvert under Belair Road. **GPS:** N39 25.653′ / W76 26.611′

   To Harford Road trailhead: Take I-695 to exit 31B MD 147 north (Harford Road) and proceed about 2.8 miles. The parking area is on the right. **GPS:** N39 25.300′ / W76 30.172′

THE HIKE

Over the river and through the woods ... to Harford Road we go?!
That's right. Between Belair Road and Harford Road lies an exceptional track of natural beauty, accessible by way of the Big Gunpowder Trail. Along the south side of the river, the trail runs through a deep gorge on a mostly flat and level trail, occasionally traversing some rocky and rooty sections. The hike described here is detailed as an out-and-back hike that heads west to Harford Road, but it can easily be done as a one-way with a shuttle since there are trailhead lots at both Belair Road and Harford Road, or it can be hiked in reverse by walking east from Harford Road to Belair Road.

This trail begins at a midpoint on the Big Gunpowder Trail and heads west, traveling only half of the total length of the Big Gunpowder Trail. However, the Big Gunpowder Trail does continue to the east all the way to Pulaski Highway (Route 40).

Start just to the left of the trail kiosk at the green gate. Follow the stone path slightly downhill and through the culvert that takes you under Belair Road. As soon as you come out of the culvert on the opposite side, take an immediate

A lush carpet of green pleases the eye.

left on a walkway that takes you over the Gunpowder River to the south side of the river. The walkway paralleling Belair Road has a black metal railing and a wall decorated with graffiti.

Now on the south side of the river, the trail pops you out on the right-hand side of the Gunpowder Lodge restaurant, in their parking lot. Walk through the parking lot and down a gravel driveway, hugging the far right side of the restaurant and the backyard of the restaurant on your left, paralleling a wood fence. See a playground area and picnic tables. Directly ahead is a worn dirt trail that heads down and immediately crosses a feeder creek. Cross this creek and the trail continues on the opposite side.

Follow the well-worn narrow path upstream through thick vegetation and lowland scenery to see small rapids, a forest floor carpeted with bluebells, and wildlife. Look for trout in the river, typically stocked in March. Cross several creeks—one is especially scenic—and be on the lookout for beaver activity.

At one point the trails heads uphill to a guardrail and paved road. Walk the road until it ends at a pump station. Walk the right side of the pump station to pick up the trail on the backside. Parts of the trail underfoot are loose sand.

Keep on keeping on! Enjoy the mindless walk and get lost in your own thoughts as the river dances alongside you. The water is typically quite clear so you can see the bottom as well as the fish darting from side to side. You might see a heron standing tall on a rock in the river.

The sound of traffic interrupts your thoughts as you get closer to Harford Road. Homes on the north side of the river now come into view. Just before you reach the turnaround point, the trail crosses under power lines way above before taking a right over a feeder creek with large rocks aiding your way across. The Harford Road parking area has space for roughly eleven cars. Now turn around and retrace your steps. So what's the advantage of hiking the trail out and back beginning from Belair Road? Working up an appetite for a giant meal at the Gunpowder Lodge!

MILES AND DIRECTIONS

0.0 The trail starts to the left of the trail kiosk at the green gate on a stone path. Walk through the culvert that takes you under Belair Road. On the other side of culvert, take an immediate left on a walkway to cross over the Gunpowder River and reach the south side.

0.1 On the other side of the walkway, arrive at the Gunpowder Lodge restaurant parking area. Walk through the parking lot and down a gravel driveway on the right side of the restaurant, keeping the backyard of the restaurant close on your left.

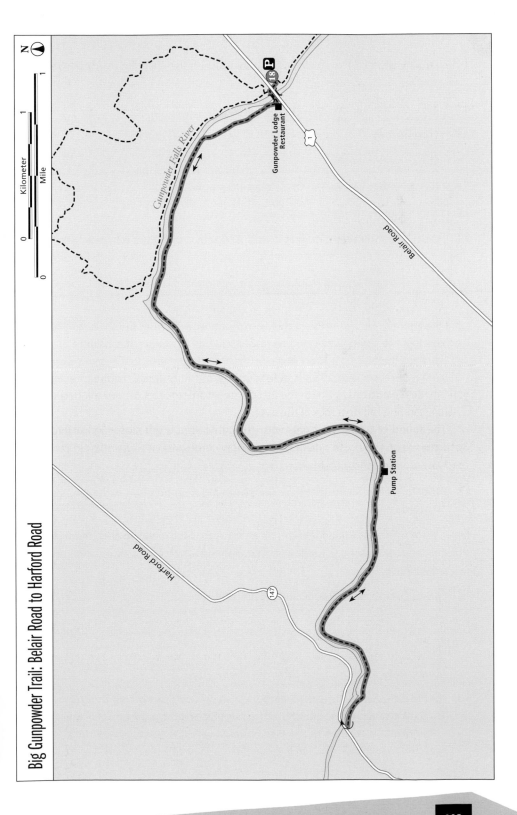

Big Gunpowder Trail: Belair Road to Harford Road

0.2 Directly ahead, follow a worn trail crossing a feeder creek on the opposite side.

0.5 Begin to hug the river on your right side.

0.9 Cross a creek.

1.5 Cross another creek.

2.9 Pass an unmarked trail on the left heading uphill.

3.0 Another unmarked trail comes in on the left.

3.1 Cross a branch about 40 feet across with big rocks piled up to aid your crossing.

3.2 The trail heads left. Walk uphill along a guardrail, and walk the road until it dead-ends at a pump station.

3.3 Walk along the right side of the pump station, following the fence to the back of the building before heading back into woods. At the back of the station, the trail splits into two worn paths. They meet up. The right side could be a bit muddy. The high road on the left might be a bit drier.

4.5 Cross a creek with large rocks.

4.7 Cross under power lines (look up, they're not obvious), and immediately after, follow the trail heading to the right and across a creek/branch followed by another stream crossing.

4.8 The trail splits. Take either side. They both meet up near the parking lot at Harford Road.

4.9 Arrive at Harford Road, which has parking for about eleven cars. Retrace your steps, now heading downstream, all the way to the parking area on Belair Road.

9.8 Arrive back at the trailhead and parking lot.

Options: You may choose to start your hike at either end of the trail at Harford Road or Belair Road or do a one-way hike by parking a shuttle vehicle at either end.

You can hike the other half of the Big Gunpowder Trail heading east to Pulaski Highway. Note that there is no parking at Pulaski Highway. In order to walk the Big Gunpowder Trail in that direction, make a left just before the culvert to follow a walkway to the south side of the river. Do not cross under Belair Road.

HIKE INFORMATION

Good eats: Gunpowder Lodge, 10092 Belair Rd., Kingsville; (410) 256-2626; thegunpowderlodge.com. A neighborhood restaurant and bar with outdoor seating.

A narrow footpath walks you through a sea of green dotted with bluebells.

Welcome to Jerusalem Mill Historic Village, home to Gunpowder Falls State Park headquarters. The mill here originally functioned as a grain mill from 1772 to 1961. The historic town buildings include a gristmill, blacksmith shop, gun shop, springhouse, and general store. This well-marked hike has much to offer, including historical sites, views of Little Gunpowder Falls, and a covered bridge.

Start: Begin at the edge of the meadow behind the Jerusalem Blacksmith Shop.

Distance: 3.2 miles double loop

Hiking time: About 1.5 hours

Difficulty: Moderate

Trail surface: Natural surface

Best season: Year-round

Other trail users: Mountain bikers, trail runners

Canine compatibility: Leashed dogs permitted

Land status: State park

Fees and permits: None

Schedule: Daily sunrise–sunset

Jerusalem Mill Museum and Visitor Center open on weekends from 1 to 4 p.m.

Maps: Trail maps available at park headquarters and the park's website: dnr.state.md.us/public lands/central/gunpowder.asp

Trail contacts: Gunpowder Falls State Park, 2813 Jerusalem Rd., Kingsville, MD 21087; (410) 592-2897; dnr.state.md.us/publiclands/central/gunpowder.asp

Other: Summer concerts, war reenactments

Finding the trailhead: From I-95, take exit 74 to MD 152 west (Mountain Road). Follow Mountain Road toward Fallston and turn left onto Jerusalem Road. Park in the lot on the right, just before the mill. **GPS:** N39 28.267' / W76 23.648'

THE HIKE

calm overwhelms you as soon as you enter the quaint and historic village of Jerusalem Mill, one of the oldest preserved mill villages in Maryland, located in Harford County. This area, rich in history, had a gun shop that supplied muskets during the early part of the Revolutionary War. Military reenactments sometimes take place here.

The calm continues as you head into the woods for a nature hike. You'll find the trailhead in the meadow to the left and behind the Jerusalem Blacksmith Shop. Look for the white blaze on the tree, just before leaving the grassy meadow and stepping on the natural trail surface. You'll be following the white-blazed trail for the first half of the loop and returning on the blue-blazed trail.

Where the trail crosses a small wooden bridge, a sign marks the site of an ice pond. It is presumed that it was once used to harvest ice in winter to later be used during the warmer months. At the first intersection with the blue-blazed trail, continue left to stay on the white trail, the Gunpowder Trail.

The next sign shares the history of the dam and start of Millrace. This dam once diverted water downstream via a race in order to power the grain mill and sawmill. The dam was abandoned around 1940 and the gristmill was converted to electrical power until it went out of operation entirely.

Visit Gunpowder Falls State Park headquarters and museum for maps and historical information.

After crossing a small stream followed by a slight uphill climb, the trail takes you away from the river to again intersect with the blue-blazed trail. This time you'll follow the blue trail to the right before passing power lines. The sound of the river rapids fades into the distance, but you'll hear the gurgle of a second small creek crossing. Follow the blue blaze on a sharp right turn downhill, heading back toward the river to follow a ridge above the river. Soon, you'll meet back up with the white trail and pass by your original starting point.

Now continue on white-blazed trail back to the center of town, and cross over Jericho Road. Head to the right over the bridge. On the other side of the bridge, head down the stairs on the left and follow the trail along the water until you reach the intersection for the yellow horse trail and the trail toward the Jericho Covered Bridge. Of course, you have to check out the covered bridge. After you've had your fill, retrace your steps to the intersection with the yellow trail. Follow the yellow trail to take you all the way back to where you started. Enjoy the smell of honeysuckle and be sure to look out for snakes!

MILES AND DIRECTIONS

0.0   Begin the trail in the meadow. Look for the white blaze on the tree. Follow the path and bear right to stay on the trail. After a few feet, make a left turn to stay on the white-blazed trail.

0.1   Reach the historical marker for the Millrace and Waste Gate.

0.2   Come to a historical marker at a wood bridge for the Ice Pond, followed by the first intersection with blue-blazed trail. Take a left at the fork and follow the white-blazed trail.

0.3   Come to the site of the old dam.

0.4   Come to a small stream crossing.

0.9   Follow the trail as it heads uphill. You will then reach the second intersection with the blue trail. Follow the blue trail to the right.

1.0   Pass by the power lines.

1.2   Continue to follow the blue trail to the right.

1.3   Come to a second creek crossing.

1.6   Reach an intersection where a trail continues straight and the blue-blazed trail takes a sharp turn to the right. Take the sharp right to stay on the blue-blazed trail.

1.7   Bear right to stay on the blue trail.

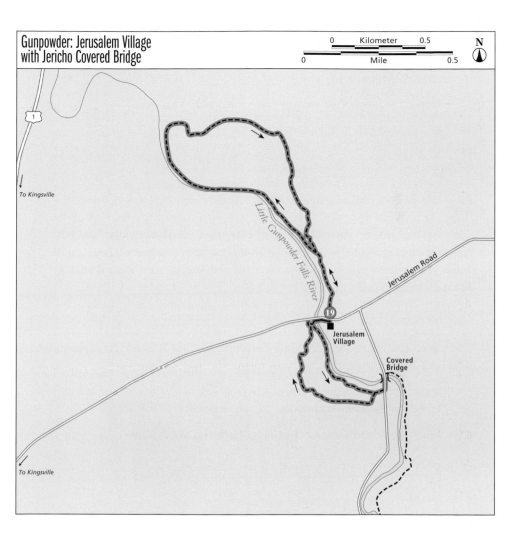

0   Kilometer   0.5

0   Mile   0.5

N

To Kingsville

Little Gunpowder Falls River

Jerusalem Road

19

Jerusalem
Village

Covered
Bridge

To Kingsville

1.8   Meet back up with the white-blazed trail.

1.9   Return to the trailhead and continue straight toward Jericho Road.

2.0   Cross Jericho Road and head to the right to cross the bridge.

2.1   After crossing the bridge follow the trail left down the stairs and back on natural-surface trail. Keep left on the white-blazed trail for views of the water from the ridge.

2.3   Cross a small wooden bridge.

2.4   Reach the intersection with the yellow trail. Stay left on the white trail to reach the Jericho Covered Bridge.

2.5 Reach the covered bridge and walk across. Retrace your route to the intersection with the yellow trail.

2.6 Take the yellow horse trail to loop you back around.

3.0 Bear right to stay on the yellow trail.

3.1 Meet back up with the white-blazed trail to again cross the bridge back to the trailhead and parking lot.

3.2 End the hike back in Jerusalem Village and the parking lot.

Options: This trail takes you on a small portion of the Little Gunpowder River Trail, however, in total, the Little Gunpowder Trail runs from Jerusalem Village south near I-95 and north to Harford Road. The total trail length from Harford Road to I-95 is 5.0 miles.

HIKE INFORMATION

Good eats: The Sunshine Grille, 12607 Fork Rd., Fork; (410) 592-3378; sunshine grille.com. Greek and American cuisine.

The trail takes hikers across a road bridge to continue toward Jericho Covered Bridge.

The varied landscape on this hike includes hillsides and stream valleys, ridge walking, and a stroll down a fire road that cuts through a pine forest.

Start: Pick up the blue-blazed trail off Bunker Hill Road
Distance: 3.5-mile loop
Hiking time: About 2 hours
Difficulty: Moderate
Trail surface: Natural surface
Best season: Year-round
Other trail users: Trail runners, horseback riders
Canine compatibility: Leashed dogs permitted
Land status: State park

Fees and permits: None
Schedule: Sunrise–sunset daily
Maps: Trail maps available at park headquarters and for purchase on the park's website
Trail contacts: Gunpowder Falls State Park, 2813 Jerusalem Rd., Kingsville, MD 21087; (410) 592-2897; dnr.state.md.us/publiclands/central/gunpowder.asp

Finding the trailhead: From I-695, take I-83 north to exit 27, Mt. Carmel Road, and turn right (east) on Mt. Carmel Road. Drive 0.5 mile to reach York Road. Make a left (north) on York Road. Drive 0.8 mile and turn left on Bunker Hill Road, just after passing Hereford High School. Follow Bunker Hill until it dead-ends into the parking lot, which holds fifty-plus cars. **GPS:** N39 36.550' / W76 40.316'

Walk up Bunker Hill Road for a few hundred feet, past a wooden gate, to reach the blue-blazed Bunker Hill Trail. There are blue blazes on either side of the road. We will hike the trail clockwise, beginning the hike on the north side of the road, then return to this spot, popping out on the blue trail on the opposite side of the road to complete our loop.

The trail begins as a narrow path through dense forest, soon to follow a nicely flowing stream branch with skunk cabbage scattered about. As the trail widens, find yourself in a picturesque stream valley surrounded by tall river birch, oaks, and hemlocks, while water flows over stepped rocks. Springtime brings a variety of wildflowers like bloodroot, hepatica, and spring beauty while the summer explodes into goldenrod and asters.

As you cross Bunker Hill Road, the same road you drove in on, you can't miss I-83 on your left. A sign on the opposite side of Bunker Hill directs you to the Charles Theret Archery Range. This trail on the opposite side of the archery is called the Mingo Forks Trail. Still blazed in blue, the surface is now a wide gravel fire road that cuts through a scenic pine forest. In just 0.25 mile from the road, find yourself among the archery stands littered throughout the woods, although

A portion of the hike follows a wide, flat fire road that leads to the archery area.

it seems to hardly be in use. The trail overall, especially the fire road section, is heavily used by trail runners, many of whom are likely members of Hereford High's sports teams.

Upon arrival at the pavilion and bathhouse area, the trail comes to a Y intersection. Follow the blue blazes, taking the trail to the right on a narrow dirt path, leaving the fire road behind.

Pass by intersections with a yellow trail, which leads to Mt. Carmel Road, as well as more creek crossings, before reaching the junction with the white-blazed Gunpowder South Trail, which heads both to the left and right. Take the white-blazed trail to the right to continue making a loop. The trail and intersection are well marked with a wooden post and the name of the trail spelled out.

On the Gunpowder South Trail, you may catch a glimpse of the Gunpowder River off to your left, but it is mostly obstructed by the thick of trees. You will catch sight of mountain laurel, dogwoods, and spicebush dotting the hillsides. In order to complete the loop, you will once again meet up with the Bunker Hill blue-blazed trail. As you cross Mingo Branch, before returning to the wooded hillsides, note that this tributary was named for the Mingo Indians, who traveled to this area from Pennsylvania.

The Gunpowder South Trail continues straight, but our hike takes us to the right, following the blue-blazed trail, to loop us back to our start. When you see a side trail come in on your left, you may choose to follow it to the lot where you parked. (You could also start the trail from this point.) To make a complete loop, continue straight ahead for a couple hundred feet to pop out at the same spot, but just on the opposite side of Bunker Hill Road.

MILES AND DIRECTIONS

0.0 From the parking lot, walk up Bunker Hill Road for a few hundred feet, past a wooden gate, to reach the blue-blazed Bunker Hill Trail. We will hike the trail clockwise, beginning the hike on the left (north) side of the road.

0.2 The trail dips down to a dry, deep creek bed and back up.

0.4 Cross a creek and climb up some stairs on the opposite side.

0.9 Walk up eight steps to reach Bunker Hill Road. Continue the blue-blazed trail on the opposite side, now the Mingo Forks Trail, on a fire road heading toward the archery.

1.3 Come to an unmarked intersection with a trail that heads off to the left. Continue straight on the blue-blazed fire road.

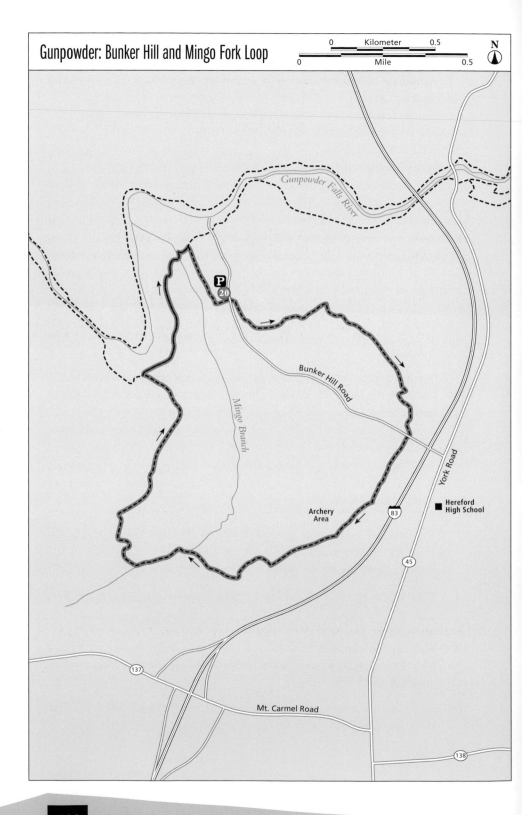

0   Kilometer   0.5

0   Mile   0.5

N

Gunpowder Falls River

P 20

Bunker Hill Road

Mingo Branch

York Road

Archery Area

83

Hereford High School

45

137

Mt. Carmel Road

138

1.5   You are now among the archery stands. The trail comes to a split near a bathhouse and picnic pavilion. Bear to the right, following the staggered blue blazes.

1.6   The fairly steep downhill path with stairs leads to a creek.

1.7   Reach the intersection with the yellow Mingo Valley Trail, which takes you to Mt. Carmel Road. Head right to follow the Mingo Forks Trail, continuing to follow blue blazes.

1.8   Cross a scenic branch.

2.0   Reach another junction with the yellow trail. Follow the Mingo Forks blue-blazed trail to the right. Soon after you may notice an open pasture hillside on the left.

2.2   Follow blue blazes off to the right on an obvious dirt trail. There is a clearing straight ahead with orange posts and a slightly used path on the left that leads to an open field. Continue to the right, following well-marked blue blazes.

2.8   Reach a Y intersection with a post that spells out the Gunpowder South Trail, which is blazed in white and heads both left and right. Go right to complete the loop.

3.2   Cross Mingo Branch.

3.3   Reach an intersection, again with the Bunker Hill Trail. Make a right on the blue Bunker Hill Trail to continue the loop. The white-blazed Gunpowder South Trail continues straight ahead.

3.4   A short side trail will dead-end into the lot where you parked. Or continue for a few hundred feet to officially close the loop from where you started.

3.5   Arrive back at the parking lot.

HIKE INFORMATION

Local attractions: Woodhall Wine Cellars, 17912 York Rd., Parkton; (410) 357-8644; woodhallwinecellars.com

Good eats: Casa Mia's Restaurant, 17417 York Rd., Parkton; (410) 357-4231; casamiasrestaurant.com

This trail is wild and wonderful! It combines the Panther Branch Trail with the Gunpowder South Trail for a scenic loop complete with wildlife, waterfalls, old ruins, and river views.

Start: Begin in the meadow at a creek crossing and wooden trail marker

Distance: 4.2-mile loop

Hiking time: About 2 hours

Difficulty: Moderate

Trail surface: Natural surface

Best season: Year-round

Other trail users: Trail runners, horseback riders

Canine compatibility: Leashed dogs permitted

Land status: State park

Fees and permits: None

Schedule: Sunrise–sunset daily

Maps: Trail maps available at park headquarters and available for purchase on the park's website

Trail contacts: Gunpowder Falls State Park, 2813 Jerusalem Rd., Kingsville, MD 21087; (410) 592-2897; dnr.state.md.us/publiclands/central/gunpowder.asp

Finding the trailhead: From I-695, take 83 north to exit 27, Mt. Carmel Road, and turn right (east) on Mt. Carmel Road. Drive 0.5 mile to reach York Road. Make a left (north) on York Road. Drive past Hereford High and Bunker Hill Road. Just before you reach the bridge on York that crosses over the Gunpowder River, you'll see parking areas on either side of York Road. The lot on the right (east side) is the preferred lot, as the trailhead is on the same side. The lot on the right parks five cars and the lot across York Road can park about ten cars. **GPS:** N39 36.832' / W76 39.538'

THE HIKE

A panther brings to mind words like wild, sleek, and beautiful. Living up to its name, you could say that this Panther Branch hike is where the wild things are. The trail has much to offer, from wildlife and waterfalls to creek crossings and river views. It's topped off with a beautiful start and finish in a large grassy meadow along the river, a popular spot for picnickers and sunbathers. This combo of the Panther Branch and Gunpowder South Trail is a real winner.

To reach the trailhead, walk down ten steps from the parking area to cross a grassy green meadow and a creek to reach the PANTHER BRANCH sign, heading to the right. At this point the white-blazed Gunpowder South Trail heads slightly left. This white-blazed trail will be our return path to this spot. Also at this spot, notice the old stone foundation of a woodstove.

For now, follow the Panther Branch Trail to the right on a packed-dirt path as it winds its way uphill and away from the river. You'll cross several creeks and pass by the occasional unmarked trail. Walk among the tall trees and a fairly open forest floor before a T intersection with the pink Sandy Lane Trail. Sandy Lane is a shortcut trail that heads left down to the river and the Gunpowder South Trail. However, you'll want to turn right and follow the blue blazes along the Panther Branch.

A marshy portion of the hike provides the perfect conditions for skunk cabbage.

21

On my last hike of this trail, someone had picked up the wooden post with the trail names and flipped it around! In situations like these, use your best judgment, a little common sense, and refer to your maps. It's possible to move the signpost, but the painted blazes on the trees don't lie.

After this intersection the trail gets wider before coming to a Y. The wider trail straight ahead might look like the obvious choice, but blue blazes staggered to the left direct us off the wider path, onto the trail on the left. Soon after, at a T intersection, you'll meet up with the wider path once again and head left following the blue blazes through a dense forest with rows of trees creating aisles and a tree-lined path. Hug the edge of a field until the trail takes a sharp turn to the left and straight through the middle of the field, heading into the forest directly on the opposite side.

On your left notice several old brick and stone foundations on the hillside as you follow a creek loaded with skunk cabbage and stepped rocks through a low-lying valley. These are remnants of former settlements and possibly those of a mill that dated back to the 1800s. This creek eventually feeds into the wide and wild Panther Branch, said to have been named for a panther that long ago lived in a cave near here. A beautiful flow of water tumbles over rocks, creating small plunges and waterfalls as it makes its way downhill.

The trail along the branch has its ups and downs while stepping over many feeder creeks before you can no longer walk the edge of Panther Branch. Do not cross the branch. The trail continues on a steep uphill to the left. When the trail levels off, you'll have a nice view of Panther Branch merging with the Gunpowder River.

Climb a bit more, wrapping around on one switchback, before heading downhill to the Gunpowder River. You are now back to water level with the junction of Panther Branch and Gunpowder River. A signpost indicates the Gunpowder South Trail heading both left and right. Take this trail left, following the river on your right, to complete the last leg of our loop.

The scenic section of river is a fantastic spot for viewing wildlife. *Plunk!* There goes a beaver, followed by the rustling sound of leaves disturbed by white-tailed deer running away and the constant sound of various birds chirping. For much of this leg, you will hug the river on the right. However, there are a few occasions when you gain some distance from the river. In one spot the water is replaced by a boggy marsh area loaded with skunk cabbage. On the other side, look for the old-timey car (looks to be a Model A), which is completely rusted over and somehow works well with the setting.

Returning to the river's edge, enjoy the sights of large boulders and small river rapids. At one point a giant fallen tree spans the entire width of the river. On the opposite side look for the stunning Raven Rock Falls, which gently cascade water down a smooth rock face.

The last mile along the river gets a bit more wild and overgrown, hopping over large rocks in the trail. A good thigh-burning uphill climb soon followed by a sharp turn to the right and back down to the river means you are nearing the end. The sound of traffic is evident as you see York Road through the trees. When you again reach the water's edge, follow it back to the meadow where you began. Throw down a blanket and take a snooze in the sun.

MILES AND DIRECTIONS

0.0 Take the steps down to a grassy meadow and cross a creek. Follow the signs for Panther Branch Trail to the right and uphill. The white-blazed trail straight ahead is our return loop.

0.3 Cross the creek and then head uphill.

0.4 An unmarked trail heads to the left on a well-worn path. Continue to follow the blue-blazed trail, bearing to the right.

0.5 Reach the intersection with the Sandy Lane Trail. The Sandy Trail goes to the left and the Blue Panther Branch Trail goes to the right. Follow the blue trail to the right.

0.7 The trail comes to a Y. Follow the blue blazes to the left, leaving the wide trail you are currently on.

0.8 Come to a T intersection and make a left, following the blue blazes, back on a wide path.

1.0 Hang a left to walk straight through the middle of this field on a grassy path, heading to the forest on the opposite side.

1.2 See an old brick-and-stone foundation on the hillside on your left.

1.5 See the remains of a three-sided structure made of stacked stone with no mortar.

1.6 Cross a feeder creek.

1.7 Now at water level with Panther Branch, see two more old foundation structures.

2.0 The trail dead-ends into Panther Branch. Follow a narrow trail left and uphill. Do not cross Panther Branch.

2.4 Reach the intersection with the Gunpowder South Trail (white blaze) both right and left. Take a left to complete the last leg of our loop, following the river.

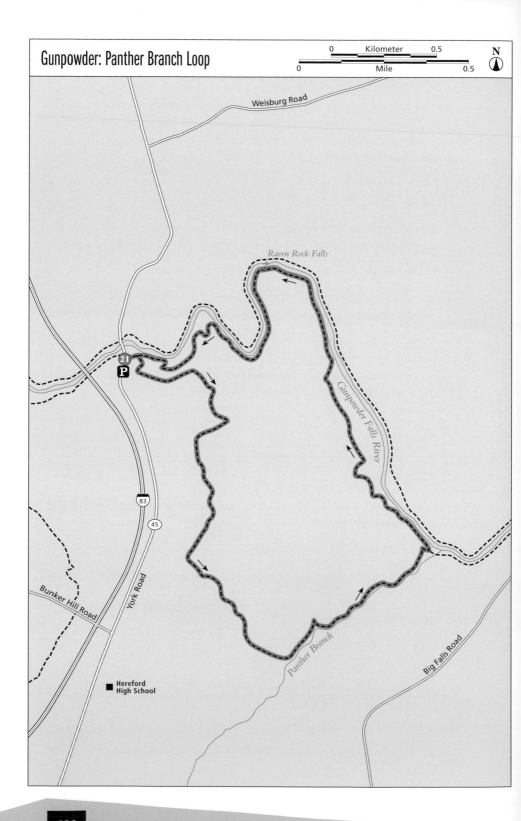

Gunpowder: Panther Branch Loop

Weisburg Road

Raven Rock Falls

21

P

83

45

Gunpowder Falls River

York Road

Bunker Hill Road

Hereford
High School

Panther Branch

Big Falls Road

0   Kilometer   0.5

0   Mile   0.5

N

2.5 Cross a creek at one of two spots, both of which join up to lead you uphill.

2.7 Look for a rusted old shed and old-time car on the right, on the opposite side of the boggy area.

2.8 Pass by the intersection with the other end of pink-blazed Sandy Lane Trail. Continue to stay straight.

3.3 Reach a giant fallen tree that spans the river and Raven Rock Falls on the opposite side.

3.8 The trail bears left and away from the river, climbing uphill.

4.0 Take a sharp turn to the right, heading back to river level, following the staggered white blazes. Again hug the bank of the river.

4.1 Return to the trailhead and cross the creek back to the meadow where you started.

4.2 Arrive back at the parking lot.

Options: The Gunpowder South Trail continues on the west side of York Road. Refer to the hike listing for Gunpowder North and South (Hike 22).

Also, the Bunker Hill/Mingo Forks Trail starts a few miles south on York Road.

HIKE INFORMATION

Local attractions: Woodhall Wine Cellars, 17912 York Rd., Parkton; (410) 357-8644; woodhallwinecellars.com
Good eats: Casa Mia's Restaurant, 17417 York Rd., Parkton; (410) 357-4231; casa miasrestaurant.com

Gunpowder: North and South Circuit

This hike is an all-day event in the Hereford area. It offers a grand tour of the Gunpowder River's south and north banks, with highlights like Prettyboy Dam and Raven Rock Falls along varied terrain, from mild river walks and rock scrambles to sloped hillsides.

Start: At the parking lot, begin at the green gate and the tree with a white blaze.

Distance: 13.9-mile loop with spur

Hiking time: About 7 hours

Difficulty: Difficult due to distance

Trail surface: Natural surface

Best season: Year-round

Other trail users: Trail runners, horseback riders

Canine compatibility: Leashed dogs permitted

Land status: State park

Fees and permits: None

Schedule: Sunrise–sunset daily

Maps: Trail maps available at park headquarters and for purchase on the park's website

Trail contacts: Gunpowder Falls State Park, 2813 Jerusalem Rd., Kingsville, MD 21087; (410) 592-2897; dnr.state.md.us/publiclands/central/gunpowder.asp

Finding the trailhead: From I-695, take 83 north to exit 27, Mt. Carmel Road, and turn right (east) on Mt. Carmel Road. Drive 0.5 mile to reach York Road. Make a left (north) on York Road. Drive past Hereford High and Bunker Hill Road. Just before you reach the bridge on York that crosses over the Gunpowder River, you'll see parking areas on either side of York Road. The lot on the left (west side) is the preferred lot, as the trailhead is on the same side. The lot on the right parks five cars, and the lot across York Road can park about ten cars. Park on the west side of the road. The trailhead is marked with a white blaze on a tree and a sign prohibiting bikes, as well as a green gate. The trail heads downhill toward Gunpowder River.

GPS: N39 36.849' / W76 39.555'

THE HIKE

An all-day outing, this nearly 14-mile clockwise loop with a spur to Prettyboy Dam passes through dense forest and across floodplains, walking narrow ledges, hopping rocks, crossing numerous creeks, and traversing steep side hills.

Here's the plan: Start at a midpoint in the river on the south side. Walk upriver, heading east, all the way up to the dam before crossing over to the north side of the river. Follow the north side of the river all the way downstream to Big Falls Road. Cross back over the river, again picking up the trail heading upstream all the way back to your starting point for one super-duper circuit!

Some of the sights includes the Masemore Road green iron bridge, built in 1898 by the Rough Iron Bridge Company, and the Falls Road iron bridge, which spans the river. Kayakers and fishermen enjoy the water, while trail runners and pet owners walk the trails. There is much deer, beaver, and bird activity so keep your eyes peeled for bluebirds, cardinals, ducks, and even eagles.

The spur trail to Prettyboy Dam is a rugged trail with roots and rocks to maneuver over and around and even some rock scrambling. This section of the hike is impressive, with rocks lining both sides decorated with creeks, springs, water chutes, and rapids. The trail fades away as it becomes a boulder and rock

Hikers experience the power of the Prettyboy Dam from its base, sitting on the Gunpowder riverbank.

field. The white blazes are a bit sporadic, but continue to hop over the rocks, with the river on your right.

The vegetation along the trail closes in on you, and you can hear the power of the water from the dam in the distance. Apparently it also exudes the power of love, as you'll find this to be a popular spot for cuddling couples enjoying the view of the dam, and you'll see hearts with initials carved into trees. The cuddling is okay. The carving is not! When one of the valves is open, it's a cool scene to see the shooting water, and you might feel some of the spray. As the story goes, Prettyboy was named for a farmer's horse that drowned in the river.

As you retrace your steps on the spur trail, you could mix it up a bit. Hop on the Highland Trail until it loops you back to the Gunpowder South Trail. (You will have to cross the iron bridge at Masemore Road to meet up with your return trail downriver on the north side). For the purpose of this hike, we will stay on the Gunpowder South Trail, retracing our steps to the iron bridge on Falls Road to pick up the Gunpowder North Trail, heading downriver on the opposite side of the bridge.

Rock formations, rocky terrain, and rugged roots are all part of the fun.

Picking up the north-side trail, you will now follow a blue-blazed path downstream. The start of the north trail is overgrown and somewhat difficult to follow over downed trees. But simply keep the river on your right. You might feel like you are blazing your own trail at times, but soon enough the path becomes more evident.

Head uphill to cross over York Road—there is a hole in the guardrail—to continue to follow the trail downstream. This road crossing at York Road is where you parked and began the hike on the south side of the river. You can end your trip here if you wish, having completed a 9-mile loop.

On the other side of York Road, look across the river to see a green open field. That field is our end point. But there is still much more to see on this river tour! In just another mile, on your left, is quite a sight to see. The tributary Raven Rock Falls flows downhill over smooth rocks.

Just before the Gunpowder North Trail comes to an end at Big Falls Road, the trail follows a peaceful section along a fire road. There is stillness in the air interrupted only by the chirps of birds. A swampy section sits off on the left lined with several bird feeders.

Cross Big Falls Road to again return to the south side of the river. Back on the white blazed trail, rock-hop across the wild Panther Branch, then pass by an intersection with the Panther Branch Trail. (If you've hiked the Panther Branch Loop trail listed in this book, you've been to this spot before.) Continue to follow the white-blazed trail, traversing several ups and downs as you now make your way back upstream. The wildlife is abundant. When you finally reach the end in the green grass meadow alongside the river, take a rest and soak in some sun. You certainly deserve it.

MILES AND DIRECTIONS

0.0   From the parking lot on the west side of the road, follow the white blazes to walk upstream.

0.1   Walk under the I-83 bridges.

0.6   The trail gradually makes a right turn at a T intersection.

0.9   On the left there is an amphitheater for the youth groups using the campground at Camp Wood. The trail heads to the right, over a wooden bridge, toward a paved road and parking lot.

1.0   To the right you can see where a bridge on Bunker Hill used to cross the river. Walk the road to the left before dipping back in the woods on the right. Immediately cross another paved road.

1.1 The Bunker Hill blue-blazed trail goes to the left. Hike straight on the south trail, heading down a few steps.

1.6 At the Mingo Forks Trail intersection, head to the right and downhill.

1.7 Take three rock hops across a creek.

1.8 The trail comes to a T and meets back up with the Gunpowder River. Hang a left, hugging the shoreline.

1.9 Pass an unmarked trail on your left.

2.1 Cross over a feeder branch on seven stumps and arrive at the parking area on Masemore Road.

2.2 On the other side of the road, toward the green iron bridge, follow white blazes for the Lefty Kreh (also Gunpowder South) Trail.

2.3 Pass the blue-blazed Highland Trail that heads off to the left.

2.9 Cross Falls Road with a green wrought-iron bridge that spans the Gunpowder. On the other side of the bridge is the wood marker for the Gunpowder North Trail. On our return trip we will cross this bridge to pick up the North Trail. For now, we do not cross the bridge but rather continue upstream, through the hole in the guardrail, following white blazes.

3.0 Rock-scramble uphill and then immediately down the other side. From here the trail becomes more rugged with nice river rapids.

3.7 Reach the other side of the Highland Loop Trail. Stay straight.

4.3 Arrive at Prettboy Dam. Retrace your steps to the Iron Bridge at Falls Road.

5.8 At Falls Road head left to cross over the green iron York Road bridge. Pick up the North Trail on the other side of the bridge, following blue blazes downstream.

6.6 Cross over Masemore Road, this time on the opposite side of the bridge.

8.0 Again see the Bunker Hill bridge that is out on your right. Cross a paved road and lot to continue on the other side.

8.7 Cross under the I-83 bridges again, this time heading downstream.

8.8 Cross a creek and head uphill to cross over York Road through a space in the guardrail to continue downstream. The opposite side of the bridge is where you parked.

9.7 Reach Raven Rock Falls on your left.

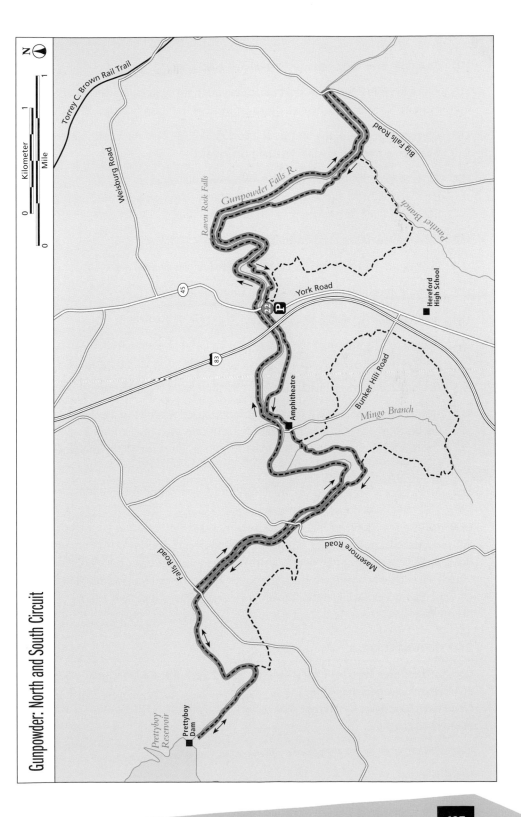

Gunpowder: North and South Circuit

N

Torrey C. Brown Rail Trail

Weisburg Road

Kilometer
0 1
Mile
0 1

Gunpowder Falls R.

Raven Rock Falls

Big Falls Road

Panther Branch

45

York Road

P 22

83

Hereford High School

Amphitheatre

Bunker Hill Road

Mingo Branch

Masemore Road

Falls Road

Prettyboy Reservoir

Prettyboy Dam

11.0 Bear right on a wide grass and gravel fire-road path.

11.3 Reach Big Falls Road. Cross the bridge on your right, walking toward a parking area. Be careful as there's a good amount of traffic and no shoulder.

11.4 On the other side of the bridge, at a ten-car lot, pick up the white-blazed trail on the river, once again heading upstream.

11.8 Cross the Panther Branch feeder creek. Immediately after the river crossing, head right to stay close to the riverbank. Then pass by the Panther Branch trail intersection on your left, blazed in blue.

12.2 Pass a yellow-blazed trail on your left.

12.4 Look right to see a rusted car on the other side of a swamp area.

12.5 Pass the intersection with the Sandy Lane Trail, blazed in pink.

13.0 Again see the Raven Rock Falls on the other side of the river.

13.3 Gain some elevation and see the river bend before heading back down to water level.

13.5 Again, leave the river, heading uphill, left, for a good thigh-burning climb.

13.8 Take a sharp right to follow the white blazes back downhill to water level. At the bottom of the hill, head to the left, upstream. Pass the Panther Branch Trailhead. Cross a creek into the meadow. Bear left through the meadow and up the stairs to reach York Road.

13.9 Arrive back at your car (take care when crossing York Road).

Options: Take the Highland Trail on your return instead of retracing your steps, and pick up the Gunpowder North Trail by crossing over the bridge on Masemore Road. Make your own shorter loop by using the various parking areas. End your loop at 9.0 miles when you pass the parking lot where started from at York Road.

Also Panther Branch and the Bunker Hill / Mingo Forks hikes are nearby off of York Road.

HIKE INFORMATION

Local attractions: Woodhall Wine Cellars, 17912 York Rd., Parkton; (410) 357-8644; woodhallwinecellars.com
Good eats: Casa Mia's Restaurant, 17417 York Rd., Parkton; (410) 357-4231; casamiasrestaurant.com

Gunpowder: Highland Loop

A short loop hike that provides access to one of the best, if not the best, sections of the Gunpowder River with pools, rapids, and chutes.

Start: Begin next to the iron bridge and follow the white blazes for Lefty Kreh Trail.
Distance: 3.0-mile loop
Hiking time: About 1.5 hours
Difficulty: Moderate due to rocky section
Trail surface: Natural surface and large rocks
Best season: Year-round
Other trail users: Trail runners, horseback riders
Canine compatibility: Leashed dogs permitted

Land status: State park
Fees and permits: None
Schedule: Sunrise–sunset daily
Maps: Trail maps available at park headquarters and the park's website
Trail contacts: Gunpowder Falls State Park, 2813 Jerusalem Rd., Kingsville, MD 21087; (410) 592-2897; dnr.state.md.us/publiclands/central/gunpowder.asp

Finding the trailhead: Take I-83 to exit 27 for Mount Carmel Road west. Take the first right on Masemore Road. Masemore Road passes the Fosters Masemore Mill and just after, find the parking area on the right. The trail starts on the opposite side of the road from the parking lot next to the iron bridge. Follow white blazes for the Lefty Kreh Trail. **GPS:** N39 36.672' / W76 40.975'

THE HIKE

t's always nice when you can mix up the scenery rather than having to retrace your steps. By combining the Highland Trail with the Gunpowder South Trail, we can do just that, all while giving you access to a fantastic stretch of river!

This loop hike begins at the green iron Howard B. Mays Bridge (1898) on Masemore Road on the opposite side of the road from the parking lot. Do not cross the iron bridge. Follow signs for the Lefty Kreh Fishing Trail blazed in white (this is also the Gunpowder South Trail).

A large rock sits in grass alongside the water and edge of the parking lot. It adorns a plaque dedicated to the Lefty Kreh Fishing Trail. It reads: "Dedicated

The trail doesn't always follow a distinct path but often takes hikers across boulder-size rocks.

to a Maryland Native son, fly-fishing pioneer, author, soldier, journalist, inventor, conservationist, photographer, outdoorsman, mentor and inspiration to count-less hopeful anglers around the world." In June 2012 Governor Martin O'Malley dedicated the Gunpowder South Trail as the Lefty Kreh Fishing Trail. Kreh is a world-renowned fly-fishing icon who has been a great influence on the sport. The Lefty Kreh Trail runs along Gunpowder Falls from the Prettyboy Reservoir to Bluemount Road in the Hereford area of Gunpowder Falls State Park.

Walk the trail upstream. In less than 500 feet, you will arrive at the inter-section with the blue-blazed Highland Trail, which heads to the left. Follow the Highland Trail but note that you will return to this spot via the white-blazed trail to complete the loop.

Begin heading uphill on a well-blazed trail with a creek down below in the valley. The trail continues with some small ups and downs and creek crossings. When you cross under some power lines, the trail continuing on the opposite side of the field becomes a much wider gravel flat path that looks to be a fire road.

After crossing a paved road and lot, the trail continues behind a green gate. Again the path narrows and you may catch a glimpse of the river. A gradual downhill becomes steeper until you come to a T intersection with the white-blazed Gunpowder South Trail. (If you were to walk left, you would reach Pret-tyboy Dam in 0.6 mile.) Take a right to continue making a loop, following the river back in the direction you came from. Look for a variety of birds on this loop, including cardinals and eagles. Beavers are also active here. It's also not uncom-mon to see a flowering dogwood and mountain laurel.

The path along the river gets rugged with rocks and roots to step over and around, and thick vegetation closing in on a narrow trail. A few steps of the trail are made of loose sand. As a result, you will be graced with a stunning section of river with giant rock outcroppings, flat rocks, and boulders on the trail and in the river, creating rapids, pools, and chutes. This is a popular catch-and-release fishing spot.

Soon, the distinct trail disappears and you'll need to rock-hop your way along the riverbank, although the blazes are still visible on this section. One final rock scramble uphill marks the end of the really rugged path. You'll see the Falls Road iron bridge. Do not cross the bridge, only cross to the opposite side of the road and walk through an open section of the guardrail to continue walking downstream.

Again, you will reach the intersection with the Highland Trail, this time retracing your steps to the iron bridge on Masemore Road and the parking lot. As you leave the lot, observe the architecture of the Fosters Masemore Mill. A plaque on the building reads BUILT IN 1797 BY NICHOLAS FOSTER AND CHRISTOPHER WALKER. THIS MILL WAS ONCE THE HUB OF AN AGRICULTURAL COMMUNITY. IT IS NOW A PRIVATE RESIDENCE WITHIN GUNPOWDER FALLS STATE PARK.

MILES AND DIRECTIONS

0.0   Begin at the green iron bridge on Masemore Road. Follow white blaze for Lefty Kreh Trail (also the Gunpowder South Trail), heading upstream.

0.1   After 500 feet, meet the intersection with the blue-blazed Highland Trail, which heads to the left. The Gunpowder South/Lefty Kreh Trail continues straight. You will return to this spot.

0.4   Cross a creek.

0.6   Cross the grassy field under the power lines.

1.1   Come to a green gate with a wooden trail post. Cross a road (named Falls Road but not *the* Falls Road) and meet up with the trail just behind another green gate.

1.3   Come to a Y intersection and make a right to continue downhill.

1.4   Come to a T intersection with the Gunpowder South Trail and make a right.

1.7   A sizable rapid marks the beginning and extra-rugged section of trail.

1.9   An unmarked trail heads off to the right.

2.1   Quickly head uphill on a rock scramble.

2.2   Cross a creek, followed by a road crossing (Falls Road). Continue to follow the white blazes.

2.4   Cross a creek.

2.8   Cross a 10-foot wooden bridge that spans a creek before returning to the start of the loop.

3.0   Arrive back at the trailhead and parking area.

A farmer who had a white colt named Pretty Boy was out in the pasture near a tributary stream of the Gunpowder River. Seeking shelter during a thunderstorm near the stream, it is said that the colt fell into the stream and perished. The tributary became known as Prettyboy in memory of the colt.

Gunpowder: Highland Loop

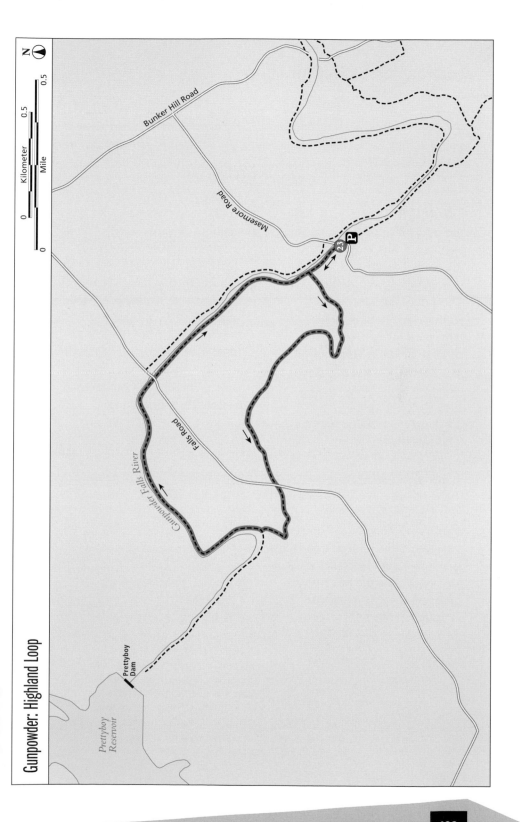

Gunpowder: Sweet Air Loop

An inspirational trail takes you through open meadows, cornfields, and dense pine forest and past a scenic pond. Nature quotes adorn the trees as you meander along the Little Gunpowder Falls.

Start: Begin your hike in the back corner of the lot at the sign that reads BARLEY POND LOOP.
Distance: 5.4-mile loop
Hiking time: About 3 hours
Difficulty: Moderate
Trail surface: Natural surface
Best season: Year-round
Other trail users: Trail runners, mountain bikers, and horseback riders permitted except on Cody Jean and Red Dot Trails
Canine compatibility: Leashed pets permitted

Land status: State park
Fees and permits: None
Schedule: Sunrise–sunset daily
Maps: Trail maps for the Sweet Air area are currently not available.
Trail contacts: Gunpowder Falls State Park, 2813 Jerusalem Rd., Kingsville, MD 21087; (410) 592-2897; dnr.state.md.us/publiclands/central/gunpowder.asp
Other: A trail kiosk with park map is located in the parking lot.

Finding the trailhead: Take I-95 north to exit 74 onto Route 152 toward Fallston. Follow it for 10.0 miles. Turn left onto Route 165 south. Take the first right onto Greene Road. In 0.2 mile make a right onto Moores Road, and in 0.5 mile, make a left onto Dalton Bevard Road. The parking lot is at the top of the hill on the right. Facing the tree line with your back to the road, pick up the trail in the far left corner of the parking lot. **GPS:** N39 32.167' / W76 30.337'

THE HIKE

One of Gunpowder's largest territories, the 1,250-acre Sweet Air area straddles Gunpowder Falls River, which is the natural boundary line of Harford and Baltimore Counties. Locals refer to this area of Sweet Air as a best-kept secret.

At the back side of the parking lot, a sign at the trailhead reads BARLEY POND LOOP, though this path is also the white-blazed Little Gunpowder Trail. We'll begin by heading to the left on this wide-open trail, which has some grass and some stone.

A meadow on the left filled with wildflowers and dandelions comes into view just before a junction with a cornfield. The trail, obviously very exposed, skirts the perimeter of the cornfield. Soon enough you'll head off into the woods of pine and tulip poplars in search of Barley Pond. Once you arrive, there is a calming sensation of a world where the fish have no cares and neither will you. Spend some time enjoying the silence, interrupted by the occasional sound of a plunk in the water.

The trail takes you across creeks and over bridges and boardwalks, with a few ups and downs along the way. A gradual downhill brings you to the river's

Fish dart through the water at Barley Pond, an exceptionally calming sight.

edge. There is a bench here if you want to get entranced by the flow of the water.

Making your way downriver, you'll pass one of several wooden signs with a quote that reads "Let nature be your teacher," while enjoying the view of small rapids and a large flat rock that juts out into the water.

At an intersection with the blue-blazed Boundary Trail, you could follow the blue trail but this means crossing over the river, which is 3 or 4 feet deep and 30 feet across. So pack some water shoes and prepare to get wet if you choose this route. For now, continue to stay straight. You will pass by several orange connector trails but continue to follow the white-blazed path.

At 3.2 miles leave the white-blazed Little Gunpowder Trail, which continues straight, and make a left on the blue-blazed Boundary Trail. A sign here directs you to the parking lot in 1.3 miles, however, we will be adding the Pine Loop to extend our circuit.

The trail becomes a wide mowed path with a large meadow on the left and houses on your right. Skirt the perimeter before coming to another mowed path off to the left, making a Y. Look closely for this left split as you start to come to the end of the field nearing a shed. Look to the left and up and across the field for a wooden post with a bird feeder on top. This is where you want to go.

Cut through the meadow, following the left side of the mowed Y split toward that post. When you reach the cornfield at the top of the hill, a sign directs you to the right for the Pine Loop. Follow the yellow-blazed Pine Loop, appropriately named, over a cushioned pine-needle path until you reach the intersection with the Cody Jean Trail. Follow the Cody Jean Trail through a gorgeous stand of white pine trees before reaching the intersection with Dalton Bevard Road (the road you drove in on). Walk across the road and back to the parking lot, passing by the Chesapeake Search Dogs Headquarters on the left.

The Chesapeake Search Dogs is a 100 percent volunteer nonprofit organization dedicated to ensuring 24/7 availability of a canine search team to law enforcement, fire services, and natural resource authorities, and emergency management agencies for the search for lost and missing persons, at no cost in the Chesapeake Bay and southern Pennsylvania regions. The final quote you will see as you leave the wooded path reads, "Enter these enchanted woods you who dare." You did, you dared, and you are a better person having experienced this little slice of paradise.

MILES AND DIRECTIONS

0.0   At the sign for Barley Pond Loop, start the trail by heading left.

0.1   Come to a meadow on the left followed by a junction at a cornfield. Take a left, following the perimeter of the cornfield on the yellow trail.

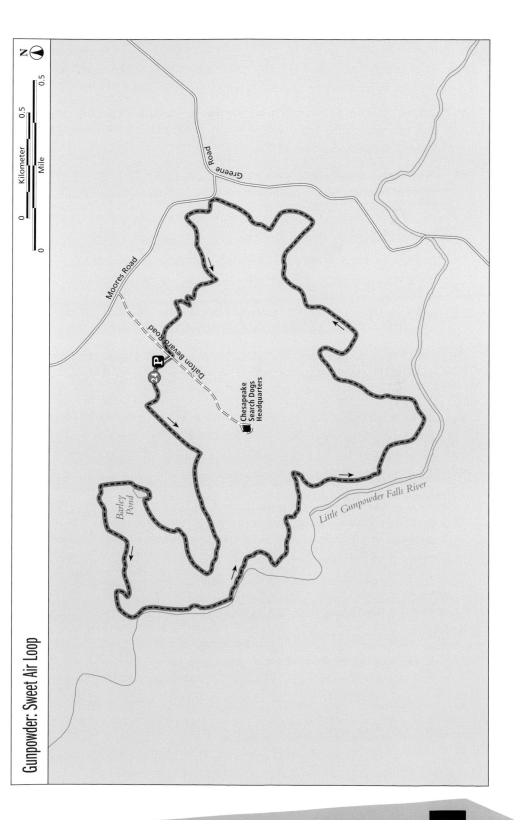

N

Kilometer
0   0.5   0.5

Mile
0   0.5   0.5

Moores Road

Greene Road

Dalton Bevard Road

P
24

Chesapeake
Search Dogs
Headquarters

Barley
Pond

Little Gunpowder Falls River

0.3 At a T intersection in the cornfield, a trail heads left toward some buildings. Take the trail to the right, continuing to follow the perimeter of cornfield.

0.6 Leave the cornfield and bear left into the woods. At a Y split, the red hikers-only trail goes to the left. Continue on the right split, still following the yellow trail, heading to Barley Pond.

0.8 At an intersection the trail headed straight goes to the river. You want to take a right to stay on the yellow trail, soon followed by a creek crossing.

0.9 An unmarked trail goes off to the left. Stay straight on the well-worn path blazed in yellow.

1.0 Reach Barley Pond. At the pond take a left to continue on the trail.

1.1 Reach a Y split. Make a left and head uphill on the white trail.

1.2 Reach the top of the hill and come to a T intersection. The white trail goes right and left. Make a left on the white-blazed trail.

1.3 Cross a boardwalk bridge followed by an intersection with the blue-blazed trail. Continue to the right, following both white and blue markers as the two trails share this path.

1.5 Here, the blue trail goes right and we continue on the white trail straight ahead.

1.7 Reach the river and other end of the red-blazed trail. The red trail goes to the right and you'll see a bridge platform with a bench (hikers-only trail). Continue left on the white trail and head downriver.

1.8 Read the sign with a quote and then cross a boardwalk. See an orange-blazed trail on the left, one of several orange connector trails that you will pass.

1.9 At an intersection the blue trail heads left. Continue to reach a second large junction. Here, you could head to the right on Boundary Trail but you must cross the river. Stay on the white trail straight ahead, do not cross the river, and continue downstream.

2.0 A John Muir quote hangs above a bench here. Check out the fallen tree with several trees growing out of it, and the small falls over a smooth rock.

2.2 A split requires horses to take the right path. They rejoin shortly uphill near the top. As you reach the top of the hill, there is an orange connector off to the left, soon followed by a wood bridge.

2.6   Pass by another bench and nature quote. Continue to stay on the well-worn white-blazed trail.

3.2   The white Little Gunpowder Trail goes straight ahead and the blue-blazed Boundary Trail goes left (to a parking lot) and right. Take a left (the sign reads To PARKING LOT IN 1.3 MILES). However, we will add on the Pine Loop. Head uphill on blue blazes.

3.4   Two trails go left. Head right here to stay on the blue-blazed trail. The trail becomes a wide-open path with green meadows on your left.

3.6   The mowed path comes to a split. Make a right at the split and immediately dip back into woods on the right. Again, pop out of the woods and back on a grassy path. Stay straight and uphill.

3.8   Skirt the perimeter of the field with houses on the right side. Look carefully for another mowed path that heads off to the left. Take the mowed path heading up and to the left. At the top of this mowed path, head toward a wood post with a birdhouse on top.

3.9   At the cornfield follow the trail sign for the Pine Loop, directing you to the right.

4.0   Follow the Pine Loop straight, followed by a right to follow the yellow blazes.

4.6   Parallel a road and continue through the wood fences. Make a right at the T intersection at the top of the hill.

4.8   The green trail goes left (hikers only) and straight to a parking lot. Stay straight, following the green trail.

4.9   At a picnic table and rock cairn, take a right on the Cody Jean Trail.

5.3   Reach Dalton Bevard Road. On your left is the headquarters for the Chesapeake Search Dogs (chesarda.org).

5.4   Arrive back at the parking lot and trailhead.

> *Chesapeake Search Dogs is a 100 percent volunteer nonprofit organization dedicated to ensuring 24/7 availability of a canine search team to law enforcement, fire services, and natural resource authorities, and emergency management agencies for the search for lost and missing persons, at no cost, in the Chesapeake Bay and southern Pennsylvania regions.*

Gunpowder: Pleasantville and Bottom Loop

Take a pleasant (no pun intended) hike through dense forest on a well-marked path. Hike some portions on the old Maryland and Pennsylvania Railroad bed, across many tributary streams, past the remains of the Ma & Pa Railroad trestle, all while enjoying floodplain and upland scenery.

Start: From the parking lot, follow the yellow-blazed trail with the river on your right.
Distance: 4.5-mile loop
Hiking time: About 2.5 hours
Difficulty: Moderate
Trail surface: Natural surface, short paved road walk
Best season: Year-round
Other trail users: Trail runners, horseback riders, mountain bikers
Canine compatibility: Leashed dogs permitted
Land status: State park

Fees and permits: None
Schedule: Sunrise–sunset daily
Maps: To date, there is not a formal published map of the area. However, a hand-drawn map is available for free at park headquarters and at dnr.state.md.us/publiclands/central/gunpowder central.asp.
Trail contacts: Gunpowder Falls State Park, 2813 Jerusalem Rd., Kingsville, MD 21087; (410) 592-2897; dnr.state.md.us/publiclands/central/gunpowder.asp

Finding the trailhead: Take 1-695 to exit 31, Harford Road northwest. Go 8.0 miles to a left on Fork Road. Go 2.5 miles to a hard right on Pleasantville Road. Go 1.0 mile and cross the steel bridge over the Gunpowder River to a small parking area immediately on the right. The trailhead is on the same side as the pull-off. The trail heads downhill toward the river from the parking area. **GPS:** N39 30.464' / W76 27.546'

THE HIKE

The concept of this loop hike is simple: Follow a yellow-blazed trail on the high road, following the Little Gunpowder Falls downstream from above until you reach gravel Bottom Road. Walk the road to the right, crossing an iron bridge over the Gunpowder. Then begin to follow the white-blazed Little Gunpowder Trail as it curves and heads uphill on the road before dipping back into the woods to now follow the river upstream.

To begin, find the trailhead on the same side of the parking lot, marked with a yellow blaze, heading downhill and downstream. With the river on your right side, the trail begins as a nice level path. Soon after the start, the trail heads to the left and uphill for views of the river below.

The Little Gunpowder Falls is the border between Baltimore and Harford Counties. On your way downstream, in less than a mile, come to the foundations of an old rail trestle that once carried passengers on the Ma & Pa Railroad and ran steam engines across the Little Gunpowder Falls.

From the foundations, the trail climbs uphill and to the left, away from the river. As you near the top, the trail bears to the right. However, a worn path heads left to get a view from another trestle foundation. As you continue on the yellow trail, it levels out and you'll now be walking the path of the former rail bed of the Ma & Pa Railroad. Several blue-blazed trails head off to the left and right, typically rejoining the yellow trail, but just stay on the yellow. Some houses will come into

Find the foundations of an old rail trestle and go back in time envisioning passengers being carried across the river on the former Ma & Pa Railroad.

view through the woods, in the distance on your left. The Maryland and Pennsylvania Railroad, known as the "Ma and Pa," ran between York, Pennsylvania, and Baltimore. Passenger service ended in 1954. But you can still envision its route as you hike the path through carved-out hillsides, past rugged rock walls and outcroppings, and above the river valley.

As the trail heads downhill, a road may be seen in the distance. The trail eventually intersects with this gravel road, Bottom Road. Walk the road to the right and pass by the intersection of Bottom Road and Laurel Brook. On the right, pass by a green gate with No TRESPASSING signs. Next, cross a bridge and pass the next intersection with Guyton Road. Once you see the scenic green steel bridge ahead, cross over and look for a white blaze on a tree. The road has now become paved, and the trail becomes a brief road walk, curving uphill to the left before dipping into the woods on the right. A few pull-offs for cars line the road. The trail on this side of the river heads upstream. You are now walking the white-blazed Little Gunpowder Trail, which you will hike all the way back to the trailhead.

Heading upstream, you will encounter many more ups and downs and creek crossings, including one particular scenic creek with water flowing over moss-covered rocks before it tumbles gently into the river. Nearing the end, the trail becomes a wide, flat ridge trail and then takes a turn downhill to the right, following staggered white blazes. A trail does continue straight ahead, but follow the blazes to return to your car. At this point the distinct rumble of cars crossing the steel bridge is within earshot before you arrive back where you began. Only this time you have popped out on the opposite side of the bridge and river. You will need to *carefully* cross the bridge to arrive back at the parking area, as cars do come fast and frequent.

MILES AND DIRECTIONS

0.0 Start the trail from the same side of the parking lot, marked with a yellow blaze. Head downhill and downstream. The river is on your right side.

0.1 The trail heads uphill to the left, away from the river.

0.2 Cross a creek and follow yellow blazes on the opposite side of the creek.

0.3 A distinct trail heads off to the left. Bear right to follow the yellow blazes.

0.5 Cross a feeder creek on a 4-foot-wide bridge and stay straight.

0.7 Cross a creek and several more stream valleys.

0.9 Arrive at the remains of foundations of a rail bridge that once crossed the river. The remains can be seen on both sides of the river. Just past the foundations, the trail splits. Take the left trail and head uphill on the yellow-blazed trail.

Gunpowder: Pleasantville and Bottom Loop

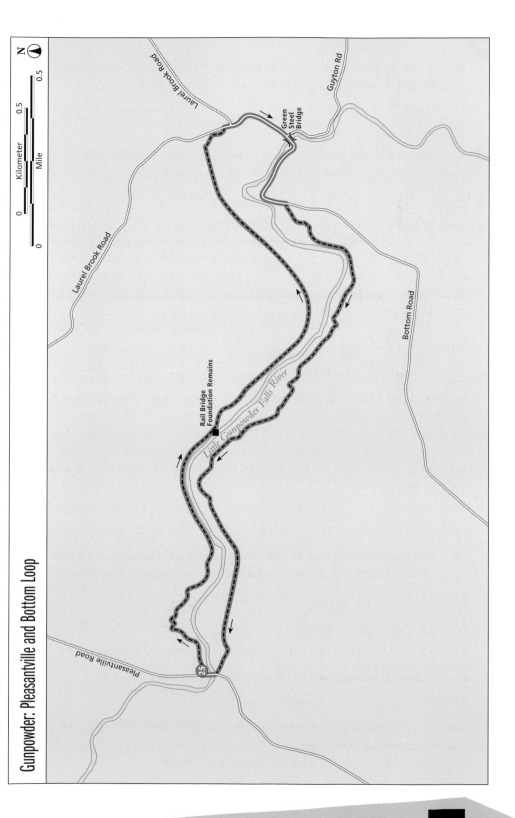

N

Kilometer
0   0.5   0.5

Mile
0   0.5

Laurel Brook Road

Laurel Brook Road

Green Steel Bridge

Guyton Rd

Bottom Road

Rail Bridge Foundation Remains

Little Gunpowder Falls River

Pleasantville Road

2.5

1.0 The yellow trail curves to the right, though there is a worn trail that heads straight up a hump of hill. The yellow is the more obvious option.

1.4 See a blue-blazed trail on your right, but continue to stay straight to follow yellow blazes.

1.7 See another blue intersection on the right. Continue to stay straight.

1.8 Note the faded blue-blazed trail on the left and the S curve of the river. Here, you may be able to see a road in the distance on your right.

1.9 Stay straight ahead on the obvious rail bed trail, though you may see a faded blue blaze in the distance and another trail heading toward the river.

2.0 The trail heads downhill to a road.

2.1 Reach the gravel Bottom Road and head to the right. Pass the intersection with Laurel Brook Road.

2.3 Cross the green steel bridge over the Gunpowder. See a white blaze painted on a tree (left side) on the other side of the bridge. The road is now paved and the trail follows the road uphill.

2.6 Leave the paved road and head downhill to the right, following the staggered white blazes.

3.7 Look down and across the river to see the same train foundations we saw heading downstream.

3.8 Cross a scenic creek.

3.9 At the top of a hill, the trail bears right and becomes a flat and wide ridge trail.

4.4 A distinct trail continues straight, though you will follow the staggered white blazes downhill to the right followed by one last creek crossing before arriving back at the bridge where you started. Cross the bridge and head to the parking area.

4.5 Arrive back at the trailhead and parking area.

HIKE INFORMATION

Local attractions: Boordy Vineyards, 12820 Long Green Pike, Hydes; (410) 592-5015; boordy.com

Good eats: Palmisano's Italian Deli Bakery, 13500 Long Green Pike, Hydes; (410) 592-9477; palmisanos.com

Little Gunpowder Trail: Sherwood Loop

Although smaller than the Big Gunpowder River, the Little Gunpowder has just as much to offer if not more in the way of bold rapids, scenic shoots, and attractive tributaries. This hike takes you through a covered bridge and follows only a short but spectacular portion of the 25.2-mile river.

Start: Begin at park headquarters
Distance: 6.4-mile lollipop loop
Hiking time: About 3 hours
Difficulty: Moderate
Trail surface: Natural surface
Best season: Year-round
Other trail users: Mountain bikers, trail runners, horseback riders
Canine compatibility: Leashed dogs permitted
Land status: State park
Fees and permits: None
Schedule: Daily sunrise–sunset. Jerusalem Mill Museum and Visitor Center open weekends from 1 to 4 p.m.

Maps: To date, there is not a formal published map of the area. However, a hand-drawn map is available for free at park headquarters and at dnr.state.md.us/publiclands/central/gunpowdercentral.asp.
Trail contacts: Gunpowder Falls State Park, 2813 Jerusalem Rd., Kingsville, MD 21087; (410) 592-2897; dnr.state.md.us/publiclands/central/gunpowder.asp
Other: Summer concerts, war reenactments, and restrooms inside park headquarters

Finding the trailhead: From I-95, take exit 74 to MD 152 west (Mountain Road). Follow Mountain Road toward Fallston and turn left onto Jerusalem Road. Park in the lot on the right, just before the mill. **GPS:** N39 27.746' / W76 23.452'

The starting point is a site to see in itself. The historic Jerusalem Mill Village is one of the oldest undamaged mill villages in Maryland. Many of the village structures are open to the public, including the gristmill, gun shop, blacksmith shop, springhouse, and general store. The hike described here will take us to the final structure open to the public: the Jericho Covered Bridge.

In total the white-blazed Little Gunpowder Trail extends between Harford Road to the northwest and I-95 to the south. The trail described here is a 6-mile out-and-back stretch with a short loop, beginning at a midpoint, at the Jerusalem Mill Historic Village, and extending south to I-95. The river forms a boundary between eastern Baltimore County and western Harford County. The trail flip-flops from the west to east sides of the river.

Cross through Jericho Covered Bridge to continue your hike on the opposite side of the river.

Start at the park headquarters and cross the Jerusalem Road bridge over the Little Gunpowder Falls. Immediately on the other side, a white-blazed natural-surface trail heads into the woods on the left, paralleling the river. The path is wide and clear with the occasional bench overlooking a scenic spot in the river. Looking to the left, you may catch a glimpse of the Jericho Covered Bridge in the distance . . . quite a nostalgic sight.

Just after you reach an intersection with a yellow horse trail, the white trail pops out on the paved Jericho Road, where you will walk through the Jericho Covered Bridge. Once across, the trail continues to follow the river on quite rugged terrain, passing by the backyards of a couple homes. Until you reach Franklinville Road, the trail takes you up and over rocks, across boulders and creeks, and around tree roots. You'll carefully place each step but have a lot of fun doing it. The rapids in this section are wild and raging. You can really get a sense of the power of the river. This short section of trail, when you leave the river and head uphill, is the only portion that could get a little tricky. You may find a trail that takes you around a trail obstruction. If you do get detoured or off-course, just know that you eventually need to get back down to the edge of the river.

At 1.8 miles the trail meets up with Franklinville Road. Hop over the guardrail and cross the bridge. On the other side, hang an immediate left to hug the river, only this time you are on the opposite bank of the river. The terrain calms down, the path becomes more open, and the walking is now quite easy.

In less than a half mile, the Little Gunpowder Trail intersects with the blue-blazed Sherwood Trail. The Sherwood Trail is a nice alternative to a straight out-and-back hike, allowing you to make a short loop, eventually connecting back to the Little Gunpowder Trail, to avoid retracing every single step. The Sherwood Trail wraps around and through Kingsville County Park, skirting the edge of ball fields and exiting the woods at a set of bleachers and a park road, just before again meeting up with the Little Gunpowder Trail.

Back on the white-blazed trail, with nice terrain and several creek hops, you can't avoid the sound of traffic and glimpses through the trees of cars whizzing by as you near busy I-95. You'll have to suck it up for a bit and focus on the beautiful scenery and not the sounds. Just be happy that you are on the trail and not stuck in traffic! Soon enough the traffic noise fades into the distance, replaced by the sound of the Little Gunpowder Falls' rushing water. Now you'll be following the river upstream.

Once you pass that same intersection with the Sherwood Trailhead, you'll be retracing your steps back across the Franklinville Road bridge, up and over some gnarly terrain, through the Jericho Covered Bridge, and back into the Jerusalem Mill Historic Village. You'll know you are getting close to the end when you start hearing the thundering sound of cars going through the bridge.

0.0 Begin the hike at the park headquarters and cross the road bridge over Little Gunpowder Falls. Follow the steps and white blazes as they head into the woods on the left immediately on the other side of the bridge.

0.5 Reach an intersection with the white trail heading to the left and a yellow horse trail heading to the right. Continue to the left to reach Jericho Road and cross through the covered bridge. Follow white blazes to the right and downhill on the immediate opposite side of the bridge, following it downstream.

0.6 Cross a feeder creek, four rock steps across, and bear right, following the river downstream.

0.7 Bear left, following staggered blazes and heading uphill.

0.8 Cross another feeder creek.

0.9 Follow the trail left and uphill, away from the river.

1.4 Look for stepped rapids on your right, though obstructed by the trees.

1.4 Follow the white blazes to the right, abruptly downhill, to reach the water's edge.

1.5 See the building foundation off to the right on the opposite side of the river.

1.6 An unmarked trail heads to the left. Stay along the river, and cross an awesome feeder creek with cool rocks.

1.8 Hop over the guardrail at Franklinville Road and cross the bridge over the river. On the other side the trailhead is on the left. Look for a blaze painted on the metal guardrail and follow the trail along the river.

2.1 Reach the intersection with the Sherwood blue-blazed trail.

2.3 Cross a paved road.

2.8 Walk next to bleachers and a ball field, cross the access road, and again follow the white-blazed trail. Leave the blue-blazed Sherwood Loop.

2.9 Cross between two baseball fields toward a wooden post with a white blaze on the other side.

3.4 Walk a paved road for a few steps uphill and follow the white blazes on the opposite side.

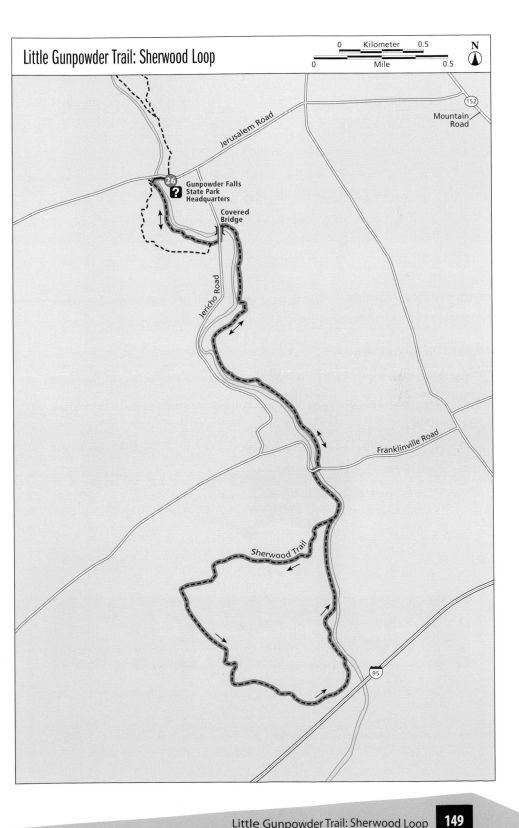

Little Gunpowder Trail: Sherwood Loop

0   Kilometer   0.5
0   Mile   0.5

N

Jerusalem Road

Mountain
Road

152

26

Gunpowder Falls
State Park
Headquarters

Covered
Bridge

Jericho Road

Franklinville Road

Sherwood Trail

95

3.6 Cross another feeder creek. In roughly 0.2 mile the river will come back into view.

4.3 Cross a scenic creek with big boulders and spills of waterfalls followed by a tiny creek crossing.

4.4 Again pass the intersection with the Sherwood Trail. Now begin to retrace your steps.

4.6 Cross back over Franklinville Road bridge.

6.0 Again cross through the covered bridge. Reach the other side and dip back into the woods (on the right).

6.4 Arrive back at the trailhead, parking area, and park headquarters.

Options: Little Gunpowder Trail toward Harford Road starts across Jerusalem Road from park headquarters, behind the blacksmith shop.

HIKE INFORMATION

Good eats: The Sunshine Grille, 12607 Fork Rd., Fork; (410) 592-3378; sunshine grille.com. Greek and American cuisine.

🌿 **Green Tip:**
Control your pets at all times. Keep your dog on a leash.
Never let your dog chase wildlife.

Prettyboy Reservoir: Hemlock Gorge

The trail plays hide-and-seek as it makes its way over giant rocks, around gnarly root systems, and across a sloped hillside before arriving at a swimming hole surrounded by natural rock walls. The fun continues through a lowland area with a carpet of green vegetation.

Start: From the parking lot, the trail begins near a metal guardrail.
Distance: 1.6 miles out and back
Hiking time: About 50 minutes
Difficulty: Difficult due to rock scrambling
Trail surface: Natural surface
Best season: Year-round
Other trail users: Hiking only
Canine compatibility: Leashed dogs permitted
Land status: Watershed Management Area
Fees and permits: None
Schedule: Sunrise–sunset daily

Maps: No trail maps available for Prettyboy Reservoir Water Quality Management Area
Trail contacts: City of Baltimore Department of Public Works, Reservoir Natural Resources Section, 5685 Oakland Rd., Eldersburg, MD 21784; (410) 795-6151; baltimore city.gov
Other: No facilities
Special considerations: Swimming is not permitted within the Prettyboy Reservoir Watershed Quality Management Area

Finding the trailhead: Take I-83 to exit 31, Middletown Road west. Go 4.6 miles to Beckleysville Road. Take a left on Beckleysville, and in 0.2 mile make a sharp right on Cotter Road. Drive 1.7 miles and make a left on Clipper Mill Road. At 0.3 mile cross the reservoir bridge, and at 0.7 mile make a right on Gunpowder Road. Pass Hoffman Cemetery on your right, then drive over the bridge crossing the Gunpowder River and park on the right side immediately after the bridge. Parking on the left is available a bit farther up. **GPS:** N39 41.387' / W76 46.851'

THE HIKE

This short hike through the Hemlock Gorge section along the Gunpowder Falls River is immensely rewarding. Don't be discouraged by the graffiti on the underside of the bridge as you start the hike.

As for the trail, well, sometimes you see it and sometimes you don't! As long as you keep the river close to you on the right, you'll be able to make your way just fine. At first your view of the river is blocked by dense vegetation, but soon enough you'll be hugging the bank of the wide river, roughly 40 feet across, on a packed-dirt path underfoot.

The trail heads uphill just briefly. On the way up look below on your right for a trail that again hugs the riverbank. Take a steep side trail that will lead downhill to meet back up with the river's edge, though the uphill path does continue. Steps after you join the trail along the water, you'll see an educational sign describing the history of the Hemlock Gorge and the Clipper Paper Mill. Though it seems out of place, it is quite interesting and informative. It tells hikers about the rich history of Hemlock Gorge at Prettyboy. The sign reads: "In 1775 William Hoffman built the first paper mill in Maryland, the Clipper Paper Mill. The Gunpowder paper mill was completed in 1776. Hoffman's daughter Carolina enjoyed playing

Massive boulders, rock walls, and a cave are cool features of this short and sweet hike.

among the hemlocks in the gorge so much that he named the area Lina's Glen. In 1925, the Glen and surrounding land were purchased by the state of Baltimore, which was preparing to expand its water supply." It explains the relationship of mammals and birds with the microclimate of a hemlock forest, specifically the flying squirrel, brook trout, and the veery, and then goes on to explain the hemlock woolly adelgid (HWA). Since the early 1990s many eastern hemlock forests died off due to HWA, a destructive bug native to east Asia. The grove in Hemlock Gorge is being treated by the Maryland Department of Agriculture to prevent infestation by the dangerous exotic species.

Behind this educational sign, cross a beautiful feeder creek with some moss-covered rocks and boulders. The trail continues on the opposite side.

One short section will require traversing a sloped hillside with no obvious trail, as you grab hold of a rock or tree trunk to keep you from slipping downhill. This little challenge is worth the big reward as you near a bend in the river. A scenic pool of water follows along the river, with both sides of the gorge lined with massive boulders and rugged rock walls. Notice a cave on your left. A small sand and gravel beach and large flat rocks offer a place to take a rest and enjoy the spills and plunges as the river flows over the rocks. Nope, you are not the first person to discover the little trail treasure! Although it's tempting to want to do a cannonball plunge, resist the urge and keep in mind that swimming is not permitted.

Once you've had your fill, continue to make out a trail as it leaves this rocky section and transitions into a narrow cut through an open and exposed lowland area, green with vegetation, filled with skunk cabbage, and dotted with colorful wildflowers. It's a drastic change of scenery. The river calms and the roaring sound of the rapids fades. A pleasant sound of chirping birds fills the air . . . or the aggravated sounds of duck calls if you happen to startle them. The sun pours onto the path, which was previously hidden by the dense forest. Continue on the trail until you reach a creek that cuts through the green landscape, feeding the river. At this point turn around and retrace your steps. However, a trail does continue on the opposite side of this feeder creek and another trail heads off to the left, should you choose to explore some more. On your return don't stress over following your exact footsteps. Again, hug the river's edge and you'll easily make the return trip.

MILES AND DIRECTIONS

0.0 Walk through an opening between a cement guardrail on the left and a metal guardrail on your right to follow a narrow dirt path, which is slightly overgrown. Head slightly downhill toward the river and the underside of the road bridge and bear left.

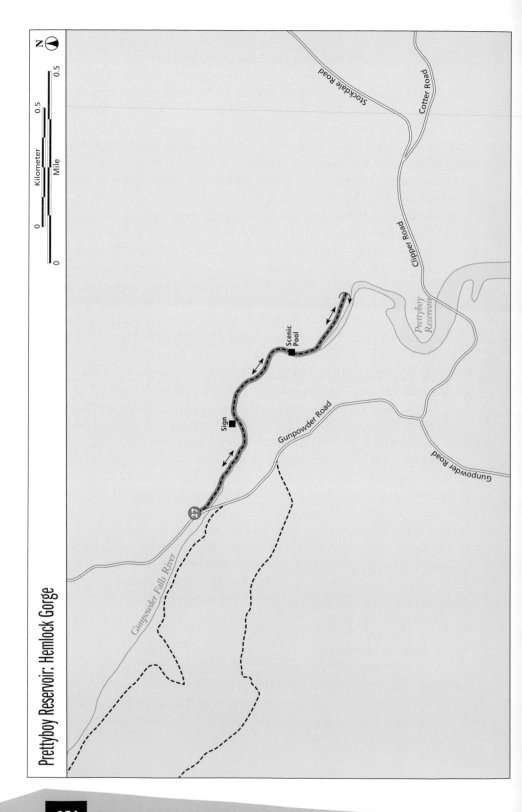

Prettyboy Reservoir: Hemlock Gorge

0.1   The trail, now in view of the river, hugs the bank.

0.2   Heading up a small incline, look down to the right to see a path that follows the river. A worn trail continues uphill, but take the steep downhill path, again hugging the riverbank.

0.3   Come to an educational sign about the history of Hemlock Gorge and the Clipper Paper Mill.

0.4   The trail fades away as you walk a sloped hillside bank.

0.5   The riverbank becomes more level and the river takes a sharp bend to the right.

0.6   Arrive at a scenic pool.

0.8   Reach a creek that cuts through an open forest floor, feeding into the Gunpowder River. Retrace your steps.

1.6   Arrive back at the trailhead.

HIKE INFORMATION

Local attractions: Just on the other side of the bridge and uphill on Gunpowder Road (before you reach the cemetery), find the trailhead for the Prettyboy Reservoir: Gunpowder Loop hike (Hike 28).

The eastern hemlock is one of the most unique species in the United States. With optimal growing conditions, one can live for over 800 years. A hemlock forest is a fragile and rare ecosystem in the mid-Atlantic region.

Prettyboy Reservoir: Gunpowder Loop

This fire-road trail offers a great deal of solitude on a wide path before leading hikers to a scenic section of river following along a narrow, rugged trail.

Start: Begin at a fire road with a sign that reads GATE 20.
Distance: 3.8-mile loop
Hiking time: About 2 hours
Difficulty: Moderate
Trail surface: Natural surface
Best season: Year-round
Other trail users: Mountain bikers permitted on fire roads
Canine compatibility: Leashed dogs permitted
Land status: Watershed Management Area
Fees and permits: None
Schedule: Sunrise–sunset daily

Maps: No trail maps available for Prettyboy Reservoir Water Quality Management Area
Trail contacts: City of Baltimore Department of Public Works, Reservoir Natural Resources Section, 5685 Oakland Rd., Eldersburg, MD 21784; (410) 795-6151; baltimorecity.gov
Other: No facilities, fishing
Special considerations: Swimming, wading, and camping are not permitted, and boats are allowed by permit only.

Finding the trailhead: Take I-83 to exit 31, Middletown Road west. Go 4.6 miles to Beckleysville Road. Take a left on Beckleysville, and in 0.2 mile make a sharp right on Cotter Road. Drive 1.7 miles and make a left on Clipper Mill Road. At 0.3 mile cross the reservoir bridge, and at 0.7 mile make a right on Gunpowder Road. Pass Hoffman Cemetery on your right, and immediately park in the pull-off on the right-hand side. Do not cross the Gunpowder Road bridge over the river. **GPS:** N39 41.204' / W76 46.683'

THE HIKE

The Prettyboy Reservoir Watershed on the Gunpowder River is the smallest and most remote of the three area reservoir watersheds. Keep in mind that the main goal of the management of the reservoir area is water quality, and recreation trails are a secondary benefit. Therefore, the reservoirs and water-quality management areas do not offer the same facilities and services you would find at a park or area specifically designed for recreation.

Just past the Hoffman Cemetery, park in the first pull-off on the right-hand side with room for maybe eight to ten cars. The trailhead is on the opposite side of the road from the parking area. Begin at two wooden posts with a silver cable strung across. A sign reads No PARKING and GUNPOWDER ROAD GATE 20.

Many of Prettyboy's trails are made up of fire roads, and they are not blazed. This trail is no exception. In all honesty the first leg of the trail is nothing to write home about with regard to scenery, however, the solitude certainly gets a thumbs up. The second half of the loop has much to offer in the way of scenery, and by using this fire road on the first leg, you are able to avoid retracing your steps, which is always a plus.

Several wide trails come in from your right, but it's not until you get to a Y split, with a grassy path off to the left and narrow dirt trail straight ahead, that you leave the fire road. Taking the narrower path straight ahead, the trail heads steeply downhill, and the sound of traffic can be heard in the distance.

Grave Run Road soon comes in to view. About 50 feet shy of reaching the road, you'll practically make a U-turn onto a lower-level trail that heads back in the direction you came from. This is where you start your return loop. However, you may want to first head straight to the road and check out River Valley Ranch. The ranch is a Christian Day Camp set up like a frontier town. It's a beautiful property.

As you make your way on the return loop on the lower trail, you will be following a small feeder creek on the left, passing by stables and the Old Town Meeting House on the property of River Valley Ranch. The creek soon flows into the Gunpowder River and the trail now follows the river.

At a split in the trail, the path straight ahead continues on a wide gravel/stone fire-road path. Another very narrow path heads slightly left, following the river. Take this low road along the river even though it may be somewhat overgrown and at times it may be difficult to make out a trail. Just stay straight, keeping the river close to you on the left. As long as you do this, the path will soon come back into view and you'll be rewarded with glorious rocks, rapids, and boulders.

The river splits around what I can best describe as an island. To the left of the island, the water turns to rapids. The right side is calm water. On the right a plank of wood will help you cross over to the right side of the split. Still keeping the river on your left, there is definitely not a trail here, as you walk the left bank and onto the island. The piles of wood mean that beavers are active in this area. After the island you will soon make out a trail or at least an open pathway between some large rocks. A cool breeze blows in the valley, the water gurgles, and ducks perch on a rock, proud to call this stretch of river their home.

Soon, the trail widens again to a fire road, leaving the river, and gains some elevation before leveling out. White-tailed deer run the hillsides here. At the two intersections, keep left, making your way back downhill and toward the river. Nearing the end of the hike, the river again comes into view for a bit before leaving the dirt path and arriving back at Gunpowder Road. The trail pops you out at Gate 22, farther downhill on Gunpowder Road from where you started. Easily the hardest climb of the day, you'll have to walk the road uphill to return to your car.

MILES AND DIRECTIONS

0.0 Begin the hike on a wide fire road, marked as Gate 20, gradually heading uphill.

0.5 A wide trail comes in from the right and heads to the river. Stay straight.

0.6 Pass another wide path on the right. Continue straight.

0.7 On your left see a large open field while walking past a row of pine trees.

1.0 A path heads off to the right. Stay straight, heading downhill.

1.1 The trail bears left, followed by a trail that comes in on the right. Pass that trail and continue straight and uphill.

1.4 The trail splits to the left and straight at a Y intersection. Leave the fire road and take the dirt path, which is the narrower of the two trails, straight ahead.

1.5 Head steeply downhill.

1.7 Grave Run Road and the River Valley Ranch come into view. Stop about 50 feet short of the road and make a U-turn onto a lower-level trail that heads back in the direction you came from following a feeder creek. This is where you start your return loop.

1.9 The feeder creek dumps into the Gunpowder River here and the trail now bears to the right, following the river.

2.2 The trail splits straight and slightly right on a wide stone path, and to the left a narrow path follows the river. Take the trail left to hug the river.

Prettyboy Reservoir: Gunpowder Loop

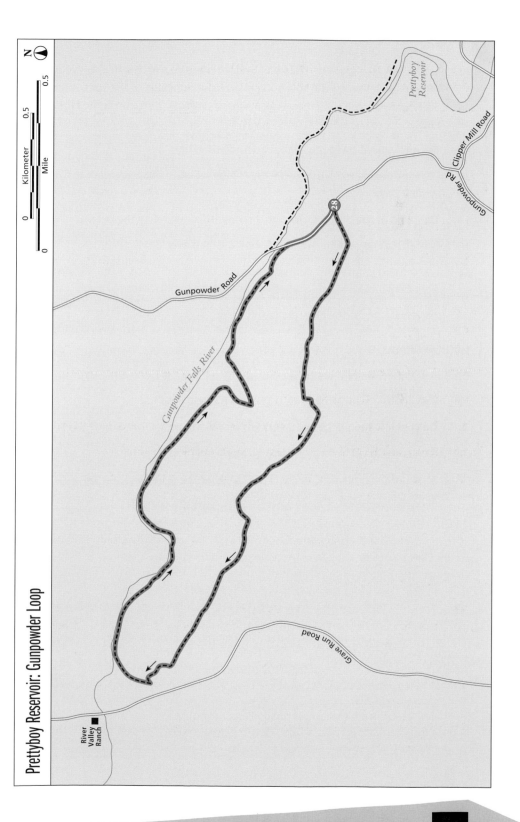

2.3 See an island in the river. Follow the right bank, keeping the river on your left. A plank of wood will help you cross to the right side of the split. After the island you will soon make out an open pathway between some large rocks.

2.6 The trail widens back into a fire road and heads uphill.

2.9 Once the incline levels out, come to a Y intersection. Follow the path to the left and downhill.

3.0 Take a left at the next intersection, continuing downhill to the river.

3.3 The fire road levels out and then levels with the river.

3.5 Leave the dirt fire road and pop out at Clipper Mill Road (Gate 22) just downhill from where you started. Walk the road uphill to return to your car.

3.8 Arrive back at the trailhead and parking lot.

HIKE INFORMATION

On the opposite side of the bridge on Gunpowder Road is the trailhead for the Hemlock Trail (Hike 27).

Maryland's Lakes and Baltimore's Reservoirs

Did you know that there are zero natural lakes in the state of Maryland? All of the state's lakes have been man-made by damming rivers. These bodies of water are sometimes called lakes but more often named reservoirs. If its primary purpose is for recreation, it's typically referred to as a lake. But if its purpose is for flood control, power, or water supply, it is usually named a reservoir. Of the reservoirs mentioned in this book, Baltimore's three reservoirs are Loch Raven, Prettyboy, and Liberty. The Baltimore City Department of Public Works (DPW) oversees the three bodies of water, totaling 477 square miles of watershed. The job of the DPW is to protect these areas primarily because they are the source of local drinking water but also because they provide natural areas for recreating. The Conowingo Reservoir, spanning Harford and Cecil Counties on the Susquehanna River, was purposed for the generation of hydroelectric power and also offers recreational opportunities.

Rocks State Park: Falling Branch

A quick out-and-back hike in the Falling Branch area of Rocks State Park couldn't be more rewarding when the destination is Maryland's second-highest vertical waterfall, Kilgore Falls.

Start: Begin at the parking lot.
Distance: 1.1 miles out and back with spur
Hiking time: About 30 minutes
Difficulty: Easy
Trail surface: Dirt path and short bridge and boardwalk
Best season: Year-round
Other trail users: Runners, horseback riders
Canine compatibility: Leashed pets permitted
Land status: State park
Fees and permits: None
Schedule: Open daily 9 a.m. to sunset Apr–Oct, 10 a.m. to sunset Nov–Mar
Maps: Trail map available at dnr.state.md.us/publiclands/central/rocksmap.asp
Trail contacts: Rocks State Park, 3318 Rocks Chrome Hill Rd., Jarrettsville, MD 21084; (410) 557-7994; dnr.maryland.gov/publiclands/central/rocks.asp
Other: Trail offers a nice swimming hole but there is no lifeguard on duty. There are no facilities such as restrooms or picnic tables.

Finding the trailhead: From US 1 north / Belair Road toward Bel Air, exit on MD 24 north / Rock Spring Road toward Forest Hill and Rocks. At the roundabout stay straight on MD 24 / Rocks Road. Turn left on St. Mary's Road. Turn right on Falling Branch Road. The parking lot is on your right. The lot fills up fast on weekends and holidays. No parking is allowed on Falling Branch Road. **GPS:** N39 41.402' / W76 25.391'

THE HIKE

n addition to the 855 acres of Rocks State Park, the Falling Branch Area makes up a 67-acre parcel of land, located 5.0 miles north of Rocks State Park. The biggest reward on this wooded hike is the second-highest natural vertical waterfall in Maryland, Kilgore Falls. Rumored as a meeting place for Susquehannock Indians, few others in recent years knew about this gem. The falls were located on private property until ownership was granted to the state of Maryland and opened to the public in 1993. This area of northern Harford County used to bustle with mills, farms, tanneries, and stills dating back to the 1700s. However, it was mostly abandoned in the 1900s once the railroad shut down and farmers didn't have a way to get their crops to Baltimore markets.

Rock-hop across Falling Branch stream to reach the base of the falls.

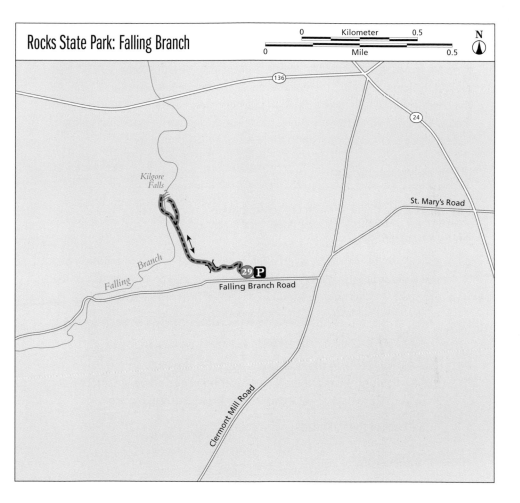

The wooded path will take you over a footbridge and boardwalk as you make your way to the falls, following Falling Branch stream, a tributary to Deer Creek. Falling Branch stream passes through a steep gorge known as Kilgore Rocks. Along the way you'll see a few hemlock trees, hardwood oak, and lots of maples. Look for white-tailed deer, red fox, wild turkey, black snakes, black racers, and a variety of birds like the woodcock. If you are really lucky, you might even see an eagle. This environmentally sensitive area is also host to a family of beavers, but be sure to enjoy the wildlife from a distance.

About halfway down the footpath, 150 feet past a bench, look to the left for the remains of what is said to be an old farmstead comprising a two-story wood-frame home with a massive chimney. The trail comes to a Y, and you can choose to go right to the top of the falls or left to a water crossing, Falling Branch stream, with nicely placed rocks and stepping stones. After crossing the stream the trail continues right to the impressive falls surrounded by huge boulders and rock formations. According to the Maryland Geological Survey, the waterfall is 17 feet tall but the rocks that form the gorge around the falls are about 34 feet high. At the base of Kilgore Falls, take a dip in the same waters where the scene from the movie *Tuck Everlasting,* starring Alexis Bledel and Jonathan Jackson, was filmed. Note that the rocks are slippery and there is no lifeguard on duty.

MILES AND DIRECTIONS

0.0   Start at the trailhead, adjacent to the parking lot.

0.2   Reach a bench.

0.3   Look down to the left to see the remains of an old stone foundation of a mill and farmhouse. When you reach the Y intersection to the top of the falls, take the trail right to continue to the top.

0.4   Arrive at the top of the falls and return the same way back to the Y intersection.

0.5   Take the trail down to the river and water crossing. Once across, follow the trail to the right. Cross a short wood footbridge and arrive at Kilgore Falls. Trace your steps back to return to the trailhead and parking area.

1.1   Arrive back at the trailhead.

HIKE INFORMATION

Local attractions: Fiore Winery of Maryland, 3026 Whiteford Rd., Pylesville; (410) 879-4007; fiorewinery.com

Rocks State Park: Hidden Valley

So simple, so scenic! Enjoy massive layers of rock and river views. This area of Rocks State Park, along an undeveloped riverbank, is located in the smallest of the three sections of Rocks State Park.

Start: From the parking lot, begin at the boardwalk on your right when facing Deer Creek.
Distance: 1.1 miles out and back
Hiking time: About 40 minutes
Difficulty: Easy
Trail surface: Natural surface
Best season: Year-round
Other trail users: Bikers, anglers
Canine compatibility: Leashed pets permitted
Land status: State park

Fees and permits: None
Schedule: Open daily 9 a.m. to sunset Apr–Oct, 10 a.m. to sunset Nov–Mar
Maps: Trail map available at dnr .state.md.us/publiclands/central/ rocksmap.asp
Trail contacts: Rocks State Park, 3318 Rocks Chrome Hill Rd., Jarrettsville, MD 21084; (410) 557- 7994; dnr.maryland.gov/ publiclands/central/rocks.asp

Finding the trailhead: From I-95, take exit 74 for MD 152. Turn left on Mountain Road. Drive 15 miles and turn right on Jarrettsville Pike. Continue 1.7 miles and at the four-way stop, continue straight onto Madonna Road. Drive 5.4 miles to the intersection of Madonna, Telegraph, and Carea Roads. There is a ten-car parking lot. **GPS:** N39 40.835' / W76 29.547'

THE HIKE

t's such a short jaunt that it's often overlooked, but what this Hidden Valley area trail is lacking in length is made up for in scenery and solitude. Unlike its "bigger brother" trails in Rocks State Park, the Hidden Valley hike doesn't have an iconic ending like the King and Queen Seat and Kilgore Falls. Rather the scenery is quite dramatic on the entire short stretch.

With room for about ten cars, the parking area alone is a welcoming site, with an open meadow and water views. It's a great spot to throw around a football or Frisbee, or plop in a beach chair with a fishing pole in hand.

From the parking area, facing the creek, a distinct trail begins on your right by crossing a short wooden boardwalk. A wide grassy path soon transitions to a narrow dirt path that hugs the edge of Deer Creek along a wide section of river. While the beginning paces are very open and exposed, it continues on into much more tree covering. The locals are well aware of this fishing hot spot, a put-and-take trout-fishing area. When asking a group of boys on the trail what they were trying to catch, their reply was "anything we can!"

The trail follows the river around a bend but soon gains distance from the water as it enters deeper into the forest, and you'll see white blazes. At a split in

Layers of rock jut out into Deer Creek along this path, a popular fishing spot.

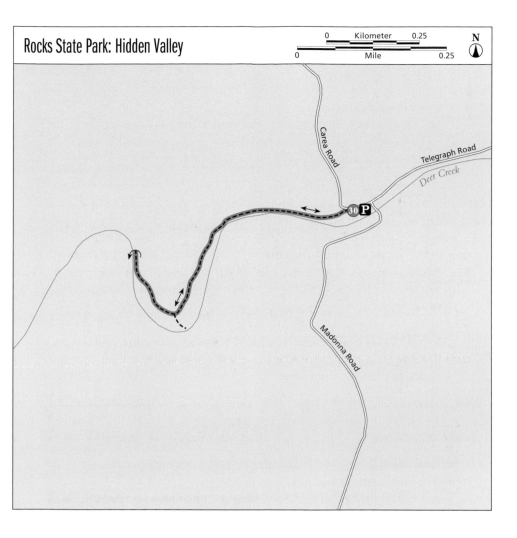

the trail, the right side continues on a white-blazed path. (To the left, a single bench and a line of rocks across the creek that create nice rapids. On the opposite side of the creek, a feeder stream flows gracefully downhill through the forest and spills into the Deer Creek. It looks like a scene out of a fairy-tale movie. Unfortunately, this area is not stable and the park is working to keep this area closed, though residents continue to reopen it. Please respect the park's efforts for your safety and the safety of the land.)

Continue on the white-blazed, hard-packed dirt trail. The trail, still narrow, follows the creek, though your views of the water will be obstructed by the forest for a short portion of the hike. The trail, sandy is sections, passes by some wild rapids and then crosses flat rocks that jut into the water on the left and massive towers of rocks on your right.

Make your way across the rocks, now scrambling over roots. The trail fades a bit and you'll find yourself sidestepping your own path. Dead-end at the rock formations, jutting out into the creek. This is a solid turnaround spot to avoid entering private property.

Out and back, look for birds' nests, butterflies, and wildflowers galore. The purpose of this hike is not strenuous exercise or an all-day outing. Rather it's a quick nature respite and a great way to enjoy a lazy summer day.

MILES AND DIRECTIONS

0.0 Facing the creek, walk over the wooden boardwalk on your right to start the trail.

0.2 Notice a gradual split in the trail, which does rejoin the main path in another 0.1 mile.

0.4 Come to an intersection. Take the trail to the right, now following white blazes.

0.6 The trail crosses flat rocks along the water's edge before it dead-ends at a rock wall jutting into the creek.

1.1 Arrive back at the parking lot and trailhead.

HIKE INFORMATION

Local attractions: Fiore Winery of Maryland, 3026 Whiteford Rd., Pylesville; (410) 879-4007; fiorewinery.com

Eden Mill Nature Center, 1617 Eden Mill Rd., Pylesville; (410) 836-3050; eden mill.org

🌿 **Green Tip:**
Pack out what you pack in, even food scraps, because they can attract wild animals.

Rocks State Park: White Trail Loop

A hike with royal status! Enjoy exceptional views from a towering rock outcropping 190 feet above Deer Creek valley. This loop hike takes you through a nice forest before culminating at this extraordinary natural feature referred to as the King and Queen Seat. This is a popular area for hikers and there is a very good chance you will see rock climbers dangling from the vertical rock faces below.

Start: From the parking lot, begin at the CAUTION sign and stairs leading uphill next to a tree blazed with purple.
Distance: 2.8-mile loop
Hiking time: About 1.5 hours
Difficulty: Difficult due to steep climbs
Trail surface: Natural surface
Best season: Year-round
Other trail users: Trail runners, horseback riders
Canine compatibility: Leashed pets permitted on hiking trails
Land status: State park
Fees and permits: No fee for the Rapids Parking Area. Day-use service charge at Wilson's, Hills Grove, and Rock Ridge Picnic Areas only; discounted for Maryland residents
Schedule: Open daily 9 a.m. to sunset Apr–Oct, 10 a.m. to sunset Nov–Mar
Maps: Trail map available at dnr .state.md.us/publiclands/central/ rocksmap.asp
Trail contacts: Rocks State Park, 3318 Rocks Chrome Hill Rd., Jarrettsville, MD 21084; (410) 557-7994; dnr.state.md.us/publiclands/ central/rocks.asp
Special considerations: Copperhead snakes have been spotted in the rocks.

Finding the trailhead: From U.S. 1 north/ Belair Road, take the exit for MD, 24 north toward Forest Hill/Rocks. In 0.3 mile, merge onto Rock Spring Road. In 2.5 miles, continue on MD 24 north/Rocks Road. Drive 4.6 miles and park in the Rapids Parking Area. Space for 25 or so cars. **GPS:** N39 38.274' / W76 24.759'

THE HIKE

S urprise, surprise. Rocks State Park has a lot of rocks! And the hike to the King and Queen Seat is no exception. Just one of the trails in the 855-acre park, this loop hike on the white trail ends at the phenomenal rock outcropping known as the King and Queen Seat, once a ceremonial gathering place of the Susquehannock and Mingo Indians, with views of the Harford County countryside below.

Right from the start, this trail will give you a good kick in the butt, with a steep uphill climb beginning on the purple-blazed trail from the Rapids Parking Area. Head up a set of stairs and rock steps, near the sign that reads CAUTION, TRAIL LEADS TO HAZARDOUS AREAS.

Take in a royal views from these massive rock formations known as the King and Queen Seat.

The rock outcroppings and house-size boulders are quite impressive, offering a nice distraction from your burning thighs. While huffing your way uphill, keep a lookout for a well-worn path, blazed in white, that heads off to your right. You'll want to take this path to begin your white loop, and if you have your head down cranking out the incline, it's possible you could miss it. If you do, you'll end up at the King and Queen rock outcropping, but ideally you want to save this glorious reward for last. Overall the trail is well marked.

The initial climb is the hardest, ascending nearly 300 feet in the first 0.2 mile. Though the ups and downs continue throughout the hike, with another good climb at the end, you will have plenty of chances to catch your breath. Take a load off on one of the well-placed benches along the way.

The trail passes by several informational signs, like one labeling information about a former stone quarry site and another detailing the former site of a Collier Pit (1785–1886) once used as the source of charcoal for the furnaces at La Grange Iron Works.

Other trail sightings include a nice overlook with a view of Deer Creek below, a rock shelf outcropping, and a cave-like formation. The hike follows some nice flat and easy trail free of rocks, interspersed with rugged trail with large, sometimes wobbly, boulders. You are always in earshot of some traffic but the dense forest does a decent job of drowning out most of it.

At 1.4 miles you could extend your hike if you choose by adding on the blue loop, but continue on white if you are eager to get to the King and Queen Seat. At about 2.0 miles you'll find yourself heading downhill, all the while getting closer to Route 24 before coming to the intersection directing you downhill to the park office and Kellog area or left and uphill to the King and Queen Seat. Yes, you have one last uphill push, though not as steep as the purple trail, until you finally reach the mother load. You can do it!

Once you've reached your reward, spend some time here taking in the view, playing on the rocks, and watching skilled climbers make their way up the vertical rock face. After you've had your royal fun at the King and Queen Seat, return to the white trail until you again reach the spot where the purple and white trails intersect. You now have a steep downhill trek to your car. Take caution, especially when the rocks are wet.

MILES AND DIRECTIONS

0.0 Follow the purple-blazed path between two wood fences on a very steep uphill trail. Note the sign that reads Caution: Trail leads to hazardous areas.

0.1 The trail takes a turn to the right as you have a giant house-size flat boulder straight ahead. Continue to climb uphill as you bear to the right.

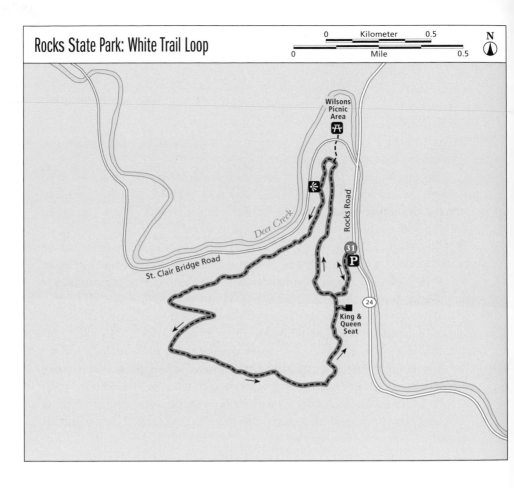

0   Kilometer   0.5

0   Mile   0.5

N

Wilsons Picnic Area

Rocks Road

Deer Creek

St. Clair Bridge Road

31

P

24

King & Queen Seat

0.2   Reach an informational sign about the stone quarry. Continue on the purple-blazed trail uphill a short way until you reach the intersection with the white-blazed trail. There are also white blazes ahead, as this is your return loop. At this point the King and Queen Seat are straight up ahead, but we save those for last. So make the right on the white-blazed trail. Look carefully for this trail, as it is easy to miss.

0.3   See a bench and an unmarked side trail that comes in from the left. Stay on the white trail.

0.7   Come to an intersection with the green trail, which leads off to the right to St. Clair Bridge Road and Wilsons Picnic Area. Stay straight on the white trail.

0.8   Off to the right you'll see a short trail to a viewpoint/rock outcropping overlooking Deer Creek.

1.2   Cross a park road via the crosswalk, following the trail into the woods directly on the opposite side.

1.3 Reach an educational sign about a Collier Pit.

1.4 A blue-blazed trail bears to the right, taking you to the nature trail and Hillsgrove Parking Area. Continue to follow the white trail, bearing left and uphill.

1.6 Pass a bench.

1.7 Reach a junction with the red trail, which heads right and left. Cross over the red trail and follow the white blazes straight ahead.

1.9 Pass another bench.

2.0 The orange trail goes off to the left. Continue straight on the white trail.

2.3 Arrive at an intersection where a sign directs you straight to the park office and Kellog area or left to follow the white trail toward the King and Queen Seat. Head left.

2.5 Arrive at an educational sign with information about the King and Queen Seat. Walk to the right toward giant rock formations on a red-blazed trail.

2.6 Arrive at the King and Queen Seat rock outcropping. Retrace your steps to the King and Queen educational sign and follow the white-blazed path behind the sign to meet up with the start of our loop, and retrace your steps on the purple-blazed trail.

2.8 Arrive back at your car and the parking lot.

Options: Add the 0.5-mile blue nature loop to extend your hike.

HIKE INFORMATION

The closest town is Forest Hill, with fast food, a few restaurants, chain stores, and pharmacies.

Local attractions: Fiore Winery of Maryland, 3026 Whiteford Rd., Pylesville; (410) 879-4007; fiorewinery.com

Eden Mill Nature Center, 1617 Eden Mill Rd., Pylesville; (410) 836-3050; eden mill.org

During the seventeenth century the Susquehannock Native Americans who lived along Deer Creek used the King and Queen Seat as the site of ceremonial gatherings. It is legend that Bald Eagle, chief ruler of the tribe, and his wife took their seats here while witnessing the marriage of their son.

Susquehanna State Park: LSHG to the Trestle Bridge

Follow the Susquehanna River downstream from the Conowingo Dam on a crushed-stone rail bed lined with vegetation and rock formations before it switches to a narrow packed-dirt trail meandering through bountiful wildflowers. The sights and sounds of nature combined with a flat surface make this a pleasing hike every step of the way.

Start: A yellow gate and trail kiosk mark the start of the trail, located at the far right end of the parking lot.

Distance: 7.1 miles out and back with spur, 4.0 miles point to point

Hiking time: About 3 hours

Difficulty: Easy

Trail surface: Crushed stone, gravel, natural surface

Best season: Year-round

Other trail users: Fishermen, birders, trail runners, bikers

Canine compatibility: Leashed dogs permitted

Land status: State park

Fees and permits: None

Schedule: Sunrise–sunset daily

Maps: Available at the Maintenance and Information Building at the park and posted on bulletin boards within the park

Trail contacts: Susquehanna State Park, 4122 Wilkinson Rd., Havre de Grace, MD 21078; (410) 557-7994 or (410) 734-9035; dnr .state.md.us/publiclands/central/ susquehanna.asp

Other: Facilities at the parking area include flush toilets, picnic tables, and trash cans.

Finding the trailhead: From US 1 (Conowingo Road), turn right on Shuresville Road. In 0.6 mile, take a sharp left on Shures Landing Road. Follow Shures Landing for 0.4 mile until it dead-ends into Exelon's Fisherman's Park and the Conowingo Hydro Station. Park at the Conowingo Dam parking lot. Facing the water, the trailhead is located at the far right side of the parking lot. The trail begins at a yellow gate and trail kiosks. **GPS:** N39 39.104' / W76 10.178'

THE HIKE

The Lower Susquehanna Heritage Greenway connects natural, historical, and cultural resources along the western bank of the Susquehanna River. It was once the towpath for the Susquehanna & Tidewater Canal, which stretched from Havre de Grace to Wrightsville, Pennsylvania, during the mid-1800s. The path you see today was originally built by the Philadelphia Electric Company in 1926 as a corridor to transport materials from Havre de Grace to the construction site of the Conowingo Dam. After two years the rail line was decommissioned, and the corridor was neglected until the Lower Susquehanna Heritage Greenway Trail was created.

The hike described here takes you on a wide crushed-stone rail trail that follows the river downstream, extending from the Conowingo Dam to Stafford Road at Deer Creek and the Flint Furnace. From there, the hike will transition to a natural narrow dirt path that continues to follow the river to the Deer Creek trestle bridge.

Smallmouth bass, northern pike, and herons aren't the only living creatures you'll find in the water. This is a hot spot for fishermen. The park is also home to river otters, painted turtles, wood frogs, screech owls, raccoons, pileated woodpeckers, beavers, and white-tailed deer. Walking the flat, level path, many small

Views of the Susquehanna River dominate the hike.

trails cut to the left to reach the water's edge, and the river is dotted with giant rocks and small islands. The old rail tracks are visible on the left side of the path.

Several educational signs along the way will give you a sneak peek into the natural and historical elements that make this trail fabulous. In the distance you'll have views of the Thomas J. Hatem Memorial Bridge over the Susquehanna River. Walk under a canopy of trees, past rugged outcroppings, marshy land, and several benches to relax and take it all in.

At about 2.0 miles a blue-blazed trail on a natural dirt path continues straight ahead, following the river. You want to take this blue-blazed trail, but first take a right on the crushed-stone path as it heads over a boardwalk bridge toward Stafford Road and the Flint Furnace.

Once you take the right turn toward Flint Furnace, you'll parallel Deer Creek, designated as a scenic river by the Maryland legislature in 1973. The name of the stream was said to have been given by the Susquehannock Indians, who fished and hunted in this area. Deer Creek is the largest Maryland tributary of the Susquehanna River.

Arrive at the Stafford Flint Furnace and read the informational sign to learn more about the history of the once-thriving town of Stafford. The town once had a school, boarding house, and post office. Most of the town was destroyed by an ice gorge in 1904. The furnace is all that remains today.

Retrace your steps to the blue-blazed trail and now continue to make your way downstream. A welcome change from the crushed-stone path, the narrow dirt trail cuts a picture-perfect path through fields of bluebells and wildflowers. This is quite a sight to see!

The site of the old rail tracks comes back into view just before coming to the Trestle Bridge over Deer Creek. Cross the boardwalk bridge, several hundred feet across, to take in the view of Deer Creek on the right and the Susquehanna on the left. On the other side, steps lead down to a rock-and-sand beach. A trail continues straight for about a half mile to the gristmill and the Rock Run Historic Area, but the trail is quite overgrown. The trestle bridge area is a *very* popular spot for fishing. There is a parking area here if you would prefer a one-way hike using a car shuttle, though the lot fills up fast. Otherwise, retrace your steps all the way to Conowingo Dam.

MILES AND DIRECTIONS

0.0   Facing the river, the trailhead is located at the far right side of the parking lot. Begin at a yellow gate and trail kiosk on a wide stone path, walking downstream with the Susquehanna River on your left.

0.5   Reach the educational sign about the geology of the area.

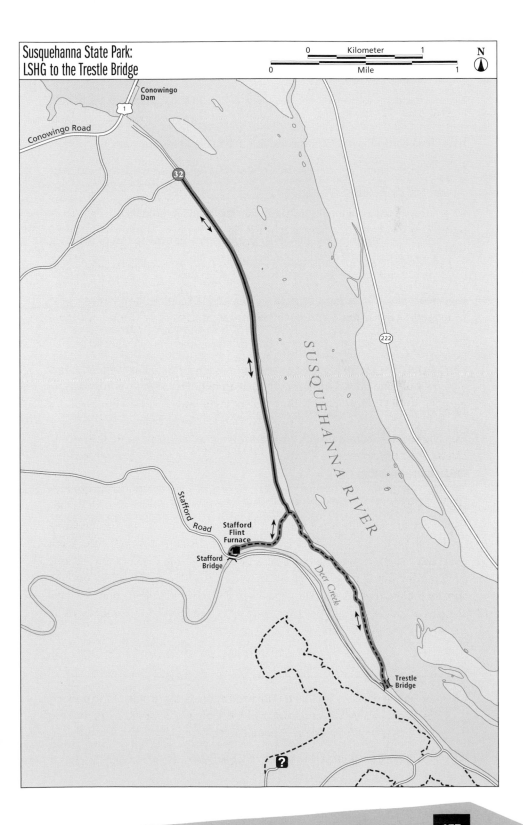

1.1   An educational sign shares information about bald eagles.

1.2   Pass a picnic table and bench as the gravel road ends and a long boardwalk begins.

1.3   The boardwalk ends and the trail is back to being a stone path.

1.4   An information sign details the Critical Area Act to reverse deterioration of the basin environment.

1.7   Read the informational sign about the forest and its wildlife.

1.9   The blue-blazed trail heads off to the left on a narrow footpath (you will take this trail on the return), but first head to the right over a 50-foot board-walk bridge to take a spur trail to the Flint Furnace.

2.3   Reach an informational sign about Maryland's Scenic and Wild Rivers program as well as the Stafford Flint Furnace.

2.4   Enjoy views from the bridge on Stafford Road, then retrace your steps.

2.8   Again cross the 50-foot bridge, and on the other side take the blue-blazed trail, bearing right, followed by a quick jog left.

4.0   Arrive at the trestle bridge over Deer Creek.

7.1   Arrive back at the trailhead and parking lot.

HIKE INFORMATION

Local attractions: Steppingstone Farm Museum, an agricultural heritage museum is located at 461 Quaker Bottom Rd., Havre de Grace; (410) 939-2299; steppingstonemuseum.org. Open weekends May–Sept 1 to 4 p.m.; small fee for adults.

Good eats: Backfin Blues Bar and Grill, 19 S. Main St., Port Deposit; (410) 378-2722; backfinblues.com

Susquehanna State Park Loop

This is a park where history, heritage, solitude, and scenery collide. Tour the historic structures along the Susquehanna River before heading into a forest of mature trees, open meadows, and past old ruins while hardly having to share the trail.

Start: Begin the hike on Stafford Road with the gristmill on your left.

Distance: 7.6-mile loop

Hiking time: About 4 hours

Difficulty: Difficult

Trail surface: Natural surface

Best season: Year-round

Other trail users: Mountain bikers, equestrians

Canine compatibility: Pets are allowed on all trails outside of the day-use areas. They are allowed in the day-use area after Labor Day and up to Memorial Day.

Land status: State park

Fees and permits: No fees for the Historic Area parking. Small fee, discounted for Maryland residents, for Day-Use Service at Deer Creek Picnic Area; daily Mar–Oct; open weekends only Nov–Feb.

Schedule: Daily 9 a.m. to sunset; historic structures open Sat–Sun from Memorial Day to Labor Day as follows: Gristmill, 10 a.m. to 4 p.m. (tours only, no grinding demonstrations due to critical maintenance); Tollhouse, 10 a.m. to 6 p.m.; Mansion 1 to 4 p.m. (volunteer-dependent). All hours are subject to change.

Maps: Available at the Maintenance and Information Building in the park on Wilkinson Road and posted on bulletin boards within the park

Trail contacts: Susquehanna State Park, 4122 Wilkinson Rd., Havre de Grace, MD 21078; (410) 557-7994; dnr.state.md.us/public lands/central/susquehanna.asp

Other: Historic sites, boat launch, campground, picnic and fishing areas

Finding the trailhead: Take I-95 north or south to MD 155, exit 89. Proceed west on MD 155/Level Road for 3.3 miles to MD 161. Turn right on MD 161/Darlington Road and proceed for 0.4 mile. Then turn right on Rock Run Road. Follow Rock Run Road to the park. Rock Run Road ends at the Historic Area. There is parking on either side of the Rock Run Grist Mill. **GPS:** N39 36.470' / W76 08.533'

THE HIKE

Just north of Havre de Grace on the lower Susquehanna River is Susquehanna State Park, heaven for active outdoorsy folks. It comes complete with history, wildlife, water views, picnic spots, a campground, a museum, and believe it or not . . . solitude! Most of the cars you see parked in the lots and up and down Stafford Road are boaters and fishermen. The park has more than 15.0 miles of marked trails ranging in level of difficulty, and the scenery is off the charts, so it's surprising that these trails aren't overpopulated. I'm certainly not complaining!

The Rock Run Historic Area, where you'll park, has a working gristmill that was built in 1800; the Carter-Archer Mansion, built in 1804; the Jersey Toll House, a collection point for travelers crossing a covered bridge across the Susquehanna; and the remains of the Susquehanna Tidewater Canal. The mansion was the birthplace of General James J. Archer.

With the Rock Run Grist Mill on your left, walk Stafford Road for 500 feet before dipping into the woods on the right. Look for a wood post on the roadside marking the Mason Dixon Trail (MDT) blazed in light blue as well as a red blaze on a tree. The red-blazed Susquehanna Ridge Trail shares a path with the Mason

Hike through open fields and rolling meadows under a wide-open blue sky on the Farm Trail portion of the loop.

Dixon Trail. The MDT is a 193-mile footpath from Cumberland County, Pennsylvania, to Chadds Ford in Brandywine, Pennsylvania, near the Delaware border. Follow this light-blue- and red-blazed path uphill on a dirt and rock path.

This colorful hike combines the red, white, yellow, blue, orange, and (again) red trails to make one giant loop through the park. As the name suggests, the red Ridge Trail takes you on a ridgeline hike with a few peeks of the river through the heavy tree cover. A fascinating feature on the white Land of Promise trail is the remains of a stacked rock wall with no mortar still mostly intact. The trail parallels this wall near an open meadow. Walk the yellow Rock Run Y trail briefly to meet up with the Blue Farm Trail.

The blue trail crosses the striking Rock Run with lots of spills and pools, a fun place to play, and then crosses the paved Rock Run Road. On the other side of Rock Run Road, follow the staggered blue blazes and wood steps heading uphill into the woods. There is a wooden sign marking Farm Road Trail. The Orange Ivy Branch trail is a nice loop off of the Farm Trail. This will add some distance along with scenery before again meeting back up with the blue Farm Trail.

The final portion of the orange Ivy Branch Trail as well as the last stretch of the Farm Trail offer a nice change of pace, walking through vast fields and rolling meadows under a big sky. You'll want to break into song, "the hills are alive with the sound of music. . . ." However this section can get tricky, as it's the only section that isn't very well marked, especially around mile 5. Be sure to carefully read the Miles and Directions below.

Not long after you leave the meadows and dip back into the trees will you again reach the red Ridge Trail, which you will take all the way back to the Rock Run Historic Area and Grist Mill to complete this circuit.

MILES AND DIRECTIONS

0.0   With the mill on your left side, walk Stafford Road uphill.

0.1   See a red blaze on a tree on the right side of road and a wooden post labeling the MDT. Leave the road and head right and uphill on a dirt and rock path.

0.6   A trail heads off to the right and uphill. Stay straight to continue on the red trail.

1.0   Come to a split in the trail marked by an old wood post. The red trail heads slightly left. Take a right to follow the white-blazed Land of Promise Trail.

1.2   Begin paralleling a stone wall on the left, following the trail through a meadow.

1.5 Cross two paved driveways, the entrance and exit roads for the Stepping Stone Museum (off of Quaker Bottom Road). The trail continues directly on the opposite side of the paved roads.

1.6 Leaving the meadow, duck into an area dense with trees.

1.8 Cross a small creek.

2.1 Come to a split in the trail. Follow it to the right to continue on the white-blazed trail. (The left side is the top half of the yellow trail that meets with the white trail.)

2.2 At a T intersection, head left to follow the white blazes.

2.5 Reach a junction. The purple trail (Historic Walking Trail) heads to the right and straight ahead. Make a left on the yellow Rock Run Y Trail.

2.7 Reach an intersection with a blue-blazed trail. Yellow continues straight, but take the blue Farm Road Trail downhill and across Rock Run and upstream on the opposite side.

2.8 Reach Rock Run Road. Walk the road left, heading uphill (blue blaze on guardrail) for 30 feet and climb the wood steps on the opposite side of the road, continuing on the Farm Road Trail.

3.1 Come to an intersection with the orange Ivy Branch Trail. Take a left. Here, the blue and orange share the trail to the left briefly before the orange trail again splits off from the blue at a Y intersection. Take a left on orange at this second split.

3.6 Take two rock hops across a scenic creek.

4.0 Notice an old stone foundation on your right.

4.4 Cross Wilkinson Road. Head right, still following the orange Ivy Branch Trail. Walk a mowed path on the field perimeter, paralleling the road that leads to the maintenance office and information.

4.6 At the end of the row of pine trees, the trail bears slightly left, continuing to walk the perimeter of a field.

4.7 Bear right when you reach a gravel road that cuts through the field. When you see the maintenance building on your right, bear slightly left and straight to continue walking the perimeter.

5.0 Come to a Y in the meadow with a very narrow but obvious worn dirt path similar to the one you are walking on. This left split simply cuts off a few steps. Once you get to that row of trees in front of you, head left along the

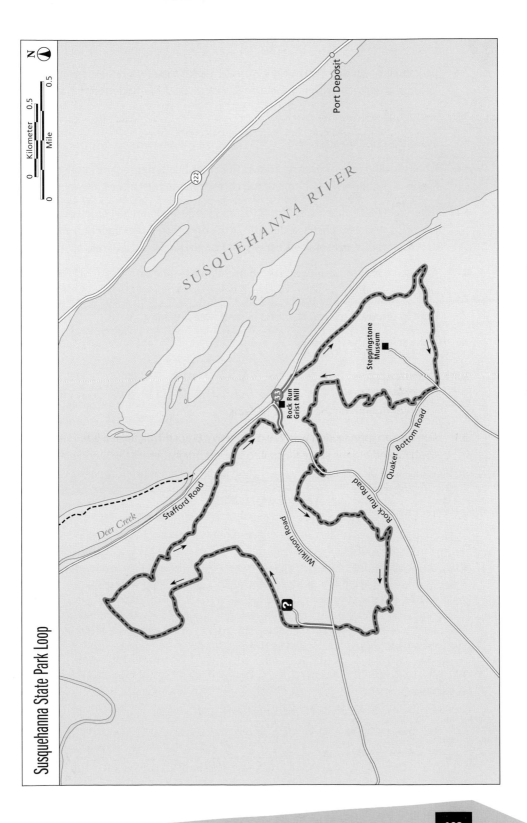

Susquehanna State Park Loop

perimeter. If you continue straight at this Y, reach the row of trees straight ahead and make a hard left. You are now back on the blue-blazed Farm Trail.

5.2 A spur trail heads off to the right.

5.5 Leave the open meadow and enter a tree-covered section.

5.6 A trail heading off to the left and down to a creek heads to the campground. Stay straight, slightly right, continuing on the blue-blazed Farm Trail.

6.1 A trail splits off to the right. This is the red Ridge Trail and will save you a few steps. A few feet beyond this split is the official trail sign directing you to the red trail, where you will backtrack a bit to get on the red trail.

6.7 A trail comes in on your right. Stay straight on the red trail.

7.4 Cross a wide creek and then bear left. Hang a left on the paved Rock Run Road to return to the trailhead and Historic Area parking.

7.6 Arrive back at the trailhead, mill, and parking lot.

HIKE INFORMATION

Local attractions: Steppingstone Farm Museum, an agricultural heritage museum, is located at 461 Quaker Bottom Rd., Havre de Grace; (410) 939-2299; stepping stonemuseum.org. Open weekends May–Sept 1 to 4 p.m.; small fee for adults.

What Is a Gristmill?

A gristmill, also known as a corn mill or flour mill, is a building used for grinding grains into flour. They were powered by wind, water, slaves, and livestock. They were most often situated next to a water source, as was the case for the Orange Grove Mill on the Patapsco River, the Rock Run Mill on the Susquehanna River, and the Eden Mill gristmill on Deer Creek. (All of these mills are mentioned in this book.) Gristmills were a major industry for small villages and towns. Communities were reliant on this source of food production for personal and economic sustainability. The flour industry in Baltimore began in the mid-1700s. By 1825 there were sixty water-powered flour mills within a few miles of Baltimore's city center. Baltimore led the American flour market from 1815 to 1827.

Elk Neck State Park: Lighthouse Trail

An easy trail with open meadows and water views most of the way leads you to the cliffs above the Chesapeake Bay and the Turkey Point Lighthouse at the tip of a peninsula of land between the Elk and Northeast Rivers.

Start: Begin at the parking lot, behind the trail information kiosk.
Distance: 2.0-mile lollipop loop
Hiking time: About 1 hour
Difficulty: Easy
Trail surface: Natural surface and crushed stone
Best season: Year-round
Other trail users: Bikers, birders
Canine compatibility: Leashed dogs permitted
Land status: State park
Fees and permits: No fees for this area of the park. Donations are appreciated.
Schedule: Daily 9 a.m. to sunset. Lighthouse tower open Sat–Sun Easter to mid-Nov from 10 a.m. to 4 p.m. Donations for the lighthouse accepted during these hours.
Maps: Trail map available on website
Trail contacts: Elk Neck State Park, 4395 Turkey Point Rd., North East, MD 21901; (410) 287-5333; dnr.state.md.us/publiclands/central/elkneck.asp
Other: Small gift shop located at the lighthouse
Special considerations: The parking lot fills up fast, especially between 10 a.m. and 4 p.m., when the lighthouse is open to visitors.

Finding the trailhead: Take I-95 to exit 100 onto MD 272. Head south toward North East and follow MD 272 for 14.0 miles. The road dead-ends into the parking lot for the Lighthouse Trail. **GPS:** N39 27.578' / W76 00.372'

THE HIKE

Elk Neck State Park encompasses 2,188 acres of dramatic landscapes including sandy beaches, marshlands, and heavily wooded bluffs overlooking the North East River, the Elk River, and the Chesapeake Bay.

At the parking lot trailhead, you are immediately rewarded with water views from the cliffs above the Chesapeake Bay. Formerly known as the blue trail, this trail still has old blue and white blazes on the trees. But you can now follow the well-marked, red-post trail markers on this easy, flat, and wide path that leads you to the Turkey Point Lighthouse and gift shop. One of seven trails in Elk Neck State Park, this is a popular hike, dotted with benches and a couple picnic tables. The path is made of crushed stone, with a short section of natural packed dirt.

At about halfway to the lighthouse, you'll reach the raptor-viewing field and an information kiosk about hawks. Migrating hawks can be seen from September to November, with peak times between 9 a.m. and noon. Seventeen species of raptors have been observed at Turkey Point. The sharp-shinned hawk is the most common. Bald eagles are seen regularly as are deer, fox, and squirrels.

Walk the stairs of Turkey Point Lighthouse for dramatic cliff-side views of the Chesapeake Bay.

Just before you reach the lighthouse, a portable toilet is located on the left. You then approach the 35-foot lighthouse situated on a 100-foot bluff at the confluence of five rivers as they meet the Chesapeake Bay. Sailboats glide through the waters and picnickers spread out blankets on the lawn for a meal with a view. Walk the forty steps to the top. On a clear day you can see for miles.

The Turkey Point Lighthouse was constructed in 1833 and had more female keepers than any other in Maryland. It's the signature landmark of the park.

In 1925 President Calvin Coolidge appointed Fannie Mae Salter to the post of lighthouse keeper. She was the last keeper of the Turkey Point Lighthouse, as it became automated in 1947. The lighthouse was decommissioned in 2000 and relit in 2002 as a "private aid to navigation." A solar-charged battery powers it.

In season, volunteers stationed at the lighthouse are happy to answer questions and share some history with visitors. On your return enjoy the wooded path on a packed-dirt surface. Kids are drawn to the swinging vines that hang from the trees, and the butterflies make the trail that much more colorful. The lighthouse destination combined with an easy path and great views of the famed Chesapeake Bay make this an ideal hike for families with children that is worth the drive from Baltimore.

Turkey Point Lighthouse and Fannie Mae Salter

A signature landmark of Elk Neck State Park is the Turkey Point Lighthouse. On the tip of the Elk Neck peninsula, it sits on a 100-foot bluff above the Elk and North East Rivers in the Chesapeake Bay. The tower itself is 35 feet tall. Built in 1833, the lighthouse guided ship captains into the C&D Canal. Of the ten lighthouse keepers, four were women—more female keepers than any other lighthouse on the Chesapeake Bay. Fannie Mae Salter (1883–1966) was the last lighthouse keeper at Turkey Point and was appointed to the position by President Calvin Coolidge. Salter took over the position of her husband, C.W. "Harry" Salter, after his death in 1925. She had been told by the Civil Service that she was not allowed to succeed her husband due to her age. Fannie Mae would not have this, so she appealed to her senator, who took it to the White House. When she finally retired in 1947, Fannie moved only 6 miles away, still in view of the lighthouse. In total Salter worked at the lighthouse for forty-five years. She died at the age of 83.

MILES AND DIRECTIONS

0.0 Begin your hike at the parking lot. As you start the trail, cliffs and views of the bay are on your right.

0.7 Reach the raptor-viewing field and kiosk with information about hawks.

0.8 Reach the Turkey Point Lighthouse and gift shop. Walk through the grass while hugging the water's edge until the trail dips back under tree cover.

0.9 Follow the blue/white trail markers onto a packed-dirt trail that leads into the trees.

1.0 Stay on the trail as it bears to the right.

1.1 The trail bears to the right once again as you continue on the loop, heading back to the trail you came in on.

1.3 Meet back up with the trail you walked in on. Retrace your route to head back to the parking lot.

2.0 Arrive back at the trailhead and parking lot.

Options: Hike the nearby Beaver Marsh Trail (Hike 35) or any of the Elk Neck State Park trails in the same day.

HIKE INFORMATION

Local attractions: The town of North East has restaurants and shops. Elk Neck State Park beach and swimming area are located on North East Beach Road. Elk Neck State Park Nature Center has educational displays and activities for all ages as well as live animals and special events like hikes and orienteering outings.

Camping: Campground with tent sites and cabins available at Elk Neck State Park.

Good eats: Woody's Crab House, 29 S. Main St., North East; (410) 287-3541; woodyscrabhouse.com

Steak and Main, 107 S. Main St., North East; (410) 287-3512; mysteakandmain.com

UnWined, 472 Mauldin Ave., North East; (410) 287-4300; unwinedmd.com

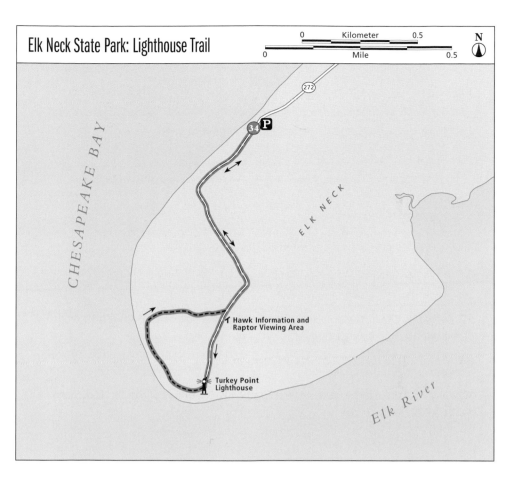

Elk Neck State Park: Lighthouse Trail

🌿 Green Tip:
Carry an extra trash bag to pack out any trash you come across on the trail.

Elk Neck State Park: Beaver Marsh Loop

This is a neat hike with unique features like a section of beach hiking, lots of wildlife, river views, and a loop around a beaver marsh pond with, well . . . beavers!

Start: Begin at the large trailhead sign at the far left side of the parking lot when facing the water.
Distance: 2.4-mile loop
Hiking time: About 1.5 hours
Difficulty: Moderate
Trail surface: Natural surface, sand-beach portion
Best season: Year-round
Other trail users: Bikers, birders
Canine compatibility: Leashed dogs permitted on the Beaver Marsh Loop
Land status: State park
Fees and permits: Small per-car fee, which is discounted for Maryland residents
Schedule: 9 a.m. to sunset daily
Maps: Trail map available on park's website
Trail contacts: Elk Neck State Park, 4395 Turkey Point Rd., North East, MD 21901; (410) 287-5333; dnr.state.md.us/publiclands/central/elkneck.asp
Other: Camping, boat launch, and a beach and swimming area are offered nearby at various parts of the park.

Finding the trailhead: Take I-95 to exit 100 onto MD 272. Head south toward North East and follow MD 272 for 10.0 miles. Turn left on Rogue's Harbor Road. Follow signs for the Rogue's Harbor Boating Facility and boat launch. **GPS:** N39 28.075' / W75 59.150'

THE HIKE

Don't be fooled by the solitude—you are definitely not alone on this hike. The birds, squirrels, snakes, ducks, and frogs will make you very aware of that! As the name of the trail gives away, the hike makes a wide, odd-shaped loop, circling a beaver marsh pond. Sometimes you have clear views of the pond and other times you are separated by forest and vegetation, but all the while, you are never too far from the marsh.

Though small, the beach section is just one of the many unique features of this hike on the Beaver Marsh Loop. Sometimes still referred to as the Orange Trail, you will see orange markings and blazes along the way, although they look to be more of a brownish-rust color to me.

At the far left and backside of the parking lot, the trailhead is located at an obvious clearing with a large trail kiosk and trail system map. The map details the trails for the White Banks Trail, Mauldin Mountain Loop, Farm Road Trail, Pond Loop, Ravines Loop, Turkey Point Lighthouse Trail, and of course, the Beaver Marsh Loop (#6).

A metal post designates this trail as a connector trail (connector trails are yellow) and reads FOLLOW THIS TRAIL TO WHITE BANKS TRAIL AND BEAVER MARSH TRAIL. The trail

The last portion of the trail takes hikers across a beach that divides the beaver marsh pond from the river.

begins on a wide stone-and-grass path with the Elk River off to the right. In less than 0.1 mile, make a left off the stone path and over a boardwalk, followed by an immediate right on a connector trail, following the sign marking WHITE BANKS AND CONNECTOR TO BEAVER MARSH. There is a faint orange blaze painted on a tree off to your right, but it is hard to see against the bark.

If you miss the first left on the connector trail, just follow the stone path until it dead-ends into the marsh straight ahead and a beach on your right. A trail heads up the hill to the left: This is the Beaver Marsh Trail. (Note that this intersection with the marsh and the beach at the end of this stone path closes the loop on your return hike.)

The connector trail ends at the official Beaver Marsh Trail, marked by rusted metal posts with square orange/brown/rust-colored markers listing the full name of the trail. Head left on the Beaver Marsh Trail. You'll have fantastic marshland views off to your right as the trail becomes narrow over packed-dirt surface.

Look for large beaver pilings and lodges, great blue herons, and ducks on this very well-marked trail. In spring the forest floor is carpeted with wildflowers while a chorus of frogs is so loud it's deafening. A wood platform with railings provides the perfect spot for viewing the marsh. Be on the lookout for black racer snakes in this area.

On the opposite side of the marsh from where you started, the trail skirts the edge of a camping area. Soon after, the trail pops out on a park road. A few tent sites can be seen along the road as well as a bathhouse. Do not cross the park road. Rather, walk the shoulder for a few steps to the right before taking a dirt trail and immediately turning to the right back into the woods.

At 2.0 miles arrive at a clay-colored beach, which separates the beaver marsh pond from the river. You can't see the beaver marsh on your left at this point, as it is blocked by tall waving beach grass. There are no trail markers to direct you here, but walk the beach to the opposite side (beware of ducks guarding their territory) and up the rock wall barrier to return to the wide gravel-and-stone path on which we began our journey. Here, the marsh is visible once again. Take a moment to again soak in the views of the fascinating landscape and habitat before following this path back to the trailhead and parking lot.

MILES AND DIRECTIONS

0.0   See an obvious open clearing and a trail kiosk with map at the left back side of the parking lot.

0.1   Make a left off the stone path over a boardwalk and an immediate right on a connector trail. This connector trail meets up with the official Beaver Marsh Trail. Take a left on the Beaver Marsh Trail.

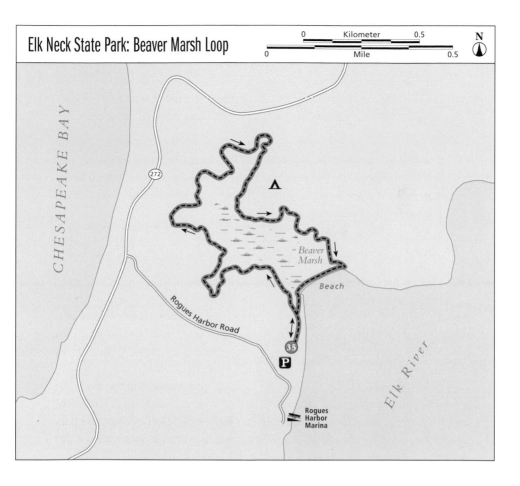

0.3 Pass a bench followed by a wooden viewing platform overlooking the marsh.

0.4 Reach an intersection to the left with the White Banks Trail. Stay on Beaver Marsh.

0.6 Pass another bench.

0.7 The trail bears to the left.

0.9 Pass yet another bench.

1.0 Cross an 8-foot wood bridge that spans a small creek.

1.2 At a trail split, head to the right.

1.3 Come to a Y intersection. The trail heading to the left is a connector trail to the Park Store Trailhead. Continue to follow the Beaver Marsh Trail to the right.

1.4 On the left the trail traces the edge of the campground.

1.8 Pop out on the park road. A few tent sites and a bathhouse can be seen on the road. Do not cross the park road. Rather, head to the right and walk the shoulder of the road for a few steps. Then follow the trail right, back into the woods.

1.9 Come to a T intersection. A yellow square label indicates a connector trail that heads to the left. The right trail is the Beaver Marsh Loop, which heads downhill to water level. After this intersection there is more of a stone pathway and then a sandy/grassy trail.

2.0 The trail opens up with an unobstructed view of the water and a clay-colored beach on your right. Walk across the beach to the opposite side.

2.2 Walk up the rock barrier wall and follow the wide gravel stone path back to the parking area.

2.4 Arrive back at the trailhead and parking lot.

Options: Hike the nearby Elk Neck Lighthouse Trail (Hike 34) in the same day.

Downed trees on the trail offer an up-close-and-personal view of their root systems.

HIKE INFORMATION

Local attractions: The town of North East has restaurants and shops. Elk Neck State Park beach and swimming area located on North East Beach Road. Elk Neck State Park Nature Center has educational displays and activities for all ages as well as live animals and special events like hikes and orienteering outings.

Camping: Campground with tent sites and cabins are available at Elk Neck State Park

Good eats: Woody's Crab House, 29 S. Main St., North East; (410) 287-3541; woodyscrabhouse.com

Steak and Main, 107 S. Main St., North East; (410) 287-3512; mysteakandmain.com

UnWined, 472 Mauldin Ave., North East; (410) 287-4300; unwinedmd.com

Maryland's Scenic Rivers

The state of Maryland created the Scenic and Wild Rivers System by an Act of the General Assembly in 1968. In passing the act, the state recognized that many rivers of Maryland, or portions of them, and their related land areas possess outstanding scenic, geologic, ecologic, historic, recreational, agricultural, fish, wildlife, cultural, and other similar resources values. Therefore, it should be the policy of the state to:

Preserve and protect the natural values of these rivers, enhance their water quality, and fulfill vital conservation purposes by wise use of resources within their surrounding environment.

The following nine rivers have officially been designated "Scenic" by the Maryland General Assembly: Anacostia, Deer Creek, Monocacy, Patuxent, Pocomoke, Potomac (Frederick and Montgomery Counties), Severn, Wicomico-Zekiah, and Youghiogheny. The section of the Youghiogheny between Millers Run and the southern corporate limits of Friendsville has been officially designated a "Wild" river.

Visit dnr.state.md.us/land/stewardship/scenicrivers.asp for more information.

Fair Hill NRMA: Orange Loop

Everything you could ask for and more! The well-marked loop trail begins steps from the Foxcatcher Farm Covered Bridge before taking you through varied terrain and scenery—past open fields, dense forest, stables, and water views of Big Elk Creek. All of this in a 5,656-acre Natural Resources Management Area located near Elkton.

Start: Begin in a field to the right of the covered bridge. A sign here reads PROTECT YOUR TRAILS, and there is a wood post with an orange blaze.

Distance: 4.2-mile loop

Hiking time: About 2.5 hours

Difficulty: Moderate

Trail surface: Natural surface

Best season: Year-round

Other trail users: Mountain bikers, trail runners, equestrians

Canine compatibility: Leashed pets allowed

Land status: Natural Resources Management Area

Fees and permits: Small fee for honor-system day pass, discounted for Maryland residents. Take an envelope, return it to the box, and rip off a car tag to hang from your windshield.

Schedule: Daily sunrise–sunset.

Fair Hill Nature and Environmental Center hours: Weekdays from mid-Mar until mid-June and late-Aug until the end of Nov, 9 a.m. to 3 p.m. Weekdays from mid-June until end of July, 8:30 a.m. to 2:30 p.m. (closed week of July 4th). Park Office hours: 8 a.m. to 4 p.m. Mon through Fri. By chance on weekends.

Maps: Available at the park office

Trail contacts: Fair Hill Natural Resources Management Area, 300 Tawes Dr., Elkton, MD 21921; (410) 398-1246; dnr.state.md.us/public lands/central/fairhill.asp. Fair Hill Nature and Environmental Center offers tours for students and day camps. Call (410) 398-4909 for more information.

Other: Facilities include a picnic pavilion and portable toilet.

Finding the trailhead: Directions to parking lot 2 (793 Tawes Drive): Take I-95 to exit MD-272N/N East Road. In 3.0 miles, turn right onto Dr. Miller Road. In 2.2 miles, turn right on MD-273 E/Telegraph Road. In 5.2 miles, turn right onto Entrance Road 1 and make an immediate left on Ranger Skinner Drive. In 0.3 mile, continue on Training Center Drive. Travel 0.5 mile and turn right on Tawes Drive. Pass the Fair Hill NRMA office located at the corner of Tawes Drive and Training Center Road. Continue 1.0 mile past the office on Tawes Drive to the covered bridge. **GPS:** N39 42.592' / W75 50.276'

THE HIKE

I n this northeast corner of Cecil County, you can spend the day playing among the 5,656 acres and 80-plus miles of trails and farm roads in the Fair Hill Natural Resources Management Area.

Formerly owned by William DuPont Jr., an avid equestrian, Fair Hill was one of the largest private land holdings in the East. DuPont used the land for horseback riding and fox chasing. The area continues to attract equestrians. Fair Hill Racetrack holds equestrian events like steeplechase, timber course, and flat races including pari-mutuel wagering. Fair Hill was purchased by the state in 1975 from Mr. DuPont's estate. About 1 hour from Baltimore and bordered by Pennsylvania to the north and Delaware to the east, the area of Fair Hill has open fields and pastures, wetlands, and mature woodlands.

This hike begins near the historic landmark Foxcatcher Farm Covered Bridge (one of two covered bridges in Cecil County) over Big Elk Creek. The bridge was constructed in 1860 and received the state's Historic Civil Engineering Landmark Award in 1994. Big Elk Creek is a stocked trout stream that runs the entire length of the Fair Hill property. In the creek you'll find smallmouth bass, sunfish, and

Find diverse scenery, from hayfields to dense forests.

bluegill. The creek is stocked every spring and fall by the DNR's Fisheries Service with adult brown and rainbow trout. (A Maryland Freshwater Fishing license is required for ages 16 and over and a Maryland Trout Stamp, allowing fishing in catch and release trout management areas).

Aside from the variety of ecosystems you'll encounter, there is also diverse wildlife here including fox, white-tailed deer, and beaver. Also be on the lookout for a bald eagle, owl, vulture, or kingfisher. Maybe you'll spot a grassland bird like a thrush or a flycatcher. Silence and solitude is possible on this hike . . . but so is horse poo. However the trail can get quite busy, as it's very popular with mountain bikers and equestrians.

The Orange Trail wanders through old-growth forest and hayfields with rolling hills and a few short climbs. The trail described here starts at the far end of the parking lot in a field off to the right of the Foxcatcher Farm Covered Bridge and behind the nature center. There is a sign here that reads PROTECT YOUR TRAILS. Heading in this direction from the parking area, you'll be walking away from the picnic pavilion to hike the trail loop clockwise.

Just a few steps into the hike, it's already time to be on the lookout for trail creatures and critters. A pond off to the left is home to muskrats, red-bellied turtles, Canada geese, American bull frogs, and green frogs. Soon, a set of stairs leads downhill to the bank of Big Elk Creek for an awesome photo opportunity of the red-covered bridge spanning the creek. The Orange Trail is very well marked, taking hikers over wooden bridges, across many creeks, along pastures, and past horse stables on a mostly dirt- and sand-packed surface. The trail dips in and out of the woods as you loop around.

On the second half of the hike, nearing the end, the trail affords fantastic views of the creek from a ridgeline high above. On the homestretch a one-way wooden bridge comes into view down below. When you reach the bridge at the bottom of the hill, you'll again see the pavilion on your right as you head back to the direction of the parking area. You will be a happy hiker having experienced the Fair Hill Orange Trail . . . now, "orange" you glad you did?

Maryland's Covered Bridges

More than one hundred authentic covered bridges have graced the state of Maryland over the past 200 years. Only six remain. Jericho Covered Bridge spans Little Gunpowder Falls near Kingsville, connecting Harford and Baltimore Counties. Cecil County has two bridges, Gilpin's Falls in Bay View and Foxcatcher Farms in Fair Hill. Frederick County proudly owns three covered bridges, Roddy Road near Thurmont, Loys Station at Loys, north of Creagerstown, and Utica Mills in Utica, near Lewistown.

Of the two mentioned in this book, Jericho Covered Bridge was constructed in 1865. The bridge is 88 feet long and 14.7 feet wide and is open to traffic. It was listed on the National Register of Historic Places in 1978. It is rumored to be haunted by the ghosts of Civil War soldiers.

The second bridge, Foxcatcher Farms, over Big Elk Creek, was built in 1860. It's 80 feet across and 12 feet wide. It was once known as Stahorn's Mill Bridge. In 1994 it received the state's Historic Civil Engineering Landmark Award. It is open for hikers, bicyclists, and horseback riders. Visit mdcoveredbridges.com and sha.maryland.gov for more information.

MILES AND DIRECTIONS

0.0 Beginning at the Foxcatcher Farm Covered Bridge, start the hike in an open field to the right of the bridge. A sign here reads PROTECT YOUR TRAILS. Look for an orange blaze on a wood post in an open field. Ahead about 50 feet on the left is a small pond.

0.1 The trail bears to the left heading into the woods, followed by a quick hop over a small creek.

0.2 Cross over a wood bridge over small creek.

0.3 Take the stairs left down to the water's edge for a great photo op of the covered bridge.

0.6 Follow the trail and orange blazes to the right. Pass an unmarked trail on the left.

1.1 The trail takes a sharp left.

1.5 Cross a cement bridge over a tiny creek with a trickle of water.

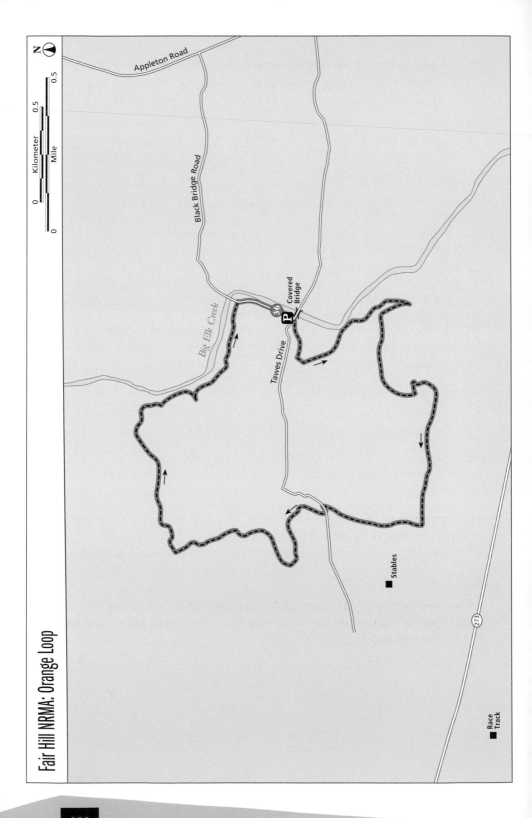

Fair Hill NRMA: Orange Loop

1.7 A spur trail to the left leads to parking lot 1 (in 0.8 mile to MD 273). Bear right to continue on the orange loop. The trail then follows the edge of a field, with stables on the left.

2.0 Follow the gravel road, which will intersect with Tawes Drive ahead. Walk the road to the left and dip into the woods on the right about 50 feet later. Following Tawes Drive on the right would shortcut the hike and return you to the covered bridge.

2.2 A horse trail goes off to the right. Straight ahead is the trail for hikers and bikers.

2.4 Cross over an unpaved road.

2.5 Reach a Y split and head to the left for hiker and biker traffic.

2.7 Enter a large field and walk the perimeter.

2.9 Leave the field and head back into trees. Then cross an unpaved gravel road.

3.3 A wide trail continues straight, but take a hard right turn to follow the orange blazes.

4.0 Reach a one-lane wooden bridge at the bottom of the hill. Pass the pavilion on your right and walk toward the parking lot.

4.2 Arrive back at the covered bridge and parking lot.

HIKE INFORMATION

Local attractions: The Fair Hill Races are an annual steeplechase horse-racing event held in May; (410) 398-6565; fairhillraces.org.

Plumpton Park Zoo, 1416 Telegraph Rd., Rising Sun; (410) 658-6850; plumpton parkzoo.org

Fair Hill Scottish Games, an annual festival featuring music, dancing, and athletic competitions; 4600 Telegraph Rd., Elkton; fairhillscottishgames.org

Good eats: Fair Hill Inn, fine dining and wine bar, 3370 Singerly Rd., Elkton; (410) 398-4187; fairhillinn.com.

Hashawha Environmental Appreciation Area: Perimeter Loop

The "land of old fields" has nothing stale about it. Hashawha offers 340 acres of open fields, pine woods, wetlands, ponds, and stream valleys. Some of the highlights include a circa 1850 historic cabin, a raptor area, a catch-and-release lake, and a visitor center. Better yet, you can have it all on a moderate 4.0-mile hike.

Start: Pick up the trail behind the trail kiosk at a sign that reads Vista Trail to Raptor Cages.

Distance: 4.0-mile double loop

Hiking time: About 2.5 hours

Difficulty: Moderate

Trail surface: Natural surface, short boardwalk, short paved portion

Best season: Year-round

Other trail users: Hikers, bikers

Canine compatibility: Leashed dogs allowed

Land status: Carroll County

Department of Recreation and Parks

Fees and permits: None

Schedule: Daily dawn–dusk. Bear Branch Nature Center hours Wed–Fri 11 a.m. to 5 p.m., Sun noon to 5 p.m.

Maps: Available at Bear Branch Nature Center

Trail contacts: Hashawha / Bear Branch, 300 John Owings Rd., Westminster, MD 21158; (410) 386-3560; ccgovernment.carr.org/ccg/recpark/hashawha/

Finding the trailhead: Take Baltimore Beltway 695 to 795, exit onto US 140 west toward Westminster. Exit right on MD 97 north toward Gettysburg / Union Mills and travel approximately 3.5 miles. Shortly after the third light, turn right onto John Owings Road and follow the signs to Hashawha. On the drive in, pass the road to the Bear Branch nature center on your right and head to the back parking lot on your left. **GPS:** N39 38.889' / W76 59.390'

THE HIKE

ashawha is a Nanticoke Indian term meaning "land of old fields." And these "old fields" will be a newly found treat to those of you who venture out to experience the trails here in northern Carroll County.

On the drive in, pass by Hashawha Lake on the left. This is certainly a focal point of the area, with a pavilion, floating dock, and wildlife-viewing area where catch-and-release fishing is permitted. Directly next to the lake lies a wetland area with some deep and some shallow marshes. Follow a boardwalk path as it winds its way through the marsh. Sightings could include geese, hawks, red-winged blackbirds, red fox, beavers, crayfish, and turtles. Lily pads float on the surface and the synchronized croaking sound of the frogs is harmonious and deafening.

From the parking lot, pick up the white-blazed Vista Trail just behind the trail kiosk. A sign here reads Vista Trail to Raptor Cages. Facing the trail kiosk, walk the path to the left. Many of the markings are wood posts with triangle trail markers. While the markings are plentiful, they can be quite confusing, making it hard to decipher what direction you are being pointed in.

Walk past Martin Cabin, a circa 1850 historic log cabin.

37

Following this hike, which combines three loop trails, you'll have something to look forward to right from the start. The first landmark is the raptor viewing area, home to several birds of prey. The birds here have permanent injuries and are unable to survive in the wild. Some of the birds you might get to see include the eastern screech-owl, barred owl, and the red-tailed hawk. They are kept here for educational use, and informational signs will give you some background on these majestic creatures.

Past the raptor area the scenery along the path leads you through pine woodland and open fields, over gentle hills, and across flowing streams. After the raptor area, continue on the green-blazed Stream Trail. It takes you down an old farm road before leaving the open field and entering a wooded landscape. The trail takes you past the historic Martin Cabin, a circa 1850 log structure that was reconstructed in the late 1990s and is now used for demonstrations.

The next portion of your journey brings you to the junction with a yellow-blazed trail. Follow the outermost perimeter of the yellow-blazed Wilderness Trail. This is where it can't hurt to have a full park map, which you can pick up in the visitor center. There are three yellow loops stacked on top of one another. By following the outermost perimeter, not only will you intersect the other two yellow loops several times, but you will also get to parallel Big Pipe Creek. Look here for trees gnawed at the base by beavers. A wide path takes you on a ridgeline hike overlooking the creek.

By staying on the outer perimeter trail, you will get the most distance out of your hike, but you can also shortcut the hike at any point by heading right at the intersections with the inner two loops. Once you've completed the yellow loop, return to the raptor area, picking up the white Vista Trail once again. Only this time, you'll be walking the other half of the white-blazed trail, which takes you through a stunning stand of pine trees that line the path, past a pavilion area, and within sight of a small pond. Finally, the trail crosses the entrance road. Before heading up the road to the parking lot, spend some time wandering through the marsh wetlands and scoping out the Lake Hashawha environment.

MILES AND DIRECTIONS

0.0   The white-blazed Vista Trail is just behind the trail kiosk. Start at a sign that reads Vista Trail to Raptor Cages.

0.2   Reach the raptor area. The white trail heads between the two cages until you see the arrows for yellow and green trail. At these markers make a U-turn to follow the green-blazed Stream Trail down a gravel utility road. Keep both cages on your left and a large field on your right. Follow the trail until you intersect with a paved road.

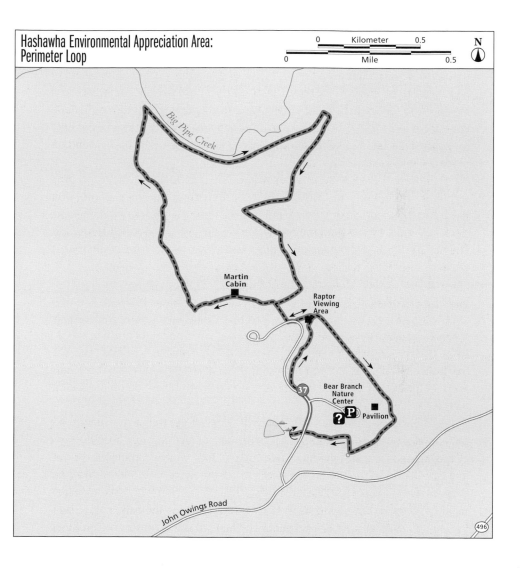

0.3 Walk a few steps on the paved road. Just before a sign straight ahead for a restricted area, make a right (north) on a gravel farm road.

0.4 See the yellow and green trail markings. (The trail loops back to this point.) Still following the green trail, leave the open field as the trail dips into the woods on a natural path.

0.5 At an intersection with the green and yellow trails, follow the green trail to head to the cabin.

0.6 At the intersection with the yellow trail, follow the yellow trail to the right over a small wooden bridge. The green trail continues slightly left.

0.7   Cross over a wooden bridge.

0.9   Reach the intersection with yellow Loop 1, which bears to the right. We are bearing just to the left.

1.2   Reach the intersection with yellow Loop 2, which heads to the right. Bear left at this intersection to continue on outer Loop 3.

1.4   See Big Pipe Creek. Following the yellow strokes of paint on the tree, take a sharp right or U-turn so the river is on your left.

2.0   An intersection with a yellow trail heads right. Stay straight here for few feet. Then follow the yellow blazes to take a sharp right back into the woods, leaving an open grassy area.

2.3   Reach another intersection with a yellow loop.

2.4   Loop 2 bears right and we bear left on the outside yellow trail. Just past that, you cross a wide-open field, making a sharp turn left to cross the field.

2.5   Intersect a path that heads to the right with a yellow marker in the distance. This trail will take you back to the cabin. Stay straight, continuing through the field—there is no yellow marker at the intersection guiding you straight. You can see the well-worn path through the field heading straight and then taking a turn to the right.

2.9   Complete the loop, arriving back at the start of the loop. Retrace your steps to the raptor area.

3.0   Once at the raptor area, follow the white trail that heads to the left when you are facing the raptor area trail kiosk.

3.4   Pass a pavilion on the right. Stay straight on white.

3.6   Head right to follow the white trail, walking through a field with a pavilion. But first look left to see a small pond. Then take a left on the gravel road. (A right takes you to the pavilion and parking lot for Bear Branch Nature Center.)

3.8   The grassy trail ends. At a parking lot, cross the entrance road to check out the lake and marsh. Then retrace your steps before walking the entrance road uphill and back to your car.

4.0   Arrive back at the parking lot and trailhead.

Appalachian Trail: Gathland State Park to Harpers Ferry

Knock out two states in 10.0 miles on a historic section of the 2,000-plus-mile Appalachian Trail (AT), which spans from Georgia to Maine. Highlights of this day hike include Gathland State Park, Ed Garvey shelter, Weverton Cliffs, the C&O Canal, and the quaint town of Harpers Ferry.

Start: Begin the hike at the white blaze painted on a post near the crosswalk with a pavilion on your right and arch structure on your left.

Distance: 10.2 miles one-way

Hiking time: About 5 hours

Difficulty: Difficult due to distance and a steep descent

Trail surface: Natural surface, crushed stone, gravel

Best season: Year-round

Other trail users: Foot traffic only

Canine compatibility: Leashed dogs permitted

Land status: National Park Service, National Scenic Trail

Fees and permits: None

Schedule: Sunrise–sunset daily

Maps: Trail map available on patc.net and in store at the Appalachian Trail Conservancy (appalachiantrail.org) at 799 Washington St., Harpers Ferry

Trail contacts: Potomac Appalachian Trail Club, 118 Park St. SE, Vienna, VA 22180; (703) 242-0315; patc.net

Other: Facilities include picnic tables, soda machines, restrooms, historic structures, informational signs

Special considerations: Weverton Cliff is rugged with a steep drop-off. Use caution in this area.

Finding the trailhead: Directions to Gathland State Park: From I-70, take exit 52 for US 340 west, US-15 south toward Charles Town, Leesburg. In 11.8 miles, take exit 2 for MD 17 toward Burkittsville. In 4.0 miles, turn left onto Seminary Lane. In 0.1 mile, turn left onto West Main Street. In 1.1 miles, turn left onto Gapland Road. In 50 feet, turn left on Arnoldstown Road. **GPS:** N39 24.353' / W77 38.375'

Directions to Harpers Ferry: From I-70, take exit 52 onto US 15 / US 340 west. For 18.8 miles, continue to follow US-340 west and turn right onto Shenandoah Street. In 0.8 mile, take the second left on Potomac Street and in 0.1 mile, park at the Harpers Ferry Train Station. **GPS:** N39 19.390' / W77 43.760'

THE HIKE

Every year, thousands of hikers set out to hike the entire Appalachian Trail from Georgia to Maine. On average, about 10 percent succeed. Even if a thru-hike of the 2,000 miles of the Appalachian Trail is not in the cards, you can see some of the most notable sights on a single day hike. This hike is described as a one-way with a shuttle. First, drop a car in the historic community of Harpers Ferry before driving 20 minutes to the town of Burkittsville (made famous by the movie *Blair Witch Project*) to start the hike at Gathland State Park, also referred to as Crampton Gap.

In addition to facilities like restrooms, a soda machine, and picnic tables, Gathland is dripping with history. The park was once home to George Alfred Townsend, a Civil War journalist. Remnants still stand of Townsend's structures dating back to the 1800s, some partially restored in the 1950s.

Begin your hike from the parking lot, with a pavilion on your right and the War Correspondents Arch on your left. The arch is a national monument dedicated to the memory of Civil War correspondents. Follow the white painted blaze on a post, across the road via a crosswalk and up the paved drive. At the top of the

Begin your hike near the War Correspondents Arch in Gathland State Park, a monument dedicated to Civil War correspondents.

hill, see another parking area. To the left, near a burial plot and mausoleum built in 1895 by George Alfred Townsend, a sign reads APPALACHIAN TRAIL SOUTH and points you in the direction of Weverton Cliff. You have now left the paved surface and are entering the white-blazed wooded natural footpath . . . the Appalachian Trail!

On the hike you may notice a Wilderness Memorial plaque on the left side of the trail on the forest floor dedicated to Glenn R. Caveney by family and friends. Caveney helped maintain this section of trail with his father.

Side trails on the AT are always blazed in blue, and there are two side trails that are especially interesting along this section of the AT. One is at 3.6 miles and takes you to the Ed Garvey shelter, a three-sided structure with a roof where backpackers can rest, sleep, and stay dry in the elements. While this particular shelter is one of the nicer ones on the AT (it has a loft!), it is typical of what an AT shelter looks like. They usually have a water source and a privy, which Ed Garvey shelter does have, in addition to a fire pit and a picnic table. Inside the shelter, you should find a trail journal, or a notebook, where hikers leave notes for other hikers to report wildlife sightings, weather reports, or simply how much fun they are having out on their hikes. After you've checked out the shelter, retrace your steps to the AT and continue south.

At 5.8 miles reach another blue-blazed side trail leading you to Weverton Cliff, with glorious views of the valley and Potomac River. The view point is only 0.1 mile from the intersection with the blue trail and it's a must-see overlook. Again, once you've had your fill of this eye-candy view, retrace your steps to the AT and head south, bearing to the left. Almost immediately upon your return to the AT, the trail takes steep switchbacks all the way down the hillside until you reach Weverton Road.

The sound of traffic is now inevitable as you cross Weverton Road, walk under busy US 340, and cross Keep Tryst Road and the train tracks before arriving at the flat, scenic, and peaceful C&O Canal towpath. Head right (upstream) on the towpath toward the town of Harpers Ferry.

Much of the canal on your right side is dried up. The sections that do have water are dark and mucky with a layer of green algae on top. But keep your eyes peeled as there are hundreds of turtles often perched in a row on logs and along the bank, or you may see a wood duck and her babies. You'll parallel the very active train tracks and rocky cliff walls on the right.

The Potomac River lies to your left, though your view is much obstructed by the trees. You'll have better views farther up the towpath. However, many side trails cut down to the river and you'll see the occasional sandy, rocky beach along the shore.

When you do get views of the river, look for lots of kayakers, tubers, and rafters heading downstream. There are many outfitters in the area that run trips down the river.

Nearing the end of your hike, leave the towpath and take the stairs to the footbridge and cross the river into Harpers Ferry. Once on the other side, you'll see white blazes leading you to the right into town, but first look to the left for a sign describing this point, the confluence of the Shenandoah and Potomac Rivers. Then, make your way into town and celebrate with a meal at one of the pubs or an ice cream. Stay and enjoy the history that surrounds you.

Harpers Ferry is the unofficial halfway point of the Appalachian Trail and home to the Appalachian Trail Conservancy, a nonprofit organization that preserves and manages the AT.

MILES AND DIRECTIONS

0.0   Start at Gathland State Park (Crampton Gap) parking lot with the pavilion on your right and War Correspondents Arch on the left. Follow the white blaze painted on a post near the crosswalk.

0.1   Reach another parking lot at the top of the paved path drive. Enter the woods to the left, just near the burial plot and mausoleum. A sign reads APPALACHIAN TRAIL SOUTH.

1.5   On the left side of the trail, reach the wilderness memorial plaque for Glenn R. Caveney.

1.8   Cross over an open area that extends left and right. A buried fiber optic cable is located here.

3.1   Reach a blue-blazed side trail on the right that takes you to a rock formation.

3.6   Reach the blue-blazed side trail to Ed Garvey shelter on the left.

3.7   Arrive at Ed Garvey shelter.

5.8   Reach the blue-blazed trail junction to Weverton Cliff.

5.9   Arrive at Weverton Cliff. Retrace your steps to the junction with the Appalachian Trail and continue south.

6.8   Reach Weverton Road and a park-and-ride. Cross the paved road heading toward the white blaze on opposite side, slightly to the left.

7.0   Walk underneath US 340.

7.2   Cross Keep Tryst Road. Walk toward the white blazes straight ahead near the brown gate and guardrail. Briefly parallel the railroad tracks.

7.3   Cross the railroad tracks and reach the C&O Canal Towpath. Head right, upstream.

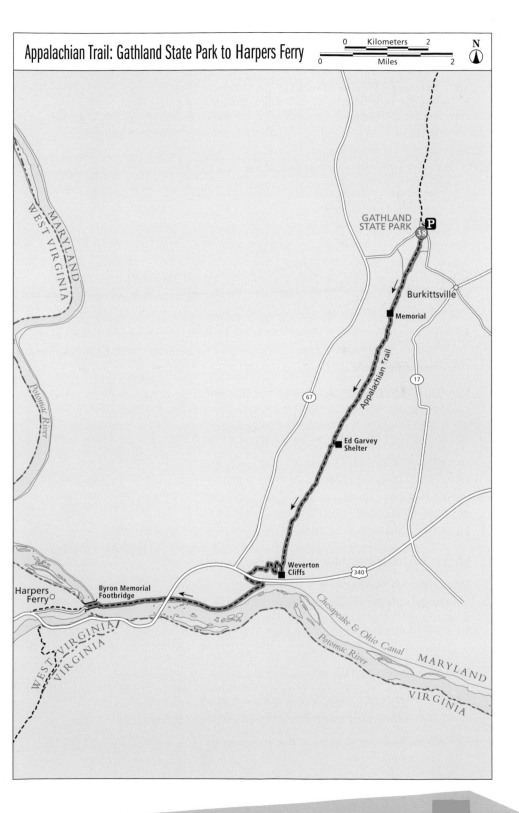

0   Kilometers   2

0   Miles   2

N

GATHLAND
STATE PARK

38   P

Burkittsville

Memorial

MARYLAND
WEST VIRGINIA

Potomac River

Appalachian Trail

67

17

Ed Garvey
Shelter

Weverton
Cliffs

340

Harpers
Ferry

Byron Memorial
Footbridge

Chesapeake & Ohio Canal

Potomac River   MARYLAND

WEST VIRGINIA
VIRGINIA

VIRGINIA

8.9 Pass under the US 340 bridge, high above.

9.5 Pass Lock 32 on the towpath.

10.0 Leave the towpath, and take the stairs up to the bridge to cross the Potomac River into Harpers Ferry on the Byron Memorial Footbridge.

10.2 On the other side of the footbridge, see staggered white blazes directing you to the right, into town. First, head left to the water to view the point where the Potomac and Shenandoah Rivers converge. Then, enjoy the historic town of Harpers Ferry.

Options: If you are looking for an overnight backpack, start at the I-70 footbridge heading south and end in Harpers Ferry for a total one-way distance of 22.4 miles. Camp at the Crampton Gap Shelter at 11.9 miles. **Directions to I-70 trailhead:** From I-70, take exit 42 for Maryland 17 north/Meyersville Road exit. Follow MD 17 for 1.1 miles, then left on US 40 west/Baltimore National Pike. The parking lot is located on the left just before US 40 crosses over I-70.

HIKE INFORMATION

Harpers Ferry has many small shops and restaurants.

Local attractions: Appalachian Trail Conservancy Headquarters and Visitor Center, 799 Washington St.; (304) 535-6331; appalachiantrail.org. In addition to the AT, the area surrounding Harpers Ferry has its own network of trails.

Harpers Ferry National Historic Park, 171 Shoreline Dr., Harpers Ferry, WV; (304) 535-6029; nps.gov/hafe/

Charles Town Races and Slots, 750 Hollywood Dr., Charles Town, WV; (800) 795-7001; hollywoodcasinocharlestown.com

Outfitters: The Outfitter at Harpers Ferry, 189 High St., (304) 535-2087

River and Trail Outfitters offers tube, kayak, and canoe rentals; 604 Valley Rd., Knoxville, MD; (301) 834-9950; rivertrail.com

Good eats: Private Quinn's Pub, 109 Potomac St., (304) 535-2322

Camping: Harpers Ferry Civil War Battlefield KOA, 343 Campground Rd., Harpers Ferry, WV; (800) 562-9497; harpersferrykoa.com

> *The official halfway point of the Appalachian Trail is near Pine Grove Furnace State Park in Pennsylvania. It's tradition for thru-hikers to take the "half-gallon challenge" by attempting to eat a half gallon of ice cream in one sitting.*

Sugarloaf Mountain: Northern Peaks and Mountain Loop

Standing out like a sore thumb, privately owned Sugarloaf Mountain is a 3,330-acre recreation area and a hikers' paradise. Combine the blue and white trails for a challenging 7.0-mile trek with elevation topping out at 1,015 feet.

Start: Begin on the blue-blazed trail, from the West View parking lot, with an old foundation on your left.

Distance: 7.4-mile loop

Hiking time: About 4 hours

Difficulty: Difficult

Trail surface: Natural surface, short paved section

Best season: Year-round

Other trail users: Trail runners; mountain bikes are permitted on the yellow trail only Mon–Fri between Memorial Day and Labor Day. Horseback riding is restricted to the yellow trail.

Canine compatibility: Leashed dogs permitted

Land status: Private land open to the public

Fees and permits: None

Schedule: Open from 8 a.m. until 1 hour before sunset daily

Maps: Map available at sugar loafmd.com and at mountain parking lots

Trail contacts: Stronghold Inc., 7901 Comus Rd., Dickerson, MD 20842; (301) 869-7846; sugar loafmd.com

Other: Picnic tables, trashcans, portable toilets; no overnight camping

Special considerations: Stay on the trails, do not wander onto private property!

Finding the trailhead: Take I-695 to MD 70 west, then I-270 south to the Hyattstown exit. Follow MD 109 to Comus, then take a right on Comus Road to the Sugarloaf Mountain entrance. Follow the signs for the mountain parking and wind uphill. Park in the West View parking lot. **GPS:** N39 15.642'/ W77 23.851'

THE HIKE

The blue Northern Peaks Trail plus the white Mountain Loop equals a good day of hiking on Sugarloaf Mountain. And yes, it's well worth the drive. The 3,330-acre property of Sugarloaf is privately owned and managed by Stronghold Inc., a nonprofit corporation organized in 1946 by the late Gordon Strong. Designated a Registered Natural Landmark, Stronghold maintains the mountain for the public's enjoyment. Sugarloaf Mountain was supposedly named by explorers and settlers who were reminded of their crystalized cone-shaped loaves of sugar.

As you drive through the main entrance of Sugarloaf, there is a parking lot at the base. But follow the sign to mountain parking and circle way up the mountain to reach the West View parking lot and the start of the blue Northern Peaks Trail. The vast views from the parking lot should be a sign that you are in for a treat.

The mountain stands alone, towering 800 feet above rolling farmland at an elevation of 1,282 feet. Well-maintained and well-marked trails make this a fairly mindless outing that allows you to focus on the surrounding scenery rather than staring at the map. Not only are the trails labeled by color but also by number at

Soaring views of the countryside can be had from White Rocks North and South overlooks.

various points along the trail. For example, the B7 milepost marker post correlates with Sugarloaf's map to determine your exact location along the trail.

The trail starts off as mild, but you will certainly break a sweat on numerous uphill climbs, descents, and switchbacks. You will get some shade as you cross creeks and boardwalks and bridges through a forest of red and white oaks, occasionally paralleling a creek. You may also see black gum, tulip poplar, black birch, and eastern hemlock. Try to spy for skunk cabbage, black-eyed Susan, mountain laurel, chestnut oak, flowering dogwood, cardinal flower, and yes, the dreaded poison ivy.

Be sure to take the super-short side trails to the overlooks of White Rocks North and White Rocks South. Enjoy a snack on the large rock outcropping and soak in the soaring views of the countryside. Quartzite is the primary type of rock on the mountain.

Keep your eyes peeled for white-tailed deer, red fox, raccoon, pileated woodpecker, flying squirrel, great horned owl, eastern cottontail, wild turkey, red-shouldered hawks, and timber rattlesnakes and copperheads. Bear, coyote, and bobcat have also been spotted here.

The highest point on the hike is 1,015 feet. A pile of rocks marks this point and there are some log benches to take a rest. Several summit-area trails will take

Take a spur trail to the remains of a fireplace and one-room building.

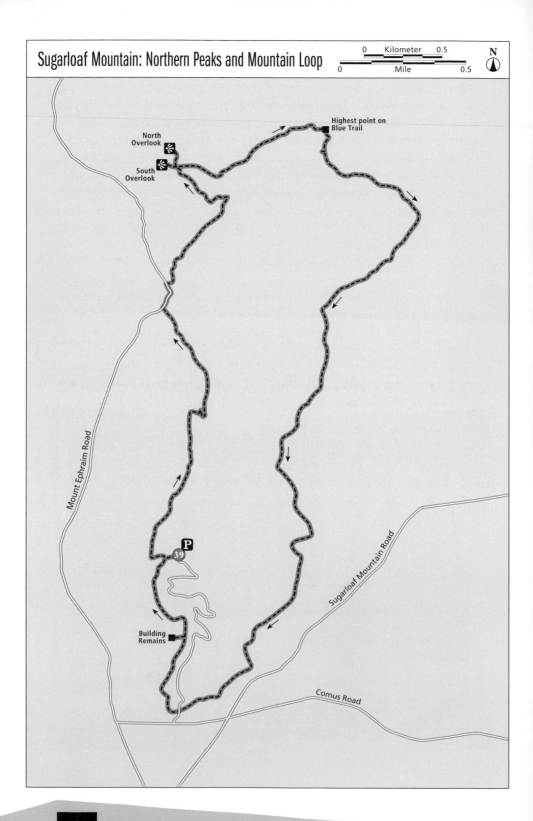

Sugarloaf Mountain: Northern Peaks and Mountain Loop

0   Kilometer   0.5
0   Mile   0.5

N

North Overlook

South Overlook

Highest point on Blue Trail

Mount Ephraim Road

Sugarloaf Mountain Road

P
39

Building Remains

Comus Road

you to the tippy top if you choose. At 5.0 miles you can choose to continue fol-lowing the blue trail or you can add some distance buy taking the white trail. The hike described here follows the white trail to add the distance. A short portion of the white trail has you walking on a park road and passing below the Westwood and Strong Mansions. This section on the park roads is the only area where the blazes are sparse.

Ahead, a spur trail will take you to the old foundation remains of a fireplace and a one-room stone building with a slate roof. Upon completing the loop, give yourself a pat on the back and maybe offer up a cheers at the nearby SMV Winery!

MILES AND DIRECTIONS

0.0 From the West View parking lot, begin at the Northern Peaks Trailhead blazed in blue. The trail immediately starts downhill, passing an old foun-dation on your left.

0.1 Take the white trail to the right (it shares a path with the blue). Note the white trail heading left, as this is where you will end the loop.

0.6 The white and blue trails split at a Y intersection. Follow blue blazes left and slightly downhill.

0.7 Reach milepost marker for B9.

1.3 Reach milepost marker for B8.

1.4 Reach Mount Ephraim Road. Walk the road downhill following the blue blazes.

1.5 Just after a curve in the road at the bottom of the hill, follow staggered blazes into the woods on your right.

2.2 Reach the intersection of two spur trails to White Rocks South and North overlooks. Visit both before continuing on the blue-blazed trail.

2.3 Reach White Rock South overlook and retrace your steps.

2.4 Reach White Rocks North overlook and retrace your steps.

2.5 Come to a T intersection. A purple trail goes to the left. Continue straight on the blue-blazed trail.

2.8 Reach the milepost marker for B6.

3.2 Reach the highest point on the Blue Trail at 1,015 feet.

3.6 Reach a five-way junction. Continue straight to follow the blue trail.

4.9 Bear left to follow the blue and white trails, which share a path.

5.0 Reach a Y intersection with the blue trail heading right and white heading straight. Now follow the white trail straight ahead.

5.5 Reach the intersection for a white diamond spur trail that goes straight to East View parking lot. Make a left here on the white-blazed trail.

5.9 Cross over a park road to continue on the white-blazed trail.

6.2 Reach the bottom of a hill and a gravel road. To the right is private property. Make a left on the gravel road, followed by an immediate right to walk the park road.

6.3 Come to two buildings, one on the left and one on the right side of the road. Do not walk between the two buildings. Before you reach the buildings, make a right, slightly uphill on a park road with a cable strung across.

6.4 Come to a T intersection with another park road. Cross this road and follow the yellow-and-white-blazed trail (slightly left) on the opposite side of road heading into the trees.

6.6 The yellow trail splits to the left. Follow the white trail to the right and uphill.

6.7 Cross a small creek.

6.8 Walk the trail to the left to visit the ruins of a fireplace and one-room building.

7.2 Continue straight on the white trail, passing the spur trail to the Potomac Overlook parking lot.

7.3 Again reach the intersection with the blue trail where you started. Hang a right to retrace your steps to the trailhead.

7.4 Arrive back at the trailhead and parking lot.

HIKE INFORMATION

Local attractions: Sugarloaf Mountain Vineyard, 18125 Comus Rd., Dickerson; (301) 605-0130; smvwinery.com

> *A monadnock is a mountain that remains after the erosion of the surrounding land. For Sugarloaf, that process took approximately 14 million years.*

Follow the Chesapeake & Ohio Canal towpath and waterway, a National Historic Park, before heading into the woods to clamber your way through a giant boulderfield playground, all while getting views of the mighty Potomac River and deep Mather Gorge—typically littered with kayakers, paddleboarders, and rappellers.

Start: Begin at the Great Falls Tavern Visitor Center.

Distance: 4.7-mile lollipop with spur

Hiking time: About 3 hours

Difficulty: Difficult due to rock scrambles

Trail surface: Natural surface and large boulders

Best season: Year-round

Other trail users: Trail runners, bikers, kayakers

Canine compatibility: Dogs not allowed on Billy Goat Trail A. Leashed pets are allowed on the towpath.

Land status: National Historical Park, a unit of the National Park Service

Fees and permits: Fees collected at Great Falls Entrance Station only.

Schedule: Open daylight hours daily sunrise–sunset. Great Falls Tavern Visitor Center open Wed–Sun 9 a.m. to 4:30 p.m.

Maps: Trail map available at nps .gov/choh/planyourvisit/upload/ GF-Map-Page-2.pdf

Trail contacts: Chesapeake & Ohio Canal Park Headquarters, 1850 Dual Hwy., Suite 100, Hagerstown, MD 21740; (301) 739-4200; nps.gov/choh

Other: Replica canal boat rides Apr–Oct Wed–Fri 11 a.m. and 3 p.m., Sat–Sun 11 a.m., 1:30 p.m., and 3 p.m.; small fee. Facilities include restrooms, visitor center, water fountains, picnic tables, and a snack shop.

Special considerations: Swimming and wading in the river are not permitted. It is possible, especially in spring, for the Billy Goat Trail A to be closed due to high water. You can call the park in advance to find out.

Finding the trailhead: From I-495, take exit 41 toward Caderock / Great Falls. In 0.3 mile, merge on Clara Barton Parkway, then in 1.5 miles turn left on MacArthur Boulevard. Drive 3.4 miles, passing several parking areas, but continue to the Great Falls parking area and park for a fee. There is more than enough parking in this lot. **GPS:** N39 00.027' / W77 14.883'

THE HIKE

The Billy Goat Trail is just downright fun! Although a bit of a drive, it's well within reach of Baltimore. It utilizes the C&O Canal towpath, a National Historical Park that runs 184.5 miles in total from Washington, DC, to Cumberland, Maryland. This hike combines ultimate rock scrambles, hiking among a boulder field, roaring waterfalls, a scenic gorge, and a flat stretch on the scenic C&O Canal. What's not to love? Well, other than all the hiker traffic; yes, it's a popular place, and for a darn good reason, so you may experience crowds and an occasional bottleneck. But it's worth it.

Begin the hike at the Great Falls Tavern Visitor Center and Museum. The trail begins as an easy jaunt down the towpath before hanging a right to follow the well-marked signs for the Billy Goat Trail Section A. The trail gets you up close and personal with the deep and scenic Mather Gorge, lined with cliffs and cut by the Potomac River. The gorge is also a playground for kayakers, paddleboarders, and rock climbers.

As you walk the towpath, the canal is on your left (look for the *Charles F. Mercer* canal boat) and the Potomac River is on your right. You'll pass several canal locks, small waterfalls, and educational signs.

Take an educational ride on a replica canal boat on the C&O Canal.

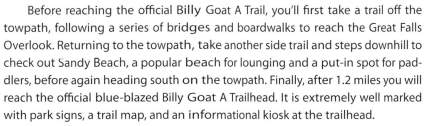

Before reaching the official Billy Goat A Trail, you'll first take a trail off the towpath, following a series of bridges and boardwalks to reach the Great Falls Overlook. Returning to the towpath, take another side trail and steps downhill to check out Sandy Beach, a popular beach for lounging and a put-in spot for paddlers, before again heading south on the towpath. Finally, after 1.2 miles you will reach the official blue-blazed Billy Goat A Trailhead. It is extremely well marked with park signs, a trail map, and an informational kiosk at the trailhead.

The Billy Goat A Trail surface is a mix of packed dirt, sand, and rock. You'll carefully place each step on this much-exposed trail. At 1.8 miles the trail ups the intensity. Here you'll see a trail marker and a sign that reads DIFFICULT TRAIL AHEAD— MANY HIKERS ARE INJURED EVERY YEAR ON THIS SECTION OF THE BILLY GOAT TRAIL. Just past this, the trail is made up of giant cliff-side flat rocks and boulders with unobstructed views of Mather Gorge. Take a snack break here to enjoy the views, and watch the kayakers below and the rock climbers and rappellers on the opposite side of the gorge. Keep a lookout for snakes.

The trail to the must-see Great Falls Overlook takes you over a bridge and above giant rapids.

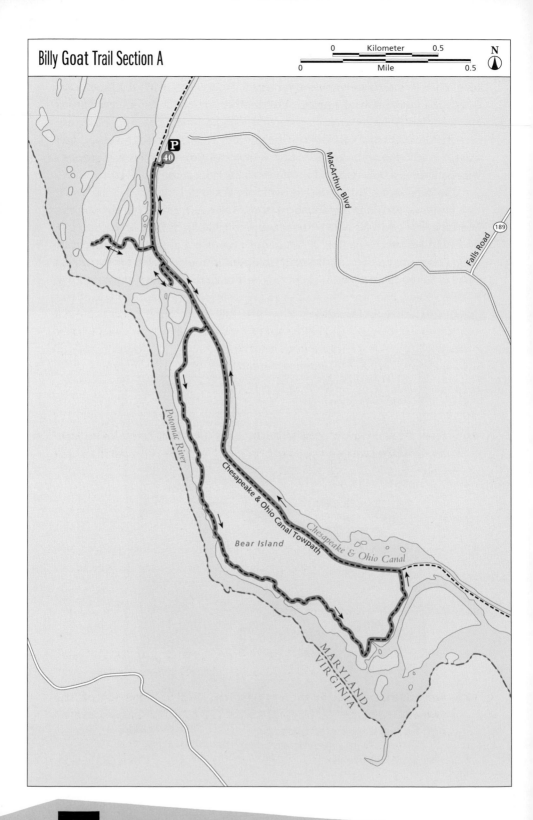

0   Kilometer   0.5

0   Mile   0.5

N

P

40

MacArthur Blvd

Falls Road

189

Potomac River

Chesapeake & Ohio Canal Towpath

Chesapeake & Ohio Canal

Bear Island

MARYLAND
VIRGINIA

You'll get a short break from the rock trail, following a flat dirt path, but then look to the sky to see where you are headed . . . up a vertical 35-foot hand-over-hand rock scramble known as the Traverse. This is often where you will experience the bottleneck of hikers.

But the rocks don't end there. On the last mile of the Billy Goat Trail, you'll pass a pond, cross over a timber bridge, walk across a small sandy beach, make a water crossing, and take one last small rock scramble up before you again rejoin with the nice flat towpath.

You'll use the C&O Canal towpath to complete a loop back to the parking area and Great Falls Tavern Visitor Center. The C&O Canal, built between 1828 and 1850 and operated until 1924, began as a passage to the west, operating for nearly one hundred years. It was a necessity for communities along the Potomac River to send coal, lumber, and agricultural products down the waterway to the market.

On this stretch of the towpath, anglers fish from several bridges. It's not unusual to see folks carrying kayaks above their heads down the towpath, trail runners, bikers, and families out pushing strollers and walking dogs. While dogs are not allowed on the Billy Goat Trail, they are allowed on the towpath.

MILES AND DIRECTIONS

0.0   From the parking area, begin the hike at the Great Falls Tavern Visitor Center. Cross the canal via a wooden bridge and follow the towpath to the left (south).

0.1   Pass Lock 19.

0.2   Pass Lock 18.

0.3   Take a side trail to the right for Great Falls Overlook, marked with a brown sign and an interpretive sign. Cross a series of bridges and boardwalks to get to the view point.

0.5   Arrive at the end of the overlook trail. Retrace your steps and head right (south) when you arrive back at the towpath.

0.9   Take an unmarked path on the right down some stairs to Sandy Beach. Again retrace your steps and head south on the towpath.

1.2   Arrive at the trailhead for the Billy Goat Trail, heading to the right off the towpath. The trailhead is very well marked with park signs, an educational sign, trail map, and a blue-blazed trail.

1.4   At a side trail intersection, continue to follow the well-marked blue blazes.

1.8 A trail marker designates an emergency exit in 0.4 mile. A sign reads Difficult trail ahead—many hikers are injured every year on this section of the Billy Goat
Trail.

2.0 Arrive at the bottom of a vertical rock scramble known as the Traverse.

2.2 A trail marker designates 0.75 mile of the Billy Goat Trail remain and a midpoint exit to the towpath is 100 yards ahead.

2.5 One long log timber bridge crosses over a creek. Immediately after the
bridge is another trail marker stating the towpath is 0.5 mile ahead.

2.7 Walk a sandy beach followed by a creek crossing that feeds the river.

3.0 Meet up with the towpath. Make a left to walk back to the Great Falls Tavern Visitor Center.

4.0 Pass Lock 16.

4.1 Walk underneath a bridge that crosses to the other side of the canal just
before passing by the Billy Goat Trailhead.

4.7 Arrive back at the Visitor Center Tavern.

Options: There are two other sections of the Billy Goat Trail (B and C). They are not
connected to each other but rather separate loops off of the towpath. This hike
details section A of the Billy Goat Trail. Add the other loops to add distance or
hike them separately. For an easy stroll, do an out-and-back on the towpath and
skip the Billy Goat Trail altogether.

HIKE INFORMATION

Good eats: Old Angler's Inn, 10801 MacArthur Blvd., Potomac; (301) 365-2425;
oldanglersinn.com

> 🌿 **Green Tip:**
> *Stay on established trails as much as possible. If there
> aren't any, stay on surfaces that will be least affected,
> like rock, gravel, dry grasses, or snow.*

Honorable Mentions

A. Baltimore & Annapolis Trail (B&A Trail)

Following the route of the old Baltimore & Annapolis Railroad, the B&A Trail extends from Boulters Way in Annapolis to Dorsey Road in Glen Burnie. It's a 13.3-mile-long linear recreational greenway following a 10-foot-wide paved path. It's primarily used by hikers, walkers, runners, bikers, and horseback riders and open year-round from dawn to dusk. The B&A Railroad was the first major direct transportation route between Annapolis and the city of Baltimore dating back to 1887. Today the trail passes through suburban neighborhoods, wetlands, and meadows and by remnants and reminders of the old B&A Short Line Railroad that used to run here, including the Severna Park Station. Facilities include public restrooms, portable toilets, water fountains, and picnic tables. Some restaurants and stores are also situated on the path. There are four parking lots along the B&A Trail. Parking is available at the B&A Trail Park Headquarters on Earleigh Heights Road. Maps and directions to all parking lots can be found on the website.

Trail contacts: 51 W. Earleigh Heights Rd., Severna Park, MD 21146; (410) 222-6244; aacounty.org/RecParks/parks/trails/bandatrailpark.cfm#.UaefeWC5f-Z

Directions to Earleigh Heights Ranger Station: From Baltimore and points north/northwest: Take I-695 to MD 10 south. MD 10 will merge with MD 100. To stay on MD 10, you must move to the right. Continue on MD 10 until it terminates at MD 2. Make a left onto MD 2 south, go to the second light (Earleigh Heights Road), and make a right. The Ranger Station is about 300 yards down on the left.

B. BWI Trail

Where the B&A Trail ends (Dorsey Road in Glen Burnie), the BWI Trail begins. The trail circles the Baltimore Washington International (BWI) Airport for 12.5 miles of paved trail and some wooden boardwalk. Okay, so maybe it's not your exact idea of "nature," but it's pretty cool and darn impressive to watch these massive people-movers take off into the sky and land in front of you. The Thomas A. Dixon Jr. Observation Area is the best spot on the trail to watch the jets come and go. And believe it or not, the trail does offer meadows of wildflowers, wetlands, and pine forest. You'll likely see some wildlife like ducks, heron, and geese in the marshy areas. There is even history here: You'll pass the Benson-Hammond House, a 200-year-old mansion, now a museum and home to the Anne Arundel County Historical Society. It stands as a reminder of a once-booming farm industry. There are two parking lots on the BWI Trail. A spur trail leads to the Linthicum Heights Light-Rail Station. Facilities include playgrounds, bike racks, and restrooms.

Trail contacts: Anne Arundel County Department of Recreation & Parks, (410) 222-7300; aacounty.org/RecParks/parks/trails/bwitrailpark.cfm#.UaesRGC5f-Z; dnr.state.md.us/greenways/bwi_trail.html

Directions to the Observation Area and Saw Mill Creek parking areas: From Baltimore and points north/northwest: Take I-695 to I-97 south. Take exit 15, MD 176 (Dorsey Road) east toward the airport. Continue on MD 176 a short distance. The Observation Area is on the left just before WB&A Road. For Saw Mill Creek Park, when exiting I-97 onto Dorsey Road, go west away from the airport. The park is on the right very near the I-97 interchange.

C. Catoctin Mountain Park and Cunningham Falls State Park

Catoctin Mountain Park, part of the Catoctin Mountain Ridge, is located in north-central Maryland in Frederick County and lies adjacent to Cunningham Falls State Park. Hiking-trail lengths range from 0.5 mile to 27 miles. Hikers will find trails ranging from easy to strenuous. The parks have hiking, camping, picnic areas, fly fishing, cross-country skiing, swimming, and canoeing. Countless highlights along the trail system include outstanding scenic vistas, wildlife, and wetlands. But a visit to the area is not complete without hiking to the 78-foot Cunningham Falls, the highest cascading waterfall in the state. This area is absolutely worth the drive—it's a little over an hour from Baltimore.

Cunningham trail contacts: 14039 Catoctin Hollow Rd., Thurmont, MD; (301) 271-7574; dnr.state.md.us/publiclands/western/cunningham.asp

Catoctin trail contacts: 6602 Foxville Rd., Thurmont, MD; (301) 663-9388 (visitor center) or (301) 663-9330; nps.gov/cato

Directions to Catoctin Visitor Center: Take the I-695 beltway to I70 west to Frederick, Maryland. Take US 15 north to Thurmont, Maryland. Take Route 77 west (the exit sign says Catoctin Mountain Park). Travel approximately 3.0 miles west on 77 and turn right onto Park Central Road. The visitor center is on the right.

D. Centennial Park

At this park you'll find paddlers cruising the water, kids playing on the playground, picnickers enjoying an afternoon, and of course, those out for an easy but scenic hike around beautiful Centennial Lake. The park itself, with 325 acres, has lots of amenities including fishing, boat rentals, a boat launch area, ball fields, picnic areas, tennis and volleyball courts, a skate area, playgrounds, an amphitheater, restrooms, and concessions.

A stroll on a paved path around the entire lake offers the best opportunity for scenery and serenity, as you may see an abundance of wildlife and wildflowers. Common to the area are great blue herons, swallows, bluebirds, turkey vultures, green herons, mallard ducks, Canada geese, bald eagles, and hawks. Also, look for rabbits, red fox, beavers, snakes, and turtles as well as monarch and swallowtail butterflies frolicking in this pleasant environment. And of course, ducks love Centennial Lake. The park is a popular spot for running races, walkathons, and triathlons. The trail sees a good amount of traffic including bikers, skaters, dogs trotting along with their owners, and parents pushing strollers. There is plenty of parking to accommodate the many visitors to the park.

The trail takes you past many park facilities, over bridges, and to the Centennial Arboretum with no fences or boundaries, rather just an uninterrupted part of the natural experience with interpretive signs and identification tags labeling the diverse species of flora and trees like hickory, oak, walnut, dogwood, and beech. The lake is home to largemouth bass, rainbow trout, and catfish. The loop hike takes you past picturesque marshes and wetlands with cattails and lily pads. Swimming is not permitted in the lake.

Trail contacts: Centennial Park, 10000 Route 108, Columbia, MD; (410) 313-7271 or (410) 313-7256; centennialmd.org

Finding the trailhead: From I-70 take US 29. From US 29, take Route 108 west, toward Clarksville. The main entrance to the park is about 1 mile on your right. The trailhead is located at the boat ramp and parking area.

E. Cylburn Arboretum

Well-manicured lawns and lush landscaping with gardens and specimen trees are the backdrop for a total of 2.5 miles of trails on the Cylburn Arboretum grounds, combined with a museum and historic mansion. Minus the slight hum in the background of the Jones Falls Expressway, you'll soon be taken over by the beauty and peacefulness of the arboretum and forget that you are in Baltimore city. The lush grounds of the arboretum boast open lawns for picnicking or simply settling down with a blanket and a book. You are surrounded by stunning display gardens.

The arboretum was once the private estate of businessman Jesse Tyson. He was the president of Baltimore Chrome Works, a company that exported chromite throughout the world. The Cylburn Mansion was originally built as a summer home for his mother and himself. Today, you can enjoy the pristine grounds and the nature museum, open by appointment and on some weekends, housing a butterfly collection, as well as displays of birds and eggs, fossils, and rocks and minerals. Explore the property to peek in the windows of the production greenhouses (not open to the public) and gardens scattered about. The hiking trails will take you through a variety of habitats.

Trail contacts: Cylburn Arboretum, 4915 Greenspring Ave., Baltimore, MD 21209; (410) 367-2217; cylburnassociation.org

Finding the trailhead: From I-83, take the Northern Parkway west exit. Turn left on Greenspring Avenue. Continue past Cylburn Avenue and take the immediate left into the arboretum. Park in the visitor parking lot on the left side of the main entrance road. Follow the walking path toward the mansion.

F. Downs Memorial Park

With 236 acres, Downs Memorial Park has many facilities, including restrooms, water fountains, a dog beach, a fishing pier, a playground, and a picnic area. Visitors enjoy expansive views of the Chesapeake Bay and Bodkin Creek Inlet. There is a total of 5.0 miles of paved hiking trails and a network of natural-surface interior trails. The Perimeter Trail takes you on a paved, curvy path through a wooded corridor and forest and marsh land. The trail is well marked with short wooden mile-marker posts placed every tenth of a mile as well as directional markers. You'll find plenty of shade as you curve your way through mature forest and marshy areas. It's not uncommon to see deer, pileated woodpeckers, turkey vultures, osprey, and black, white, and red squirrels. If you hear some sort of critter making scurrying sounds among the leaves, it's a good chance you've found some skinks. These lizards scurry about. Look for the juvenile lizards with blue tails and the plump adults with red and brown heads. The park is home to three species of native orchids, ferns, red maple trees, mountain laurel, dogwoods, black walnut trees, white, black, and chestnut oak trees, and wildflowers like wood aster and spotted jewelweed. Other highlights of the park include a dog beach, Downs Park Fishing Pier, and Mother's Garden, a Victorian-style garden. The park is named for John (Jack) Downs, a public servant of the county, as a tribute to his dedicated service to the residents. Downs served as county councilman in this district.

Trail contacts: Downs Memorial Park, 8311 John Downs Loop, Pasadena, MD 21122; (410) 222-6230, events line (410) 222-6239; aacounty.org/RecParks/parks/downs/#.UsrxvrSW5Mk

Finding the trailhead: Take I-695 to I-97 south. Then take exit 14 to MD 100 east. Take a slight right on Mountain Road east. Drive 3.7 miles and continue on Pinehurst Road. Follow signs to the park and take a right into the entrance at Chesapeake Bay Drive.

G. Eden Mill Park, Nature Center, and Museum

Eden Mill, located in Harford County, has more than 5.0 miles of trail with views of wetlands, creeks, meadows, and forest. The wildlife is bountiful with inhabitants like fox, rabbit, deer, beavers, bluebirds, and turtles, just to name a few. A trail map is available on the website. Eden Mill is also home to a historic gristmill that's rumored to have a resident ghost! The mill, both gristmill and sawmill, sits on the bank of Deer Creek and last operated in 1964. The park and trail are open daily from dawn to dusk. The Nature Center and Grist Mill Museum are open Mon–Fri 9:00 a.m. to 4:30 p.m., Sat noon to 5 p.m., and Sun 1 to 5 p.m. (4 p.m. Nov–Mar).

Trail contacts: Eden Mill Nature Center, 1617 Eden Mill Rd., Pylesville; (410) 863-3050; edenmill.org

Directions: From US 1 north, turn left onto Mountain Road. In 5.8 miles turn right on Baldwin Mill Road. In 9.4 miles turn left onto Fawn Grove Road. In 1 mile turn left onto Eden Mill Road.

H. Federal Hill Park

This hill on the south side of the Inner Harbor in the town of Federal Hill affords one of the best views of Baltimore, overlooking the prosperous cityscape. Federal Hill is an iconic Baltimore landmark. In 1788, 4,000 people feasted here to celebrate Maryland's ratification of the US Constitution. The hill was once a lookout occupied by Union troops during the Civil War. It became a public park in 1880. Amenities include a basketball court, playground, and walking paths.

A steep set of stairs will get you to the top. Walk the tree-lined brick paths encircling the hill to see monuments like the one commemorating the Battle of Baltimore and statues of War of 1812 heroes like Lt. Colonel George Armistead and Major General Samuel Smith. You'll see old war cannons, and several benches are placed for taking a load off your feet and taking in the city surroundings. Federal Hill Park is just across from the Maryland Science Center. The neighborhood of Federal Hill is a hot spot with trendy restaurants, boutique shops, and lots of nightlife options.

Trail contacts: Federal Hill Park, 300 Warren Ave., Baltimore; (410) 396-5828; bcrp.baltimorecity.gov/ParksTrails/FederalHillPark.aspx

Directions: From I-95 south, take exit 55 for Key Highway. Follow Key Highway, and Federal Hill Park will be on your left.

I. Liberty Reservoir Watershed

Located in western Baltimore County and eastern Carroll County, Liberty Reservoir is owned by the City of Baltimore Department of Public Works and was constructed for use as a public water supply. It is primarily fed by the North Branch of the Patapsco River. The Liberty Dam was completed in 1954. The reservoir is open to the public year-round, from sunrise to sunset, for hiking, biking, fishing, paddling, horseback riding, and bird watching. Camping and swimming are not permitted.

There are 9,200 acres of watershed that surround the reservoir. Most of the trails are fire roads, and they are not blazed or marked. Overall, the watershed trails are lightly used and little known, though there is an obligation to let you know that this large piece of preserved nature exists for explorers and adventurous hikers. Numerous public roads provide access points to this area.

Trail contacts: City of Baltimore Department of Public Works, Reservoir Natural Resources Section, 5685 Oakland Rd., Eldersburg, MD 21784; (410) 795-6151; baltimorecity.gov

J. Ma & Pa Heritage Trail

The Maryland and Pennsylvania Railroad stretched between Baltimore at North Avenue and Howard Streets, on to Towson, through Long Green Valley, and into Harford County. It ended at Market Street in York, Pennsylvania. Today, the Ma & Pa Heritage Trail in Harford County is a rail trail located on portions of the former railroad corridor. There are three sections, though they are not connected, for hikers, walkers, joggers, and bikers to enjoy: 1) the 1.9-mile Bel Air section, 2) the 1.4-mile Edgeley Grove section, and 3) the 1.7-mile Forest Hill section. There are active efforts in place to connect the trails. Once that happens, the total length of the trail system will be approximately 8.0 miles one-way.

The trail passes parks and ball fields, playgrounds, and even a dog park on a combination of a crushed stone, packed dirt, and paved surface. Cross over boardwalks and bridges with scenery that includes red maples, tulip trees, and sycamores, gardens, and marshland. In the Bel Air section, near the tunnel that runs under MD 24, a piece of railroad track was laid next to a display board explaining the history of the Ma & Pa Railroad. This *Daybreak* sculpture, an Eagle Scout project, is a nice reminder of the once major railroad for the owner's of the counties' canneries, quarries, and mines.

Trail contacts: Ma & Pa Heritage Trail, 702 N. Tollgate Rd., Bel Air , 21014, (410) 638-3528; mapatrail.org

Directions to the Bel Air section: Directions from I-95 and MD 24 (exit 77B): Take MD 24N toward Bel Air. Turn right on Baltimore Pike / US 1BR. Drive 0.4 mile and turn left on Archer Street. Turn right on Thomas Street and make an immediate left on Williams Street. Drive 0.5 mile to the trail parking lot on left. From here, the trail extends 3.3 miles to Edgeley Grove and Annie's Playground.

K. Patterson Park

This 137-acre public park located in Baltimore city isn't considered a hiking destination but rather a fine green space with paved paths in a prime location convenient for many city dwellers. The park is heavily used by social sports clubs and is popular with dog owners taking their pups for a walk. Boat Lake, where fishing is permitted, is a highlight of the park. It's home for ducks, herons, turtles, and frogs. The Park's Pagoda (originally known as the Observatory) was designed in 1890 by Charles H Latrobe. After a total restoration, it stands proud as an iconic city landmark. Climb the stairs for great views of Baltimore's neighborhoods from noon to 6 p.m. on Sunday from mid-April to mid-October. In the park you'll find sports fields, tennis courts, playgrounds, a dog park, a swimming pool, and an ice-skating rink. Concerts and festivals are held at the park. See a map of the paths on the Friends of Patterson Park website. The figure-eight path noted on the map is 1.92 miles in length and a perimeter path is 2.1 miles.

Trail contacts: Friends of Patterson Park, 27 S. Patterson Park Ave., Baltimore; (410) 276-3676; pattersonpark.com

Directions: Take I-95 south toward Baltimore City. Take exit 59, Eastern Avenue, and bear right off the ramp (west) toward Highlandtown. Continue on Eastern Avenue for 2.5 miles—the park is on the right.

L. Rock Creek Park

Leaving Baltimore and heading into DC, Rock Creek Park, an urban nature park, is a nice option for a day trip. Take a visit to the nature center, which houses a children's Discovery Room, live turtles, fish, snakes, and a bird observation deck. Here you'll also find a map of the trails. Just behind the nature center is a self-guided interpretive trail called the Woodland Trail, and the Edge of the Woods Trail, a 0.25-mile accessible trail, starts at the front door of the nature center. There are 32 miles of trails in total. The two main trails are the Western Ridge Trail and the Valley Trail, with several connector trails that allow for loop hikes. The 1,700-acre park has a mix of natural surface and paved paths. All types of outdoor enthusiasts use the trails including hikers, runners, bikers, and horseback riders. After your hike, check out the astronomy programs led by rangers at the planetarium. Check out the website for program days and times.

Trail contacts: Rock Creek Park, 5200 Glover Rd. NW, Washington, DC, (202) 895-6070 for visitor info or (202) 895-6000 for park headquarters, nps.gov/rocr/index.htm

Directions: From I-95, take exit 27 for 495 west. Take exit 30 for US 29 south. Continue on Colesville Road. At the roundabout take the third exit onto 16th Street NW. Turn right for Military Road. Turn left on Glover Road. The Nature Center and Planetarium is on the right.

M. Savage Park

This Howard County park has 2.8 miles of interconnecting trails. Other amenities include ball fields, pavilions, playgrounds, tennis courts, and volleyball courts. The Savage Mill Race Trail extends for 1.4 miles along the Little Patuxent River, passing through the grounds of an old cotton mill. Along the rail trail, check out the historic structures of Bollman Truss Bridge, the last remaining of its type. It was built in 1869 and moved to Savage in 1887. Savage Mill is a renovated cotton mill that was originally built in the 1800s. Today it houses restaurants and specialty shops.

Trail contacts: Savage Park, 8400 Fair St., Savage, MD, 20763; (410) 313-4700; howardcountymd.gov/savagepark.htm

Directions: From MD 295 south, take the exit for MD 32 west. Take exit 12 A-B for US 1 south. Keep left for Washington Boulevard, then keep right for US 1 south. Turn right on Gorman Road and follow it to the Bollman Truss Bridge.

Appendix

CLUBS AND TRAIL GROUPS

Mountain Club of Maryland, 7923 Galloping Circle, Baltimore, MD 21224; (410) 377-6266; mcomd.org. The oldest hiking club in Maryland (established 1934), Mountain Club of Maryland is the premier hiking group in the state. The club is a Baltimore-based volunteer organization centered on hiking. They lead hikes, camping trips, canoeing outings, and other outdoor activities in addition to maintaining sections of the Appalachian Trail.

Maryland Outdoor Club, marylandoutdoorclub.org. This 100 percent volunteer-run organization hosts all types of outdoor activities oriented toward young professionals in the Baltimore and Washington, DC, area, but is open to anyone. Take part in outings like hiking, biking, backpacking, rafting, and camping.

Baltimore Outdoor Sierrans, Greater Baltimore Group, Maryland Chapter Sierra Club, maryland.sierraclub.org/baltimore/bos. The Baltimore Outdoor Sierrans hosts social outings for young people, generally between the ages of 25 and 45, interested in enjoying the outdoors and having a positive impact on the environment. Sierra Club membership is not required.

Meetup Groups, meetup.com. Search on "hiking" and "Baltimore" to find a plethora of hiking and outdoor groups, each tailored to a specific niche. Here you can find groups geared toward hiking with dogs, or hiking in a particular area of Maryland, entrepreneurs who are also outdoor enthusiasts, and groups specific to age and experience.

About the Author

Heather Sanders Connellee was born and raised in Baltimore. She has a serious case of wanderlust, and her love of travel and the outdoors has taken her all over the United States and around the world. While her heart is in the outdoors, home will always be Baltimore, though the trail was her "home" during her six-month journey hiking the Appalachian Trail. Heather is the former editor of *American Hiker* magazine and former trail programs manager for the American Hiking Society, where she spearheaded National Trails Day® and the National Trails Fund and lead various volunteer trail groups. When she's not writing about the outdoors and travel for various publications, she enjoys hiking, backpacking, rock climbing, kayaking, biking, and anything and everything outdoors. Heather and her husband, Grant, along with their dog and cat live in Harford County, Maryland. Their most recent adventure was summiting Kilimanjaro, but the bucket list doesn't end there. Heather is Vice President of Marketing and Development at Leffler Agency Inc., a Baltimore-based advertising firm. Heather is also the author of FalconGuides' *Best Easy Day Hikes Baltimore*. As long as the world goes 'round, she'll be rounding the world.

Mike Ciesielski

> The world is a book and those who do not travel read only one page.
>
> —St. Augustine.

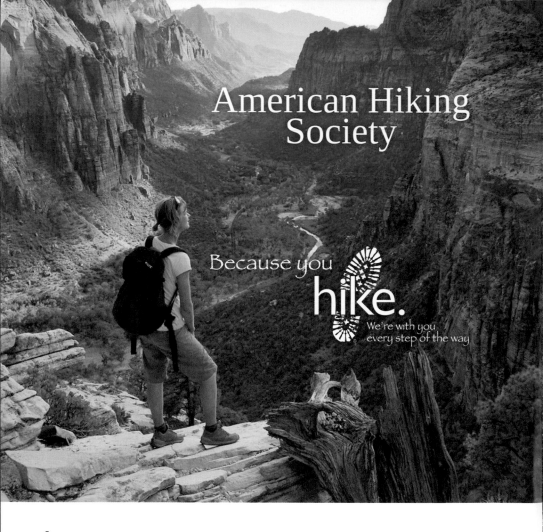

American Hiking Society

Because you **hike.**
We're with you every step of the way

As a national voice for hikers, **American Hiking Society** works every day:

- Building and maintaining hiking trails
- Educating and supporting hikers by providing information and resources
- Supporting hiking and trail organizations nationwide
- Speaking for hikers in the halls of Congress and with federal land managers

Whether you're a casual hiker or a seasoned backpacker, become a member of American Hiking Society and join the national hiking community! You'll enjoy great member benefits and help preserve the nation's hiking trails, so tomorrow's hike is even better than today's. We invite you to join us now!

American Hiking Society